D1257346

HARRIET SHELLEY
FIVE LONG YEARS

TO HARRIET * * * * *.

WHOSE is the love that, gleaming through the world,
Wards off the poisonous arrow of its scorn?
Whose is the warm and partial praise
Virtue's most sweet reward?

Beneath whose looks did my reviving soul
Riper in truth and virtuous daring grow?
Whose eyes have I gazed fondly on,
And loved mankind the more?

Harriet! on thine:—thou wert my purer mind;
Thou wert the inspiration of my song;
Thine are these early wilding flowers,
Though garlanded by me.

Then press unto thy breast this pledge of love;
And know, though time may change and years may roll,
Each flowret gathered in my heart
It consecrates to thine.

Dedication, Queen Mab.

HARRIET SHELLEY
FIVE LONG YEARS

LOUISE SCHUTZ BOAS

LONDON
OXFORD UNIVERSITY PRESS
NEW YORK   TORONTO
1962

92
S 5452 b

Oxford University Press, Amen House, London E.C.4

GLASGOW   NEW YORK   TORONTO   MELBOURNE   WELLINGTON
BOMBAY   CALCUTTA   MADRAS   KARACHI   LAHORE   DACCA
CAPE TOWN   SALISBURY   NAIROBI   IBADAN   ACCRA
KUALA LUMPUR   HONG KONG

© *Louise Schutz Boas 1962*

Printed in Great Britain

PREFACE

THE story of Harriet Shelley can at last be put into proper perspective as an inextricable part of the life of Percy Bysshe Shelley, his 'purer mind' in the first flush of his development as a thinker and a writer, to whom he dedicated his first important poem as his 'inspirer'. She lives on in the sadness of much of his later verse when he was 'half in love with easeful death'. She has been belittled and begrimed in an effort to lay her ghost, her story coloured by Victorian prejudice, by misguided hero-worship or hatred of her husband. Shelley's detractors shaped it into a stick to belabour him, his admirers into a whip to lash her. In the attempt to make a Victorian gentleman out of an impassioned poet the biographers needed fuel for their fires; they threw in Harriet's reputation. Having decided that his separation from her was 'pivotal' in any estimate of him as man and/or poet, believing that the 'Great' must be the 'Pure'—in the narrow smugness of Victorian morality—they were compelled to disparage her. For them Shelley sprang full-formed from the brow of Mary Godwin, his second wife; Mary's biographer, Mrs. Marshall, solemnly asserted (in 1889) that until he met her Shelley was 'childlike'; his rupture with Harriet 'ended his boyhood'; with Mary, 'like Undine' he acquired a soul.

The most determined detractor of Harriet, after Godwin who had a vested interest in exonerating his own daughter, was Mary's dedicated daughter-in-law, Lady Shelley, who set up a Shelley shrine in her home, complete with relics. Outraged by the *Life of Shelley* (1858) in which Thomas Jefferson Hogg glorified himself, Lady Shelley published first a small volume, *Shelley Memorials* (1859), and then gathered together the documents, letters, journals, etc., in the possession of her husband, Sir Percy Florence Shelley, together with some she borrowed from Lady Dorchester, for publication. Restricted by Lady Dorchester to a privately printed issue (more than the reputed 'twelve only'), she annotated with marginal notes enforcing her interpretations. Seemingly a miscellany artlessly put together,

v

MAY 29 '62

THE HUNT LIBRARY
CARNEGIE INSTITUTE OF TECHNOLOGY

Shelley and Mary is a contrived eulogy; disregarding any earlier documents, Lady Shelley began with July 1814 when Shelley and Mary were 'united'; Lady Shelley even in her private moments must have had difficulty in accepting the fact that Mary lived with Shelley over two years without benefit of clergy. Her annotations negated any untoward suspicions and reinforced her portrait of a poet resembling the feminized portrait by Amelia Curran which still decorates so many volumes of Shelley's unfeminine poetry, a picture less like him than the fanciful painting by Joseph Severn, sitting among the ruins of the Baths of Caracalla in Rome, writing *Prometheus Unbound*. Lady Shelley excised from copies she distributed passages which on second thoughts seemed to her inappropriate.

Edward Dowden, selected as the official biographer, resisted her pressures, refusing to strip Harriet's character bare; Trelawny, the friend of Shelley's last year (1822), cried out in his old age, when he had passed away, 'who will there be to stop her?' (i.e. Lady Shelley). That she burned papers and letters concerned with the separation from Harriet, Dowden knew. He fought with his conscience but gradually yielded to Lady Shelley's coadjutor, Richard Garnett. The letters between these two gentlemen trying to be gentlemanly in their denigration of Harriet make an amusing study in self-justification, Victorian smugness, and determined prejudice. Two knight-errants came forward, Thomas Love Peacock in the time of Hogg's *Life* and Lady Shelley's *Memorials*, and the American Mark Twain (Samuel Clemens) after Dowden's *Life*. Twain's *In Defence of Harriet Shelley* is dictated by righteous anger.

Today it is not necessary to denigrate Harriet to exonerate Shelley or Mary; it is not necessary to prove that he did not love his first wife in order to prove that he did love his second. The modern pattern of marriage and divorce is such that Shelley's views no longer seem fantastic. Love we recognize today as no respecter of marriage; whatever causes the deep emotion of love, making another essential for one's very life, it is an undeniable force driving old men into incongruous behaviour and young men into impulsive action, and both often to desperation. Today it can be said that neither of Shelley's marriages was perfect, that he never found that perfection of mind and body which was his ideal. Today we know that genius is often restive; that men sometimes outgrow the wife of their youth, and endeavour to re-create the first raptures with another; that divorce is the outcome of such emotional direction, and that after divorce a wife and a husband may build up a new relationship. Whether we approve of divorce or not, it is part of modern living.

Anticipating the twentieth century, Shelley expected Harriet to accept the translation of Utopian theories into present action. As an advocate of free speech, a free press, universal suffrage, universal education, the limitation of private fortunes (accomplished today by income taxes and death duties), the study of science, the establishment of an association which should, starting in Ireland, spread widely, grouping finally into an international association, he was a century ahead of his time. Harriet, very young yet already socially conscious, was converted to all his free views; he undertook her education first when she was fifteen and a half. Under his tutelage she read history and philosophy—a host of difficult and serious works beside reflective novels, and the journals of the day such as Cobbett's *Political Register* and Leigh Hunt's *Examiner*. Robert Browning, having been shown by Thomas Hookham, Shelley's friend and publisher, Harriet's letters to him, wrote to Dowden, then writing his *Life of Shelley*, pointing out that the young woman who wrote these intelligent letters, who read widely, studied Latin, read Horace's *Odes* and sang songs from Mozart, had been misrepresented; he himself would not make this public but, of course, Dowden would. Dowden, a victim of two-way morality, could not present Shelley as anything but 'good'; therefore Harriet must have been 'bad'; he therefore struck a balance; he patted her on the head for having been a good little girl, and he permitted Shelley to have been happy with her for a time; but he erroneously continued to state that he had 'positive proof' of her eventual misconduct. He had no such proof. Even Peacock's defence of Harriet was turned to her discredit by Lady Shelley.

For all people who deal with Shelley are, like Harriet herself, and Hogg, Shelley-possessed. Today we can permit our heroes to have flaws; indeed part of the public will not have a hero who is not aberrant.

Had the story of Harriet not ended tragically it would anticipate many a modern tale of schoolgirl- and schoolboy-marriage, of mutual study and endeavour, and parting. Today they could remain friends, as Shelley then suggested. But the twentieth century was far in the future; in 1814 there were no universities for women, no occupational therapy for deserted wives. Harriet had not tried to become a writer, and was not trained to be a journalist. She had accepted the Godwinian idea that one's life must be used for some worthy purpose. Because she could find no use for her living, because with Shelley her life had been happy and useful, because her life's springtime had blossomed with him into a glowing summer, and without him had declined to a bleak winter, her life came to an abrupt close four months after her twenty-first birthday.

No portrait or miniature of Harriet exists. Her descendants searched in vain for letters to or from her, and for her burial certificate. The only direct descendants of Shelley, the Esdaile family of Cothelstone, Somerset, have up to the present retained the Notebook in which Shelley's early poems were written, many of them as yet unpublished. Mrs. Lettice Worrall, great grand-daughter of Shelley and Harriet, kindly searched for Shelley's books, some of which it is known Harriet kept, though she sent him others; but she found none. Mrs. Worrall kindly showed me Harriet's wedding ring, a flat band of minute diamonds and turquoises, Shelley's matching tie-clip, and his christening shirt. These were Ianthe Shelley's, which had been kept for her by Eliza Westbrook Beauchamp.

Unfortunately Hellen Shelley, the young sister who had been at school with Harriet, kept no letters of Harriet's to her, and destroyed the letters of Shelley given her by the family solicitor; these presumably were those which Leslie Hotson in 1929 found copied in the records of the Court of Chancery. Hogg, though he had many letters from Harriet, one in Latin, published none and left none at his death (at least there were none in the sale of Hogg papers). Peacock published none to him.

Harriet's letters to Mrs. Nugent and one to Mrs. Newman are preserved in a beautifully bound volume in the Huntington Library, San Marino, California (HM 20178-20198); permission was kindly given to quote from these. The letter quoted on page 168 is in the British Museum (Ashley 5021).

Harriet's letters to Miss Hitchener together with Shelley's, and Miss Hitchener's to Shelley and to Harriet are in the British Museum, Add. MSS. 37496. Her letter to J. Frank Newton of June 1816 is Add. MSS. 37232. Permission to quote from these letters has been given by the Trustees of the British Museum.

The letters to and from Miss Hitchener and those to Miss Nugent have been privately printed, but can be best consulted in the Julian Edition of Shelley's *Works*.

Harriet's so-called 'suicide letter' is in private hands; permission to consult it was kindly given, but did not include the right to make use of it. The letter as illustrated is reproduced with the kind permission of E. Swift Newton for the Estate of A. Edward Newton, and is taken from A. Edward Newton's *Greatest Book in the World* and from the sale catalogue of the A. Edward Newton library.

Eliza Westbrook's letter to John Williams is quoted from the original letter in the Caernarvon County Hall; permission to quote this and a letter of Mr. Madocks has been kindly granted by Breese, Jones, and Casson of Port-Madoc, and by the County Archivist, Caernarvon.

Shelley's 'Lost Letters to Harriet' including the letter to Eliza Westbrook are quoted with the kind permission of Leslie Hotson and of the *Atlantic Monthly*.

Thomas Hookham's letter to Shelley with the news of Harriet's death is in the Berg Collection of the New York Public Library where I was allowed to examine it, through the kindness of Mr. John D. Gordan.

Unpublished letters of Sir Timothy Shelley were consulted in the Horsham Museum, Horsham, Sussex.

The hitherto unpublished stanzas from the 'Esdaile Notebook' are printed with the kind permission of the Clarendon Press and Neville Rogers, Esq.

My thanks are due to Ernest Benn Ltd. for permission to quote from their Julian Edition of Shelley's *Works* (10 vols.), vols. v, viii, ix, and x; to Routledge & Kegan Paul Ltd. for permission to quote from Roger Ingpen's *Shelley in England*; and to The Bodley Head Ltd. for permission to quote from *New Shelley Letters*, W. Sidney Scott, ed., and for permission to reproduce from that book the silhouette of T. Jefferson Hogg.

I am indebted to the late Mr. Charrington and to Miss Charrington for their hospitality in letting me view gardens and house at Field Place; to Capt. Livingstone-Learmonth for his hospitality at Tanyrallt, and for pictures, as well as for a most plausible explanation of the attack upon Shelley which my account reflects; to Messrs. Hunton & Son, Bracknell, for permitting me to see and roam about in 'High Elms' at Bracknell which was doomed to destruction; to R. N. Ellis-Davies, Esq., of Craig Wen, Caernarvon, for showing me furniture made for the Shelleys at Tanyrallt. Cwm Elan and Nantgwillt vanished when the Birmingham reservoir was built, flooding the countryside.

I am grateful to the secretary of St. George's Church, Hanover Square, for her patience and help. Through her suggestion I investigated the possibility that Harriet Shelley might have been buried at the graveyard used by the church on Bayswater Road (then Uxbridge Road), where as late as 1890 there was a stone with the name Shelley among stones of the proper date; but the Chapel of Ease and many of its stones were struck by bombs and little remained; meanwhile I came to accept Roger Ingpen's discovery of the burial record of Harriet Smith at Paddington Parish Church as that of Harriet Shelley.

To Lady Mander I am most grateful for her kind permission to reproduce the portrait of William Godwin as he was when Harriet knew him. The portrait of Charles, 11th Duke of Norfolk, as he was when Harriet and Shelley were his guests, is reproduced from an engraving by Williamson published in July 1813; the original drawing by W. C. Ross was exhibited at the Royal Academy in 1811. Miss Pettman of the National Portrait Gallery kindly provided this information.

For permission to reproduce the picture of Clapham Common I am indebted to the Trustees of the London Museum, Kensington Palace; for the pictures of Dublin, Edinburgh, and Hyde Park to the Trustees of the British Museum.

To Dr. Eleanor L. Nicholes I am indebted for the information of the preservation of the Tremadoc Embankment and the ambitious plans for improvement in the current years.

To Edmund Blunden I am indebted for many a kind suggestion, and to Neville Rogers for stimulating discussions of Shelley, and for the reading of some of Shelley's unpublished poems to Harriet.

The Boston Athenaeum, and, in especial, Miss Margaret Hackett have been most kind; and I have to thank warmly the London Library and the British Museum.

My warmest thanks are due to Miss Sylva Norman, without whose encouragement, and finally her insistence, this book would never have been finished and submitted to a publisher.

LOUISE SCHUTZ BOAS

November 1960

Postscript. In the Ingpen Papers in Berkeley, California, is evidence that the social standing of the Westbrooks was higher than usually represented. From 1807 onward *Boyle's Court Guide* listed Harriet's father among the 'fashionable' residents of London, close neighbour to a General, a Viscountess, a Dowager Countess and Beau Brummell (no longer in full glory).

Ingpen had proof that Sir Bysshe eloped only once; his second wife was twenty-seven, her mother was present at the marriage, and she was not a great heiress. He made public neither the elopement of Shelley's married sister Mary, nor the 'unpleasantness' between Lady Dorchester and Lady Shelley which prevented publication of *Shelley and Mary*.

Unpublished also are three letters from Harriet to John Williams, one of August 1813 authorising Mr. Nanney to 'sell the furniture at Tanyrallt'; two, August and October 1814, requesting him to send her 'Boxes' to London.

October 20, 1813: Harriet Shelley to Catherine Nugent:

A little more than two years has passed since I made my first visit here to be united to Mr. Shelley. To me they have been the happiest and the longest years of my life. The rapid succession of events since that time makes the two years appear unusually long. . . . Tho' my age is but eighteen yet I feel as if I was much older.

November 20, 1814: Harriet Shelley to Catherine Nugent:

. . . here I am, my dear friend, waiting to bring another infant into this woful world. Next month I shall be confined. He will not be near me. No, he cares not for me now. He never asks after me or sends me word how he is getting on. In short, the man I once loved is dead, this is a vampire.

November 9(?), 1816: Harriet Shelley to Eliza Westbrook:

When you read this letr. I shall be [no] more an inhabitant of this miserable world. . . . God keep watch over you all, you dear Bysshe, and you dear Eliza. . . . My children . . . are too young to regret me.

February 12, 1839: Mary Wollstonecraft Shelley in her *Journal*:

Poor Harriet, to whose sad fate I attribute so many of my own heavy sorrows, as the atonement claimed by fate for her death.

CONTENTS

ILLUSTRATIONS

CHAPTER I

Fair in Form and Pure in Mind

A most intense young man,
An ultra-poetical, super-aesthetical
Out of the way young man!

W. S. GILBERT

THE most ordinary thing that extraordinary young man,
Percy Bysshe Shelley, ever did in the course of his short
life was to fall gradually and imperceptibly in love in the
springtime with an extraordinarily pretty girl, and, in late summer, elope with her. Their marriage took place in 1811 shortly
after his nineteenth, her sixteenth, birthday. In the ordinary
course of events they would never have met, or, meeting, have
gone beyond such words as might have passed between any girl
and her school-friend's brother. In the stratified class-conscious
society of early nineteenth-century England there was a gulf
between Harriet Westbrook, daughter of a retired coffee-house
proprietor and vintner, and Percy Bysshe Shelley, heir to a large
fortune and a baronetcy. Mr. Westbrook's fortune was of considerable size, but it had not been inherited; he had made
it from his coffee house off Grosvenor Square, and possibly
augmented it from money-lending. It enabled him to educate
his daughter in a proper school where her closest friend was a
daughter of Timothy Shelley, Member of Parliament, a country
gentleman belonging to the branch of an old family, and himself the heir to Sir Bysshe Shelley. Sir Bysshe's title was a somewhat new honour (1806); his vast fortune was the accumulation
of his inheritances plus that of his first wife. Though Sir
Bysshe's father had been in trade, that had been long ago, and
in another country—America—and he had not profited from
it. Mr. Westbrook's money had not acquired respectability

B   1

from age, and he had not retired to a country estate. When
Harriet had been about ten he had settled his family in a handsome house in a fashionable district of London, in the parish
to which his wife had belonged when they married, and in
which they had remained: St. George's, Hanover Square. He
had also a summer home in the Welsh spa, Aberystwyth.

Though proudly conscious of his position as heir to a title and
a landed estate, Shelley had pronounced democratic principles
which influenced him to give preference to those whose birth
did not equate with his; his close friends tended to be his
social and economic inferiors as if in his relationships with
others he liked to be the benefactor.

When he first met Harriet Westbrook he was still at Eton,
she at Mrs. Fenning's School (later Miss Hawkes') across the
Thames on the north side of Clapham Common, where
Shelley's sisters, Mary and Hellen, were also resident, Mary
almost two years younger than Harriet, Hellen two years
younger than Mary. There is no record of Harriet's first impression of the tall, curly-haired, fashionably dressed, gay-
spirited young man who came to the school, a willing messenger
from Field Place, his father's estate near Horsham, Sussex.
When he came to the school in April 1810 he was four months
less than eighteen, Harriet four months less than fifteen. His
first impression of Harriet, either then or on some similar visit,
was remembered by his sister Hellen years later: his outspoken
admiration, his calling Harriet's hair, 'a poet's dream'. At
school it was believed that if there should be a fête Harriet
Westbrook would be Venus.

In April Shelley and his oldest sister, Elizabeth, had been
visiting with their cousins, the Groves. To Harriet Grove, a
year his senior, Shelley had been especially devoted. When he
first met Harriet Westbrook his cousin Harriet had not yet
defected from him. She was undeniably pretty, resembling
closely Shelley and his sister Elizabeth. But Harriet Westbrook
was undeniably lovely.

Early in January 1811, taking with him Harriet Grove's
brother Charles, Shelley called upon Harriet Westbrook at her
father's home, to bring her a gift from Mary who was not to

return to school after the holidays. Whether this was of his contrivance or his sister's is irrelevant; with it he established his acquaintance with Harriet Westbrook and became known to her family. He immediately made sure of her as a correspondent by ordering his publishers to send her a copy of his new novel (his second), *St. Irvyne, or the Rosicrucian*.

If Harriet was unusually beautiful, Shelley was unusually fascinating. Harriet was not unlike the women of his own family, but Shelley was unlike any one Harriet had ever known. Circumstances contrived to throw them together, when he had been removed from the sphere of his mother, his sisters, and his cousin, leaving him in an emotional vacuum to be filled by Harriet Westbrook, beautiful, docile, and near by. Springtime, propinquity, and loneliness were more potent than any scheming of Harriet's older sister. Disappointed in the behaviour of his mother, his sister Elizabeth, and his cousin, Shelley was to turn to Harriet Westbrook for companionship, and for the satisfaction of forming someone in the likeness of his ideal woman. Her circumstances were far from humble; her father kept a proper household, with horses and carriages; his had been a reputable well-known coffee-house, the Mount, in Lower Grosvenor Street. Though coffee-houses had not maintained their earlier importance as clubs, and although alcohol was served, they were eminently respectable; otherwise Shelley would not have appointed one as his meeting place with Harriet in August 1811.

John Westbrook, twenty-nine,[1] vintner, of the Parish of St. Mary, Lambeth, had in 1780 married Ann Elliott, twenty-three, of the Parish of St. George, Hanover Square, by special licence, a more costly and fashionable method than the reading of banns on three successive Sundays. St. George's, a fine structure, its name a compliment to George III, included among its parishioners the titled, the opulent, and their numerous servitors, maids and menservants, artisans, and workmen. Ann Elliott and John Westbrook signed their names in the register in the handwriting of educated people. In later years when Shelley's father and his tight-lipped lawyer perforce had dealings with Mr. Westbrook they found him a man of dignity; not even the

carping William Whitton could cavil at him, though toward
Harriet's older sister Eliza he showed active dislike and resentment.

Of Mrs. Westbrook little is known beyond the dates of her
marriage and of her death (1819), and that she bore four children, all daughters, of whom only the second, Eliza, and the
youngest, Harriet, survived.[2] Eliza was christened at St.
George's 8th August 1783, Harriet the 27th of August 1795.
Harriet's mother had been thirty-eight, her father forty-four at
her birth. The only existent description of Mrs. Westbrook is a
fanciful one in Hogg's *Life of Shelley*, characteristically disparag-
ing; he pictured her (she was then fifty-three):

as dignified as silk and satin could make her . . . fully capable of
sitting all day long with her hands before her, but incapable of aught
besides, good, or bad, except possibly of hearing herself addressed
as Mamma.

How else would a middle-aged mother in 1811 have dressed
and sat to receive a young man of superior social position paying
a call upon her daughter? From this description by Hogg, who
never met her, Mrs. Westbrook has been judged incompetent.
Harriet's reference to her sister as 'my more than Mother', a
girlish appreciation of the possessive and protective love of an
older sister, has been used to support this misinterpretation.
Mothers were of small consequence under paternalistic rule.
Fanny Burney's novels were dedicated to her father, 'the Author
of my being'; John Stuart Mill (born eleven years later than
Harriet) kept deliberate silence in his *Autobiography*, deleting
before publication the sole reference to his mother. Little, therefore, can be inferred about Mrs. Westbrook; that Eliza ran the
household is patently untrue, since she was spared to join
Shelley and Harriet and remain with them.

In the early days of friendship when young people show their
interest in each other by exchanging confidences—embroidered
by fancy—Harriet had little to tell Shelley, and was the better
listener to all he poured forth of himself, his background, his
family, his accomplishments, his hopes, his plans. Until she met
Shelley, Harriet's life had been without complication, bounded
by school, her father's home in London, his summer home in

Wales, and the country through which they drove on the way
to Aberystwyth. Shelley did not yet know the exquisitely lovely
hills and valleys, the rivers and bays of Wales; of these she
could tell him. At Aberystwyth the sea is limpid green and blue,
the bay ringed with hills varied in shape and colour. Aside from
the duty of drinking the waters of the chalybeate springs, and
bathing in cold or warm spring waters, there were country
pleasures: driving, walking, riding; admiring the hilltop views;
studying the ruins of the castle, originally built in the early
twelfth century, fought over by Henry V, blown up by Crom-
well; picking up on the beach pink and red jasper, agate, cor-
nelian, and amethyst, to be polished by the local lapidaries and
set in brooches and rings.

London, Shelley knew better than Harriet; on his visits to his
cousins, the Groves, he had enjoyed its manifold diversions: the
opera, theatre, concerts, lectures, museums, balls, and parties.
Harriet's life had, as she wrote to Miss Hitchener in March
1812, been narrow:

My knowledge has been very confined on account of my youth, &
the situation in which I was placed. My intercourse with mankind
has therefore been much less than you may imagine; when I lived
with my Father, I was not likely to gain much knowledge, as our
circle of acquaintance was very limited, he not thinking it proper that
we should mix much with society. In short, we very seldom visited
those places of fashionable resort & amusement which from our
age might have been expected. 'Twas but seldom that I visited my
home, school having witnessed the greater part of my life. But do not
think from this that I was ignorant of what was passing in the great
world; books & a newspaper were sufficient to inform me of these.
Tho' then a silent spectator, yet did I know that all was not as it
ought to be; I looked with a fearful eye upon the vices of the great
& thought to myself 'twas better even to be a beggar, or to be obliged
to gain my bread with my needle, than to be the inhabitant of those
great houses when misery and famine howl around. I will tell you
my faults, knowing what I have to expect from your friendship.
Remember my youth and if any excuse can be made, let that
suffice. In London you know there are military as well as everywhere else. When quite a child I admired these Red Coats. This grew
up with me & I thought the military the best as well as most
fascinating Men in the world, though at the same time I used to
declare never to marry one. This was not so much on account of

their vices as from the idea of their being killed. I thought, if I
married anyone, it should be a Clergyman. Strange idea, this, was
it not? But being brought up in the Christian Religion, 'twas first
gave rise to it.[3]

Here Harriet revealed the innocence of her daydreams, and her
fears. Her father's house was at 23 Chapel Street (now Aldford),
a short street between Park Lane and Grosvenor Chapel which,
facing it, gave it its name. Across Park Lane was Hyde Park
where the future George IV rode with his friends and his loves,
but not with his wife from whom he vainly sought divorce. As
Prince of Wales and then as Prince Regent, he furnished a
plenitude of gossip: his health, his quarrels with his wife, his
devotion to his daughter, his mother, and his many sisters, his
love affairs. His father, George III, had been mad and had
recovered, but was again mad, a sad old man kept out of sight
at Windsor Castle where he played the piano and talked with
angels, and read Shakespeare to his patient queen, imagining
himself King Lear. The Jubilee 1809–1810 passed with increas-
ing demands for a Regency; the Queen felt her eldest son's
celebration of his father's fiftieth year on the throne to be in
reality a celebration of his own emergence as Regent.

In the great houses on Piccadilly and Park Lane lived the
grand ladies and gentlemen of his circle, many of them, as even
innocent schoolgirls knew, of highly questionable morals. Their
fantastic gambling debts, their promiscuous loves, their extravagances, their rapid round of pleasures could not fail to attract
the attention of young people outside their orbit in spite of (or
because of) the warnings of parents and clergymen. It is odd
that those who think well of the world do not enjoy it, while
those who think ill of it can enjoy it so thoroughly. Those who
think well of human nature take too high a view of what life
should be to enjoy it as it is; they tend to live in angry discontent,
neither people nor the times accepting their correction. Frank
hedonists, thinking poorly of human nature, accepting its imper-
fections as inevitable, can, like the powerful Whigs of the early
nineteenth century, develop an enormous zest for living, for the
exciting game of politics, of love, of daily activity. In his old
age Lord Melbourne looked admiringly at a portrait of his

mother, speaking of her with warm affection, and then he added: 'But she was not chaste, not chaste'.[4]

Chastity was a virtue upon which middle-class fathers insisted. A man of strict morals, Mr. Westbrook took care to warn his daughter against the vices of high society lest in her innocence she pine to become part of it. He also took the precaution of sending his beautiful daughter to boarding school, away from the admiring glances of young men who even in church were not unobservant. Vain Harriet never was; yet no girl was ever yet wholly unaware of freely proffered admiration, even if not vocalized. Any young girl might dream of becoming, like the heroine of a novel, the wife of a lord to be carried into one of those great houses and the land of romance. If Harriet had such dreams, they were dissolved, perhaps by her good sense, more probably by the admonitions of her parents. As she phrased it, she would not be an inhabitant of a great house, while 'misery and famine howl around' (surely the verb is Shelley's?). It sounds as if her father or the servants had pointed out to her the beggars whose wretched lot was in sharp contrast to the conspicuous waste of the darlings of fortune. Docilely she agreed that it would be better (i.e. morally more praiseworthy) to be a beggar or a lowly wage-earner, poor but honest, than to be a social butterfly apathetic to human misery. It is an amusingly innocent juxtaposition of beggar and needlewoman; she had apparently been told that respectable girls, forced to earn their bread, were scarcely better off than beggars, which unfortunately was quite true. And this hard fact influenced her in the rejection of a soldier as a possible husband: soldiers' wives were all too often widowed, and as widows forced to earn their living. It was therefore a simple matter of logic, in a world in which Napoleon was triumphantly in power. Clergymen, on the contrary, did not go to war; and clergymen were much admired and respected, especially by ladies. Harriet's naïveté exposed her fundamental desire for security; for women, security came almost exclusively through marriage. Until she met Shelley, Harriet had not been disrespectful of the clergy or questioned the tenets of the church. Her education in freethinking was enthusiastically undertaken by Shelley.

Their correspondence in 1811 was never made public. The content of Shelley's letters to Harriet at this time can be surmised from his letters to others; he habitually revealed himself, his background, his thoughts, his beliefs. From childhood he had been a teller of tall tales; his narratives of home, family, school, Eton, and Oxford lost nothing in the telling. He was the oldest child of Timothy Shelley of Field Place, Sussex; there were five other children, of whom only the youngest was a boy. His father's home was considerably larger than Mr. Westbrook's London home; it was a broad-fronted house facing extensive gardens. The estate included several farms, hunting preserves, great wooded areas, and a large pond. As a child Shelley had learned to ride, to shoot (he was always an expert, in later years proud to hold his own with Lord Byron); he had not learned always to tell the truth.

At six, having acquired the rudiments with his sister Elizabeth under a governess, he rode daily two miles to Warnham to learn Latin from the rector. Warnham was a sleepy little village devoid of interest for the child save for the tombs and tablets commemorating his ancestors; on the tombstone of his great-grandmother he read: 'She was born in Newark, in North America'. From this sprang an early interest in America, fostered, too, by the American garden at Field Place, a delightful greenery where American trees, shrubs, flowers, and fruits flourished, a perpetual reminder of the romance of his great-grandfather who as a young man had gone to America to make his fortune. He had not, however, acquired hoards of gold, and after the death of his older brother, had been recalled. His wife had been Joanna Plum, either the widow or the daughter of a New York merchant. As the records of Christ Church, Newark, were burned during the American Revolution, nothing is known of her family. The inscription on the tombstone in Warnham shows her to have been almost six years her husband's senior.[5]

In 1811 her son, Sir Bysshe Shelley (he had acquired a baronetcy for his political services to the Duke of Norfolk) was living near Field Place in the market town of Horsham, in a rather charming house of moderate size on the bank of the narrow river, near the church. Legend has wrongly placed him in a mean cottage, attended by a lone servant. It was his steward who accompanied him nightly to the local inn where he gathered politically useful gossip.

At the age of eight, newly arrived from America, he had received a sizeable legacy from his grandfather: two thousand pounds in cash, beside jewels, silver, linen, books, and certain property rights in the Manor of Streatham. Three years later at the age of eleven he had inherited from his grandmother another fortune: all her moneys in cash, mortgages, loans, land in East Grinstead, half her best linens, and all her jewellery. She must have feared his American blood and birth as detrimental to his status as an English gentleman, for she charged her executor with the task of educating him 'in a handsome manner, and with a scholastick and gentlemanlike education, so that he may be fitten to be bred up or put to the Law or some other gentlemanlike science or employment'; he was on no account 'to be sent or putt to sea'. A further bequest, from a great-uncle, contingent upon his not marrying until the age of twenty-three, the handsome Bysshe forfeited by eloping at the age of twenty-one with a sixteen-year-old girl of large fortune. Before he was thirty he was a widower with two daughters and one son, Timothy.

Nine years after the death of his wife he married Miss Perry, then twenty-seven, and was again left a widower with children, four sons and two daughters, who, as their father developed the gentlemanly vice of avarice, allied themselves with their mother's more aristocratic family, the Sidneys of Penshurst. Shelley regaled his friends with tales of his grandfather, gratuitously presenting him with a third marriage for which there is no evidence. He expatiated upon his grandfather's peculiarities, his penuriousness, and his failure to make generous provision for his grandson and ultimate heir. Sir Bysshe had three main interests: politics, money, and his castle. At his death (four years after Shelley first called upon Harriet) money was found to the extent of thousands of pounds stuffed in sofas, chairs, and pockets. His 'Folly' was a castle by the sea, Castle Goring, which early in 1811 had been building for almost twenty years; it was never completed. Its huge expense—eighty thousand pounds had been absorbed in its construction—pre-empted much of Sir Bysshe's available resources and gave him an excuse for a lack of generosity toward his children and grandchildren. Beyond paying for the printing of his grandson's early poems he ignored requests. Goring Castle was of greater importance.

Facing the English Channel it stood in extensive grounds. It was a strange creation, part Gothic, part Palladian architecture. One façade, the north-east, was a copy, reduced in size, of the Duke of Norfolk's Arundel Castle; its opposite, the southwest façade, was designed after a villa near Rome. The Gothic front stood squarely upon the flat earth; the Roman front with its six-columned portico was on slightly rising ground, with a long flight of low steps leading down to gardens. Obviously its erection satisfied Sir Bysshe's dreams of grandeur, as his grandson's were satisfied by descriptive verse.[6]

Shelley's tales of Field Place, of his sisters and cousins, of the ponies and horses, the games, the parties, the visitings; of his childish pranks, including performances of magic rites—all this to Harriet was the tale of a Prince Charming. The tradesman's blood in his veins was thoroughly diluted with that of the landed gentry. The Duke of Norfolk not infrequently dined at Field Place, taking interest in the boy who would in time enter Parliament under his aegis. It was a story to dazzle a girl who knew of life on such a scale only in the pages of a novel. It was not all told in consecutive narrative; it was pieced out bit by bit in the self-revelation ordinary enough between boy and girl who are making strides in the friendship which easily merges into love—not sudden, violent, inexplicable love, but the love that comes from a community of thought, an exchange of sympathies. Their earliest letters would naturally have contained childhood reminiscence, the *lingua franca* of youth seeking common ground, yet emphasizing unique reactions to experience.

At the age of ten at Sion House Academy Shelley had found the discipline of the masters and the older boys harsh after the gentle society of his sisters and the household's deference to the heir. He had not fitted into the school pattern; his mind was inordinately active and original, his sensitivity heightened, his interest in sports nil. It is not necessary to believe all his tales of

fights and rages and unhappinesses, or in those recalled by schoolmates when posthumous fame mounted. It is certain that he was
over-sensitive to physical pain; that he reacted violently against
bullying; that he built up lasting ideas of tyranny and freedom,
and turned for solace to the acquisition of knowledge, deter-
mining to be 'wise/And just and free, and mild', and to dedicate
himself to perpetual warfare against injustice and oppression,
decrying all violence save that of the spirit against evil.

At twelve Shelley had entered Eton. Whatever his rebellions,
his protests against the fagging system under which lesser boys
served greater boys until in turn they had lesser boys to serve
them, he became attached to Eton where boys who were future
bishops, barristers, judges, and political leaders fancied themselves as authors. Many little volumes of verse, sententious
pamphlets, and lurid thrillers were published by Eton and
London booksellers. In March 1811 Shelley's first novel,
Zastrozzi, appeared with 'P.B.S.' on the title-page as author.
Charles Richard Sumner, two years Shelley's senior, had dis-
creetly refused to let his initials appear on the title-page of his
thriller, *The White Nun, or the Black Bog of Dromore*; his publisher
had to compromise with 'By a Gentleman of Note', which did
not indicate vanity, 'Note' being merely 'Eton' spelt back-
wards.[7] Sumner received five pounds for his novel; Shelley,
claiming to have received thirty for the copyright of his, gave a
banquet to his Eton friends. It was customary for the older boys
to meet in informal groups to read aloud original verse and prose,
as well as passages culled from extra-curricular reading, all
copied into notebooks called 'Sylvas'. Shelley's difference from
others at Eton at this time has been over-emphasized; in literary
effort and accomplishment he was a conformist, not unlike the
future Bishop Sumner. He did not yet know that he was a poet,
and his verses were no more remarkable than those of his fellows.

In April 1810 he entered his name at Oxford, and in October
he came into residence at University College, established there
by his father who renewed his own youth; he introduced his son
to his old haunts and servitors, and to the son of his former
landlord, as a possible printer and publisher. This was a larger
world than Harriet's at Mrs. Fenning's School where young

ladies did not write novels; neither did they study Greek and
Latin—French, geography, and national history took the place
of the classics as mental discipline. Although before Harriet's
birth, in 1792, Mary Wollstonecraft had vigorously advocated
higher education for women, and their inclusion in public life,
there was as yet no serious effort to obtain either for them.
Genesis and *Paradise Lost* had defined woman's position; if God
had meant women to be intellectual He would have made Eve
from Adam's head. It was a man's world; yet there were signs
of change. Two or three years before Shelley urged Harriet to
learn Latin, and drew her into serious discussions, William
Lamb (later Lord Melbourne) was soberly instructing his mad-
cap wife, Caroline; on his journeys alone he wrote out lengthy
translations from the classics for her to collate with the original
texts and then write her opinion for him. At home he read
Shakespeare and Hume with her. Charles Richard Sumner also
expected intellectual companionship in marriage. In his letters
to his fiancée he explained that whereas domestic arrangements
were the wife's affair—mending, cleaning, supervision of children and servants—yet these

feminine matters need not be discussed and should not be brought
to a man's attention; they should be managed behind the scenes.
Nor can I conceive anything greater than the disappointment of that
man who admires a woman for her mental resources and cultivation
of mind but finds on marriage that she degenerates into a mere
'intendante de la maison'.

Part of the fascination which Shelley had for women was his
deference to their understanding, his treatment of them as
mental equals, his tacit assumption that it was not better to be
the mother of a great man than to be a great woman. No one in
Harriet's sphere had ever suggested that she could be a person
in her own right, or that she should extend her learning into the
realm of man's wisdom. Shelley demanded that she share his
intellectual questionings; that if she did not agree with him she
should refute his ideas. There is no subtler compliment.

How often Shelley wrote to Harriet or how often he saw her
between January and April in 1811 it is impossible to know; he
normally besieged his correspondents with lengthy epistles. He

was often in London that January; his Oxford friend Hogg, who had expected Shelley to join him there, saw nothing of him. Shelley did not reveal to Hogg his growing interest in Harriet Westbrook, though he had written profusely of his abortive love for his cousin Harriet Grove. It is not likely that he told Harriet Westbrook why her friendship and her corre- spondence were essential to him as balm to his self-esteem, deflated by family tension and parental reproaches. It would have been impolitic to tell the young girl to whom he was offering the heady wine of intellectual speculation that she was a substitute audience replacing the cousin whose companionship and confidence he had recently lost.

For the past two years Shelley had been devoted to Harriet Grove. Between October 1809 and August 1810 his cousin, a year his senior, had been drawn into a publishing venture, a volume of verses in an edition of fifteen hundred copies, printed in Horsham, published by Stockdale in Oxford in September, advertised and offered for sale as *Original Poetry by Victor and Cazire*,[8] and quickly withdrawn when Stockdale identified 'St. Edmond's Eve', the fourteenth of the seventeen poems, as a plagiarism from M. G. Lewis's *Tales of Terror*. Shelley or his sister Elizabeth may have transcribed the poem from memory, forgetful of its source and believing it original. Shelley assured Stockdale the error was his 'co-adjutor's'. It was, however, too exact a transcript to be overlooked or excused. If a copy reached Harriet she would have read this borrowed tale of a haunted and vanishing Canon who had caused the death of his wife, and also the lines from Shelley to Harriet Grove:

> He loves thee, and dearest one never, oh! never
> Canst thou cease to be loved by a heart so sincere.

This hardly reflects the transports of passion which Shelley poured out in letters to Hogg in December and January. Be- tween the writer of these profuse letters, wrapt in Gothic woe over Harriet Grove's defection, and the young man who came to Chapel Street in January, there would seem to be a wide gulf, but Shelley was then as always of mercurial disposition. For Harriet Grove his spirit was steeped in gloom; for Harriet Westbrook it soared.

THE HUNT LIBRARY
CARNEGIE INSTITUTE OF TECHNOLOGY

Even thus early Shelley was a professor *manqué*; so impelling
was the force of his ideas that he burned to communicate them,
to win proselytes. To Harriet Grove as to his father the ideas
developed in association with Hogg at Oxford seemed startling
and dangerous. Like a proper young lady she showed his letters
to her father who promptly forbade further correspondence.
Shelley was outraged at his cousin's docility; she who had known
and loved him, who had been his companion and confidante,
had lapsed into orthodoxy and was so far lost as to accept a
suitor of her father's selection. To Hogg on January 6th and
11th Shelley poured out his despair: his lone vigils in the churchyard, his meditations on death, a vial of laudanum in his hand.
On the 11th he also wrote to Stockdale, ordering from him a
copy of *St. Irvyne* [9] to be sent to Miss Harriet Westbrook.

His estrangement from Harriet Grove, followed by separation from his favourite sister, Elizabeth, at first sympathetic,
then pliant to her father's prohibitions, made a new friendship
almost imperative—and Shelley and Hogg both prided themselves on their susceptibility to 'female excellence'.

Shelley was in need of a sympathetic listener. All through the
holidays he had been engaged in a debate with his father which
had become acrimonious. Imbued with a keen desire to pene-
trate the secret of reality, to probe the nature of belief, Shelley
shocked his father. Not illiberal in his views, Timothy Shelley
had settled his own questionings and expected his son to accept
his conclusions. He believed in the supremacy of man's reason;
so did his son; hence they came to an *impasse*, along divergent
paths of the Enlightenment. For Shelley's father there was a
mechanistic universe which, analogous to a watch, had been
set going by a supreme mechanician and allowed to run by its
own immutable law. It was a neat and satisfactory solution for
the problem of the beginning of the world and the existence in
it of evil. For Shelley the world was not a perfect mechanism;
perfection lay ahead. He demanded *proofs* of the existence of a
supreme mechanician. For him man was the measure of all
things, man who had immense capabilities, who was naturally
good, who could *will* evil from the world. He could quote the
Bible more accurately and extensively than his father; he could

quote Paley upon whose *Evidences of Christianity* his father relied; he could quote many another philosopher who was only a name to his father.

His mother felt it necessary to protect the younger children, as he informed Hogg:

My mother imagines me to be on the high road to Pandemonium; she fancies I want to make a deistical coterie of all my little sisters.

It was more exciting to convert Harriet Westbrook to free-thinking. Before he returned to Oxford in late January she had had time to read and discuss *St. Irvyne* with him. It was not the sort of novel usually read by schoolgirls, a novel of mystery and crime, terror and passion. Confusing as the story is, it is revelatory of Shelley's view of life, love, and morals; it also reveals his essential innocence. Embedded in the absurd posturings of his larger than life characters are his earnest beliefs, including definite views on the true basis of love, and the limits of its endurance. Young, inexperienced, fascinated by the author's magnetic personality, Harriet may not have comprehended the special pleading of the complicated tale.

As literature *St. Irvyne* is worthless; as a preview of Shelley's mature sentiments, upon which he was to base his conduct, it is invaluable. The stock ideas of the Gothic novels he had admired were reproduced with more consistency than the flamboyant characters and the blood-and-thunder plots. In both Shelley's novels plots, possibly borrowed from obscure sources, exist for the sake of the underlying ideas. The Gothic novel was a recognized *genre* with fixed conventions, Shelley's immediate model being *Zofloya or the Moor* by 'Rosa Mathilda' (Charlotte Dacre). Action was usually in the distant past, in remote places of 'horrid' scenery untamed by man, suitable for deeds of violence by people of uncontrolled passions, with free use of poisons, poignards, dungeons, caverns, and tortures. The stock ingredients were sin, villainy, virtue, mystery, murder, madness, persecution, and beauty, compounded with pseudo-philosophic ideas on tyranny, love, woman, marriage, and religion. Dearer to Shelley than the precipice-hurlings and poisonings were the radical views: the evils of conventional marriage; the virtue of free union, man and woman held together not by a church ceremony, but by love and *a community of intellectual interests*; the tyranny of parents and rulers; the supreme importance of *mind*. Like Verenza in *Zofloya*, Shelley's heroes (and villains) could not really love a woman's body if they did not respect her mind. In his first novel, *Zastrozzi*, Verezzi was cloyed after a month's voluptuousness with Matilda. Before their physical union he had prized the 'elegance of her mind'; together they had enjoyed books, music, discussions; the neglect of these when passion engulfed them ended these beautiful evenings. Shelley's innocence cries aloud in both his novels with their passionate men and women living alone and unobserved for weeks or months, parting chastely to retire 'to their respective rooms' when 'the lateness of the hour warned them to separate'. 'At last arrived the hour of retiring—morning came,' and they met at breakfast.

St. Irvyne, mistakenly regarded as a disjointed tale held together by a hasty welding of its two plots, achieved cohesion by the studied contrast of two love stories, a contrast between a love springing from, and sated by, physical passion, and an enduring love of gradual development, based upon a community of sentiments and intellectual interests. Here was much for Harriet to ponder upon as spring unfolded with Shelley more and more at her side. Twitted by Hogg, to whom he was boasting, he declared that he was not in love, if he knew what love was. Indeed he had not been pierced by Cupid's arrow at first sight; neither had he been so smitten by his cousin Harriet Grove, with whom he had thought himself desperately in love. The love now developing for Harriet had been foreshadowed in *St. Irvyne* where it was true and lasting. Sudden love was the theme of the first part of the novel; its delights were transient:

Yet the love with which Wolfstein regarded Megalena, notwithstanding the strength of his expressions, though fervent and excessive, at first, was not of the nature which was likely to remain throughout existence; it was like a meteor at midnight, which glares amid the darkness for awhile, and then expires; yet did he love her now; at least if heated admiration of her person and accomplishments, independently of mind be love.

But the love of Fitzeustace and Eloise was genuine; their *minds* were congenial. Their story is developed in chapters seven, nine, eleven, and twelve. Chapters five and six are inexplicably absent. Chapters one to four, eight and ten are concerned with the story of Wolfstein, Megalena, and Ginotti.

In the first chapter there is a murder followed by a relentless pursuit, not, as in today's crime fiction, by minions of the law or some wise amateur detective; the pursuer is a man of mystery, the Rosicrucian of the sub-title. In the end he proves to be not only two characters, Ginotti and Nempere, but also the figure that fascinated Shelley, a man cursed with eternal life. Of this gift for which he had sold his soul he would disburden himself by its transfer to Wolfstein. Wolfstein, to save the beautiful captive Megalena from a fate worse than death, had murdered the bandit chieftain. Having fallen in love with Megalena at first sight himself, he fled with her, shadowed by Ginotti who again and again crossed their path. In a mansion outside Genoa Wolfstein swore fidelity to Megalena, a vow kept even when love vanished. Beautiful Olympia, failing to win his love, killed herself to prevent his killing her at Megalena's bidding.

In the eighth chapter Ginotti reappeared, and in the tenth he explained himself: his intellectual curiosity had impelled him to search into the 'latent mysteries of nature'—a curiosity the young Shelley had shared. Ginotti, however, had delved farther into magic rites than Shelley. Moreover, he had fallen into the sin of living to himself, unmindful of others, the sin abhorred by Godwin, and, through his teaching, by Shelley.

Chapter ten, besides revealing the character of Ginotti, his absorption in science, his rejection of the deity, his suicidal tendencies, gives an extraordinarily vivid description of a man in the presence of the devil. This would have been of special interest to Harriet who at the time she read *St. Irvyne* had troubled dreams of the devil of whom she was 'dreadfully afraid'. Shelley rescued her from such fears; but in his novel the devil was a vital and menacing power, claiming Ginotti in the hurried 'Conclusion' after the twelfth chapter. Wolfstein, protected by the fact that he had loved and been loved, escaped 'the power of hell' though he 'expired'—either by spontaneous

C

combustion or the contamination of Ginotti's terrible end. Before the double deaths Wolfstein had stumbled over the lifeless body of Megalena—neither he nor Shelley could find 'any visible cause ... for her death'. Sinful as Wolfstein and Megalena were, their love on an ignoble plane, yet they were mutually faithful, and joined in death.

Interrupted by chapters eight and ten the story of Eloise advanced to a 'conclusion' abruptly revealing Wolfstein as her brother, Ginotti as her seducer under the name of Nempere. Eloise, though the mother of an illegitimate child, remained 'pure'. In 1891 there was to be a storm of outraged protest over Hardy's use of 'pure' for his Tess; in 1811 Shelley's daring went unnoticed, so small was his public. The unity of the novel depended upon this purity, upon the contrast between pure and spurious love; the love of Wolfstein and Megalena was spurious as was the love of Nempere and Eloise, but the love of Fitzeustace and Eloise was 'pure'.

The great flaw in the character of Ginotti was his rejection of love, his exclusion of it from his life; this rather than his insatiable curiosity threw him to the devil. Having, as Nempere, won Eloise by a pretence of love, he lightly gave her, in payment of a gambling debt, to the colourless Englishman Mountfort, as artificial a character as inexperience could create. Nempere designated her 'a beautiful girl of easy virtue', whereas the author saw her as 'injured innocence'; the Chevalier Mountfort, quickly sharing his view, addressed her as 'suffering angel'. She responded by calling him 'generous benefactor'. Though habitually 'licentious', the Chevalier did not make love to her, serving only to give her refuge in his 'cottage ornée', to introduce her to Fitzeustace, his poet-friend so much in love with love that he had never found 'a congenial female', and to fight a duel with Nempere.

Eloise's story plays variations on the theme of love: filial love for her dying mother, trusting love for her seducer, true love for her soulmate. It began as novels of seduction ordinarily ended, with the 'poor outcast wanderer', her heart torn by the 'vice and unkindness of the world', returning on a 'dark, autumnal, and gloomy' night to her childhood home. Timidly she knocked at the door which, contrary to a reader's expectations, opened, 'and an instant's space beheld her in the arms of a beloved sister'. From this hospitable welcome to the Château St. Irvyne the story of the preceding five years is developed in flashbacks, ending discrepantly and disconcertingly with Eloise embarking for England (she had been orphaned in Switzerland), married to Fitzeustace, enjoying 'that happiness, which love and innocence alone can give'. In his final flourish the young author forgot his intention of restoring his heroine to her home and family without the degradation of the marriage ceremony.

Fitzeustace, like Shelley, was a firm anti-matrimonialist. An offer of marriage would have been an insult to Eloise's intelligence. Living with Mountfort and Eloise in a Swiss valley perfumed with rose and jasmine, Fitzeustace had at last found idyllic love. When he declared his love, Eloise (who was obviously pregnant) asked: 'Know you not that I have been another's?' To this he responded that as he would have her free from prejudice against a free union, so he would be free from prejudice against the victim of a libertine. Her soul remained 'uncontaminated by the frailty of the body in which it is enshrined'. Hence he could gaze upon her child with delight and 'the affection of a father'. The union of Fitzeustace and Eloise, its joys enhanced by 'mental enjoyment', was not *pleasure*, but *happiness*. The even tenor of their life was interrupted by his father's summoning him to England. To take her with him— and he could not endure separation—marriage was inescapable. Marriage was 'an human institution, and incapable of furnishing that bond of union by which alone can intellect be conjoined; I regard it as but a chain, which, although it keeps the body bound, still leaves the soul unfettered; it is not so with love'. Still to lovers like themselves it would be 'harmless'; they would only be 'yielding to the prejudices of the world . . . and procuring moral expediency, at a slight sacrifice of what we conceive to be right'. Harriet would have been wise to read this back to Shelley in the late spring and summer of 1811 when he talked of their union without benefit of clergy.

As a basis for intimate discussion with Harriet nothing could have served Shelley better. By their suspicious attitude toward their son, by their anxious protection of their daughters from him, his parents unconsciously fostered close intimacy with Harriet. To instruct others in the truths which seemed self-evident to him was as necessary to Shelley as breathing. In Harriet he found a faithful disciple, sharing his vital and excited interest in matters of the world, in political and social justice, in the problem of wealth and poverty; and beyond the concrete problems, those of a philosophical nature: good and evil, the bases of religion with its concomitant danger of superstition. At first he frightened Harriet as he had his cousin, but Harriet Westbrook was made of sterner stuff than Harriet Grove. She was also already more deeply attached to him.

Until Shelley argued with her she had not known of the evils of organized religion; now she learned that there were twenty thousand clergymen supported by the government, out of the pockets of those who went to church and those who did not go; those who belonged to the Established Church and those who were of other sects or religions or of none. Harriet had not known that dissenters, Catholics, and Unitarians, along with freethinkers and atheists, suffered political disabilities; they could not be members of Parliament, nor could they attend Oxford or Cambridge. The process by which Shelley enlightened her and converted her to freethinking is best told by herself, in a letter written in March 1812 to Elizabeth Hitchener:

You may conceive with what horror I first heard that Percy was an Atheist; at least, so it was given out at *Clapham*. At first I did not comprehend the meaning of the word; therefore, when it was explained I was truly petrified. I wondered how he could live a moment professing such principles and solemnly declared that he should never change mine. I little thought of the rectitude of these principles; and when I wrote to him I used to try to shake them, making sure he was in the wrong, & that myself were right; yet I would listen to none of his arguments, so afraid I was that he should shake my belief. At the same time I believed in eternal punishment, and was dreadfully afraid of his supreme Majesty the Devil: I thought I should see Him if I listened to his arguments. I often dreamed of Him, and felt such terror when I heard His name mentioned: this was the effects of a bad education; and living with *Methodists*. Now, however, this is entirely done away with, & my soul is no longer shackled with such idle fears.[10]

Here is a clear picture of a 'prejudiced' schoolgirl, her mind entrenched in the orthodoxy of home and school, filling letters with asseverations of faith. She would listen to none of his arguments: *would* not listen; the habitual preciseness of her grammar indicates that she meant exactly what she said, that she was *unwilling* to listen. Shelley overcame her reluctance; he persuaded her that an atheist did not have horns and a cloven hoof; that an atheist might be a better man than a church member. He showed her that one's religious beliefs were only mental clothing, put on at birth by parents, the style shaped by environment; for what made any one a Mohammedan or a Buddhist or a Christian but the accident of birth? Man's behaviour, not the creed he mumbled in church, made him virtuous.

Absorbing as the proselytizing of Harriet was, Shelley had other irons in the fire. At Oxford he had become involved in close friendship with a fellow student who had preceded him at University College by a few months without, apparently, making friends. He succumbed at once to the fascination of Shelley, drawn to him by a magnetic force he neither could nor wished to resist, a force that operated upon him during his long life, and established his immortality. Though Thomas Jefferson Hogg later wrote many essays, and competent articles for the *Encyclopædia Britannica*, and though he published one novel (in 1812), and a travel book, he is immortalized only by his *Life of Shelley*.

Shelley was influenced by him at Oxford, and partly detached by him from Eton friends. Hogg had not been at Eton. He came from Stockton-on-Tees, south of Durham, and was destined for the law, the established profession of his family. He had taken delight in arguing Shelley into his own atheistical conclusions. Among their joint pranks had been the publication in November 1810 of a small volume of verse, mostly worthless, with here and there a melody foreshadowing golden phrases of Shelley's later lyrics. The *Posthumous Fragments of Margaret Nicholson* did not, as they hoped, 'sell like hot cakes' in spite of the impropriety of two of its poems. The improprieties may possibly have been Hogg's contributions; Shelley said at the time that part of one poem was written by 'a friend's mistress'; he expunged that poem from the copy sent to his mother. There is no record of Harriet's receipt of a copy.

The supposedly dead Margaret Nicholson was alive in Bedlam, a mad washerwoman who years before had attempted to stab the King, George III. There are some felicities of phrase, some competent heroic couplets; there are Shelleyan diatribes against war, praises of peace, love, and concord, and the dream of freedom from oppression:

> Kings are but dust—the last eventful day
> Will level all and make them lose their sway;
> Will dash the sceptre from the Monarch's hand
> And from the warrior's grasp wrest the ensanguined brand.

Such sentiments helped the sale no more than the calculated passion of the *Fragment,* an epithalamium for Francis Ravaillac and Charlotte Corday (who did not happen to be contemporaries). There was also a love lament, too specific to be a reference to Harriet Grove with whom Shelley had certainly not enjoyed 'passion's wildest ecstacy'. By the time he entered into correspondence with Harriet Westbrook this volume of verse was no longer important to him. Into a pamphlet, aided and abetted by Hogg, he was putting the summation of all the arguments he had used in his letters to Harriet, and in the anonymous or pseudonymous letters with which he bombarded clergymen.

On the 9th of February 1811 there was advertised in the *Oxford Herald* as speedily to be published, *The Necessity of Atheism.* On the 13th an advance copy was sent to a London friend, Edward Fergus Graham, who was to 'cut out the title page, and advertise it in eight famous papers'—an order soon rescinded. The author's name was not on the title-page. The laws of blasphemous libel were in operation; with all his willingness to flout authority Shelley was never ready to risk prosecution when he could avoid it by anonymity. He sent the pamphlet to 'all the Bishops'; its future high value as a rare item did not save it from the episcopal wastebaskets. Jacob Wood, Master of St. John's, Cambridge, kept his copy—St. John's had a reputation for liberality of thought; he kept it along with a medley assortment, which in one volume he presented to the college in 1839, carefully writing a table of contents on the fly-leaf. Of the eighteen items he commented on only the final one, a *Parish Priests' Manual*, of which he wrote: 'From the Author. This admirable little tract was sent me from the unknown author by the Revd. H. H. Norris of Hackney. J. W.'[11]

The first item in the volume is indexed on the fly-leaf as ' 1. Atheism necessary'; there it remained until ferreted out over a century later, to be sumptuously bound and exhibited in a glass case. Shelley would have preferred it to have been worn to shreds in students' hands. It had not impressed the Master of St. John's as 'admirable' or as dangerous; it was merely one of the miscellaneous pamphlets thrust upon him between 1792 and 1828.

Having only just read *St. Irvyne* which concluded with an affirmation of belief in God (Ginotti in vain struggle to save himself from the Devil recanting his disbelief), Harriet would have been astonished at its author's now appearing in print as an atheist, had he not prepared her, in letter and in conversation, marshalling the arguments of *The Necessity of Atheism* presented to the public as if it were a Euclidean hypothesis proceeding logically to its *Q.E.D.* She was not shocked by it nor did she mark her copy as Shelley's father did his, 'Impious!'[12] She was converted to the views his father considered both false and dangerous. Mr. Shelley felt that his son's heresy stemmed from his close association with Hogg. Without doubt the acceleration of Shelley's scepticism was fostered by Hogg, who was part author of the pamphlet. So Hogg informed his parents, and Shelley his father, to whom on the 29th of March he wrote:

You well know that a train of reasoning and not any great profligacy has induced me to disbelieve the scriptures:—this train myself and my friend pursued. We found to our surprise that (strange as it may appear) the proofs of an existing Deity were as far as we had observed defective.

We . . . embodied our doubts on the subject and arranged them methodically in the form of 'The Necessity of Atheism', thinking thereby to obtain a satisfactory or unsatisfactory answer from men who had made Divinity the study of their lives.

The foreword, called 'Advertisement', ran:

As a love of Truth is the only motive which actuates the Author of this little tract, he earnestly entreats that those of his readers who may discover any deficiency in his reasoning, or may be in possession of proofs which his mind could never obtain, would offer them, together with their objections to the Public, as briefly, as methodically, as plainly as he has taken the liberty of doing.

Thro' deficiency of proof,

AN ATHEIST.

The use of the singular, 'author', means one or both of two things: that Shelley was prepared to take full responsibility, and that Hogg with his characteristic cynicism was not interested in circulating the pamphlet. Hogg was never a crusader; Shelley passionately was.

The pamphlet was brief, its argument threefold: there are three bases for belief in a creative deity, the senses, reason, and the testimony of others. For the few who have had direct revelation, who have seen God, belief rests upon the evidence of their senses. Reason finds it more credible that the Universe has always existed than that it was created; the generative process, which is incomprehensible, is even more incomprehensible if attributed to Deity. The testimony of others may be contrary to reason and hence not credible. It is easier to believe in a Universe that had existed from all eternity than to believe in a Being capable of making it. To consider the generative power as an 'eternal, omniscient, Almighty Being' obscures the issue.

There are, then, no certain proofs; hence belief is 'a passion of the mind, and no degree of criminality can be attached to disbelief'. Nor can society be harmed by the admission of the deficiency of proof:

Truth has always been found to promote the best interests of mankind . . . [*sic*]. Every reflecting mind must allow that there is no proof of the existence of a Deity.

Shelley spread copies invitingly in the window of a local bookshop, where it was quickly spotted by a passing Fellow. Outraged by its title and contents, he insisted, without giving the bookseller time to peruse more than a few shocking passages, that there be an immediate bonfire. Though he salvaged one copy the bookseller was not fortunate enough to live until that one copy was worth his entire stock-in-trade. The authorities of Shelley's college could not overlook such flaunting of attack upon orthodox belief, belief to which all students subscribed upon entering their names at their colleges, signing at that time the thirty-nine articles of the Church of England.

As Shelley had openly and personally arranged the display in the window and on the counters of the shop, he was summoned before the Master and Fellows of University College. Refusing to answer the questions put to him, refusing to disavow authorship or to retract the views expressed, he was expelled. Hogg, summoned for questioning, readily admitted implication, and was also expelled. Rather relishing the excitement, the two young men set off next day in the London coach, settling down in lodgings to await their fathers' displeasure. Their rooms were on a narrow street running from Oxford Street toward Piccadilly. Its attractions were two: a gay wallpaper of vines and ripe grapes, and the name Poland Street. Shelley had read with enthusiasm Mrs. Porter's novel *Thaddeus of Warsaw*, his heart rejoicing when he read on the first page that the hero was the grandson of Sobieski, the 'first Polish nobleman who granted freedom to his peasants'. There was another attraction for Shelley which he did not mention to Hogg: it was within easy distance of Harriet Westbrook's father's house in Chapel Street. As yet Hogg had heard nothing of Harriet.

Parental wrath broke. Shelley's father, forewarned by Stockdale's report of Hogg's detrimental influence on the writings Shelley was asking Stockdale to publish, was none the less unprepared for anything so serious as expulsion. Hogg's father, expecting less for his son than the Parliamentary career planned for Shelley, was less outraged; philosophically, though sadly, he accepted the situation; his son had forfeited his right to a university education and would have to study law without it. The fathers agreed upon the necessity of separating the two young men, and the desirability of keeping them away from the younger members of their families, lest they corrupt them with radical ideas. Mrs. Hogg wrote strongly admonitory letters to her son, as did their clergyman. But the Hoggs did not cry aloud to the world their son's misdemeanour as Timothy Shelley did his son's. No one within the sound of *his* voice could be unaware of the pamphlet, the expulsion, the ingratitude of a pampered son. He rushed up to London to talk his son into a better frame of mind.

He was not successful. How much of these stormy interviews, how truthfully reported, Harriet heard can only be surmised, or how great the strain upon her sympathy as she realized that Shelley was defying his father. He convinced her that he was in the right, his father a pig-headed man unable to follow a logical argument. Shelley had no intention of taking his father's advice, even before he knew what it was; he did not alter when he did know. He would *not* go to Field Place, study with a tutor, and return to Oxford, apologizing for his conduct; he would *not* make a tour of the continent. He refused flatly to dissociate himself from Hogg, though both fathers deprecated the young men's effect upon each other. Parents might keep them apart, but they intended to correspond.

As in the winter holidays, father and son were involved in bitter argument, each certain that he was supremely reasonable, the other absurdly obstinate. Mr. Shelley pressed his point: as the intricacies of a watch postulate a skilled watchmaker, so the intricacies of the universe postulated a skilled universe-maker; God as the great Artificer was a reasonable man's solution to the puzzle of the world. His son, starting also with Reason, took a divergent path: what proof was there that the world had been *made*? why could it not have *evolved*? why could it not have been always in existence? Why could not his father, if he were so sure of his theory, *prove* it? He irked his father, being better read, more nimble in argument, more resilient, and equally obstinate, until Mr. Shelley retreated to Field Place, more baffled than ever; in despair he turned over the handling of his rebellious son to his solicitor, William Whitton, a dry man with little sympathy for impetuous, idealistic youth.

At the end of three weeks Hogg obediently departed, leaving Shelley alone, unable or unwilling to come to terms with his father. Even when he offered his father terms that were not impossible, he offered them as demands, and in such a manner that his father instinctively refused; the contrite apology he demanded he could not obtain. To his chagrin, solitude and absence from Hogg produced no change.

Solitude was both necessary to Shelley and abhorrent to him. He needed it for reflection, for the formulation of the ideas that crowded his mind, and for their expression in forceful verse and prose. He needed an audience and found one in Harriet West-brook. He played with the plan of becoming a surgeon like his cousin John Grove, and attended lectures at St. Bartholomew's with Charles Grove, having firmly rejected the law, the church, the army, the navy. The more his father urged him to settle upon a profession, the less inclined he felt to undertake a way of life not attractive to him. He was, as he reminded himself, his friends, his acquaintances, his father and grandfather, heir to six thousand pounds a year. He expected to be provided for. Until provision should be made for him he was adrift in London, dependent upon a kind-hearted uncle (Captain Pilfold of Cuckfield), and the small sums his sisters spared from their pocket money, sent him through Harriet Westbrook, who received them from Hellen. One wonders if they were ever augmented surreptitiously by Eliza Westbrook, who now came under Shelley's spell. Scarcely had Hogg left London on his way to a law office in York, than Shelley sent for Eliza and Harriet—he was ill, and they came to see him on the 18th of April. Boastfully he wrote Hogg of this visit, and of his going to Chapel Street, and to Harriet's school, walking with her, he said, for two hours on Clapham Common. Hogg was now to hear much of Eliza and Harriet.

Mr. Westbrook's purpose in keeping his daughter in school beyond the ordinary leaving age might well have been to protect her from the gaze of the beaux who rode in Hyde Park, so close to Chapel Street. A very different young man now walked with her on the Common, along the Nightingale Walk shaded by trees, a tall, handsome young man with thick curling hair, who in his eager talk stooped until his head was almost level with hers; an elegantly dressed young man who wore his silk pantaloons, his fine waistcoats carelessly—from November to March Shelley had run up a heavy tailor's bill at Oxford. It was bewildering to listen to his impetuous discourse. Vitally interested in ideas, he was vitally interesting as he expounded them. It was impossible for her to resist his charm—his father, well aware of it, soon ceased to deal directly with him, turning him over to his impervious lawyer.

Many years later Mary Shelley wrote:

I do not believe that his being was regulated by the same laws that govern the existence of us common mortals—nor did any one think so who ever knew him.[13]

Fascinated herself, Eliza did not shield Harriet from the sunshine of Shelley's presence. If her thoughts strayed beyond friendship, she can scarcely be blamed; they were an attractive pair, and the magic of youth, of spring, of emergent love stilled misgivings.

Of moderate height, Harriet was exquisitely formed. In his old age Hogg recalled her vividly as she was the following September:

I also saw—and for the first time—his lovely bride, bright as the morning—as the morning of that bright day on which we first met; bright, blooming, radiant with youth, health, and beauty.[14]

In his novel, *The Memoirs of Prince Alexy Haimatoff*, written the next year in a period of separation and estrangement, Hogg described Harriet repeatedly as each of the successive loves of Alexy. In his novel *Nightmare Abbey*, written in 1818, Thomas Love Peacock, who was in close association with Shelley and Harriet from 1813 on, pictured Harriet in Marionetta who

knew nothing of the world and society beyond the sphere of her own experience. Her life was all music and sunshine, and she wondered what any one could complain of in such a pleasant state of things. She loved Scythrop [Shelley], she hardly knew why.

Of Harriet herself Peacock gave the clearest existent portrait:

I remember her well. . . . She had a good figure, light, active and graceful. Her features were regular and well-proportioned. Her hair was light brown, and dressed with taste and simplicity. In her dress she was truly *simplex munditiis*. Her complexion was beautifully transparent; the tint of the blush rose shining through the lily. The tone of her voice was pleasant; her speech the essence of frankness and cordiality; her spirits always cheerful; her laughter spontaneous, hearty and joyous. She was well educated. She read agreeably and intelligently. She wrote only letters, but she wrote them well. Her manners were good; and her whole aspect and demeanour such manifest emanations of pure and truthful nature, that to be once in her company was to know her thoroughly. She was fond of her husband, and accommodated herself in every way to his tastes. If they mixed in society, she adorned it; if they lived in retirement, she was satisfied; if they travelled, she enjoyed the change of scene.[15]

Only in added maturity did she, when Peacock knew her, differ from the girl whose company Shelley so often sought in the spring of 1811. Eliza did not contrive their meetings; she did not prevent them. By her coy hints she came nearer to discouraging than encouraging Shelley. Later when he blamed her for having manœuvred the match, he was only partly right. As Eliza watched that spring she saw an enchanting young man aflame with more than the radical ideas he was expounding to Harriet. He was too young, he was at odds with his father, he was neither a student nor a man of the world; he had no private fortune, no income, his future dependent upon two sturdy lives, his father's and his grandfather's. From one point of view he was a poor match for the beautiful daughter of a well-to-do man. Yet he might make up his quarrel with his father and with his university, complete his education, enter Parliament, and in time inherit title and fortune—and Harriet might be Lady Shelley. Eliza willingly helped romance; her help was hardly needed.

It was spring—and spring in London with its pearly mists, its blossoming parks, the ethereal light that illumines the vistas at the ends of its narrower streets, is itself enchantment. Spring and propinquity were heady wine. Unlike today's young people Shelley and Harriet were seldom alone; with the reserve of their times the magic of touch was not added to that of sight and sound. There were for schoolgirls no provocative perfumes, no alluring cosmetics. They were not needed. It was pleasure to behold each other, to catch the quick response to every utterance, as they slipped unawares into love. Here were two attractive teenagers, drawn together by natural emotional need, by Harriet's admiration of him, by his of her and her beauty, by his need of her as audience, as disciple, as woman. Harriet took first the place of his sister Elizabeth, then that he had thought to fill with his cousin Harriet.

Until he went to Field Place in the middle of May, he was constantly in Eliza's company, spending, as he wrote to Hogg on the 8th of May, most of his time at Chapel Street, seeing Harriet whenever she came, visiting her at school whenever he could. With Eliza he went to church, taking the sacrament which he found 'soothing' in spite of his atheism. At the West-brooks' he had facilities for study and for writing, and a willing audience in Eliza whose education in freethinking he had undertaken, though with less ardour than that of Harriet whose mind was keener, her receptivity toward his ideas flattering.

Shelley's intellectual pursuits and excitements must be kept in mind in any interpretation of their relationship. For a young man to instruct the girl he was courting (Shelley did not at first realize that he was courting) was not unusual in the day of limited education for girls. In New England a few years earlier a theological student had in correspondence with his fiancée taken her through Euclid, proposition by proposition (the letters[16] still exist), and they married and lived happily. Shelley visualized Harriet as assistant in his schemes for the improvement of a troubled war-torn world, for the establishment of peace, the abolition of war and tyranny. Inasmuch as his ideas were anathema to his parents, his sister, his cousin, he found it soothing to be treated with respect. Eliza, though prejudiced in favour of orthodoxy, conceded that he *might* be right; Harriet's assent was unconditional.

There is a legend that Harriet dropped at school one of Shelley's letters which an instructress promptly read. Its impiety scorched the hand that held it and nearly blinded the eye that (one can imagine with what avidity) perused it. To conventional schoolmistresses a virulent case of small-pox would have seemed less dangerous than a touch of atheism. On the 25th of April Shelley reported to Hogg that he had just returned from visiting Harriet at Clapham where

They will not speak to her; her schoolfellows will not even reply to her questions; she is called an *abandoned* wretch, and universally hated, which she remunerates with the calmest contempt. My third

Clapham Common, 1810

sister, Hellen, is the only exception. She, in spite of *infamy*, will speak to Miss Westbrook, because she cannot see how she has done wrong.

Hellen's support of Harriet aroused his hope of converting her; he declared her a

dear little girl; she would be a divine little scion of infidelity, if I could get hold of her. I think my lessons here must have taken effect.

Why could he not 'get hold of her'? Had his father asked the schoolmistress to keep him from Hellen? Later on he wrote to Hellen at Field Place, sending the letters under cover to a gardener whom he asked to place them in a certain tree for her to find; the gardener did not comply with his request.

If Shelley was not allowed to see Hellen at school, would he have been allowed to see Harriet, equally under the school's care and rule—especially if a teacher had read one of his letters? Many years later a schoolmate 'remembered' that Harriet had been expelled, which seems untrue in view of the fact that she was scheduled to return in the autumn of 1811. It seems more probable that Shelley had not been prevented from seeing Hellen, but that an eleven-year-old sister did not attract him with the same force as the fifteen-year-old school beauty to whom he was expounding his cherished views, his ardent plans. Extraordinary these were, more than a century ahead of his time. His friendship with Harriet was not extraordinary, merely the interest of boy and girl ripening imperceptibly into love, the only compulsion a natural emotional and physical urge. Because it was not a sudden seizure at first sight, because she was, however beautiful, not the fairy princess of a boy's dreams, he did not at first recognize it as love. In *St. Irvyne* he had pictured just such a love developing from propinquity and a community of interests.

Eliza had also read *St. Irvyne*.

CHAPTER II

A Marriage is made

. . . when the power of imparting joy
Is equal to the will, the human soul
Requires no other heaven.
Queen Mab

T HERE had been a month of friendly meetings and com-
munications before in mid-May Shelley went to Field
Place, where he was bored. His mother, though outwardly sympathetic, was unwilling to give ear to her errant
son; she restricted conversation to trivialities and the weather.
Elizabeth was convalescent from scarlet fever, and her brother
did not endear himself to anyone by his sharp criticism of
'these country physicians'. Reading to Elizabeth, writing
lengthy letters to Hogg and to the Misses Westbrook, writing
verses and metaphysical essays filled his days.

Somehow his father got possession of a letter from Eliza
Westbrook which concluded:

You will not take any notice to your sister, Mary, or indeed to any
of your family, of your intimacy with us; for particular reasons
which I will explain to you when next I have the pleasure of seeing
you.

The letter had opened with acknowledgment of a letter from
Shelley:

I am obliged to you for your proposition in regard to Harriet, but
I am in hopes that she will leave school for good—there has been
another misunderstanding between the friends at Clapham, which
has rendered the situation of my sister so completely uncomfortable
my Father has now determined upon her not returning there again;
he talks of wholly retiring into the country, but not to any distant
part. It is so much my wish to leave this busy scene that I shall do
all in in my power to expedite his plan.[1]

Eliza did not succeed in expediting that plan for several years, but she must have succeeded in alarming Mr. Shelley, who could not confront his son with his discovery of that intimacy unless he admitted to having intercepted or found and *read* without permission a private letter.

Until he went to Wales in mid-July Shelley was in and out of London, a four-hour journey from Horsham by stage-coach, thirty-five miles over an excellent road. From Chapel Street some time in May, while Eliza at his instigation was reading Voltaire's *Dictionnaire philosophique*, he wrote a not insignificant letter to Hogg who regarded the allowance of two hundred pounds a year which Shelley had wrested from his father as niggardly. Shelley called Hogg a 'grandee' for putting six hundred as the proper figure. Hogg's prospects were far less than Shelley's; why should his wants be far more? Shelley took a circuitous path to reach a subject very much in his mind at the moment: did this figure represent Hogg's needs at some time in future for the cherishing of a loved one 'in the indissoluble, sacred union of Love'? Twenty-four lines of not very successful love verses followed, suggested less by Hogg's hypothetical involvement than by Shelley's own dreams and the state of his emotions. By this devious route he arrived at the centre of his thoughts and delivered a diatribe against marriage. This was not misogyny; on the contrary his anti-matrimonialism was based upon deep admiration for all the women in his young life, from his mother to Harriet. It was the *ceremony* and the conditions of marriage he deplored; the law required that the ceremony be under religious sanction, and a wife became the chattel of her husband. Pretending that the union of which he was thinking was Hogg's, he burst into invective:

A kind of ineffable, sickening disgust seized my mind when I think of this most despotic, most unrequired fetter which prejudice has forged. . . . Yes! This is the fruit of superstition.[2]

Eliza's thoughts were not the only ones to stray: Shelley's were surely concerned with his possible union with Harriet, not the mythical union of Hogg with Elizabeth Shelley, for whom, unseen, he, at Shelley's instigation, had developed a passion.

D

Elizabeth chose to remain unseen, returning to him unopened two long passionate letters (which he preserved all his life).[3]

On the next day Shelley wrote again to Hogg, reporting that he had had a letter from 'Miss Westbrook the elder':

The younger is in prison [i.e. in school]; there is something in her more noble, yet not so cultivated as the elder—a larger diamond, yet not so highly polished.

The detractors of Eliza, taking their cue from Hogg and from Shelley in his final reaction against her, overlook this tribute to her as a cultivated person and remember only his strictures against her as 'affected', as simpering of '*l'amour*'. In the summer of 1811 Shelley's feeling for her was friendly and warm.

He was at this time under the influence of a highly romantic love story which he read in June and re-read in July: Sydney Owenson's *The Missionary*, a lush tale he admired greatly; he soon put it into Harriet's hands. It was one of those popular exotic tales which gave the illusion of being instructive; here one learned a little of the history of Portugal, and much about the beauties of the Vale of Cashmire; about the strange customs of the Orient, and about Brahminism, interwoven with the seductive loveliness of veiled maidens and the pride of princes on slender Arabian horses. Love at first sight, with insurmountable barriers between the lovers, mystery, dangers, were all in the remote past; the wild tale acquired respectability through the introduction of historical facts, a little learning gleaned from authoritative sources carefully footnoted. Though Shelley disparaged the novel to Miss Hitchener (for whom he played the part of a mature adult), he was voluble in its praise to Hogg, using it to afford release from the emotion surging within him. Luxima, the heroine, was 'divine', Luxima was 'an angel', with Luxima he was enamoured; this applied also to Harriet whose beauty was no less striking and who was angelically enduring contumely from her schoolmates through her loyalty to him. Save for her dark tresses, Luxima was not unlike Harriet: attractive, virginal, with a perfect figure; modest, sensitive, with a bewitching sadness, a blushing and eloquent countenance:

The changing tints of her complexion resembled the dissolving tints of an iris.

Luxima moved with such grace that she seemed to glide like a disembodied spirit; graceful Harriet was, but she could not match Luxima, clad in white draperies, gliding in and out of grottoes. Harriet did not, like Luxima, offer the titillation of the forbidden and the alien. Luxima was a Brahmin priestess; Hilarion who loved her was a Christian monk. The situation bore no resemblance to that of Harriet and Shelley, yet in Luxima Shelley could see Harriet, also pure, gentle, and kind as well as beautiful. She was not an alluring Oriental, only a charming English girl in whose glance love was reflected as it was now in his. Praise of Luxima, as he uttered the wish that she were in actual existence, served as a safety valve for his love of Harriet which he was not ready to admit to Hogg.

For he was torn between his preoccupation with Harriet and his loyalty to Hogg, to whom he had sworn eternal affection as first in his heart. Shelley impulsively committed himself to his friends, always at the moment of correspondence eager to express unalloyed devotion. He liked to believe that Hogg was first in his affection; even more, he liked Hogg to believe this. He delayed admission of the true state of his emotions (if, indeed, he was fully aware of them) lest Hogg think him disloyal. In chronicling his days he wrote confusingly.

In his letter to Hogg on the 21st June he said that he had been invited by Mr. Westbrook to Aberystwyth, adding incongruously that he would stay a week in London with Mr. Westbrook and then join Hogg in York. Shortly thereafter he informed another friend that he was about to go to Wales 'where I purpose to spend the summer'; he would 'pedestrianize' in order to observe 'the manners and disposition of the peasantry'—it was a journey of over two hundred miles. A day or two later he wrote Hogg that he would see him in York on his way to Wales, where, however, he might not go.

By the middle of July he was in Wales, at Cwm Elan, in Radnorshire, the magnificent ten-thousand-acre estate of his cousin Thomas Grove: hills and dales, brooks and cataracts and woods, natural beauties with which he was not in tune.

He was intent upon meeting with the Westbrooks on their way to Aberystwyth. Meanwhile he settled down to the reading of a novel sent him by Harriet, *Adeline Mowbray*, by Mrs. Opie.

Here is proof that before he left for Wales he had broached the subject of love to Harriet. With Hogg he had debated the question of marriage; Harriet's pressing him to read Mrs. Opie's novel was her answer to his arguments against the marriage ceremony as evil compared to the virtue of a free and 'pure' union. His disclaimer to Hogg that 'if I know anything about love, I am not in love', was followed by the wish that such images as Luxima in *The Missionary* could be embodied.

Adeline Mowbray was highly pertinent. Fortunately neither Harriet nor Shelley was aware that it was a *roman à clef* satirizing the anti-matrimonialism of Mary Wollstonecraft and William Godwin.[4] The hero's name, Glenmurray, kept the initial, but Shelley did not recognize in him Godwin who was already the object of his veneration.

Mrs. Opie showed that whereas a free union might be abstractly more virtuous than marriage under the existent laws, it was not practicable in an imperfect society, which was what Godwin himself had declared in the preface to his novel *Fleetwood*. Mrs. Opie's hero, like Godwin and like Shelley, believed the marriage ceremony, by which a woman lost all rights as an individual, was insulting. A husband could control his wife's property and her earnings. Divorce, difficult for a man, was almost impossible for a woman; absolute divorce permitting remarriage could not be granted by the House of Lords except when approved by the Ecclesiastical Court; an average of only two such divorces a year had been granted over a period of thirty years. These were the facts that Shelley put before Harriet. She countered by sending him *Adeline Mowbray*, the sad tale of a young woman who had been converted to anti-matrimonialism.

It was original in that the heroine was seduced not by a villain, but by a book in which the virtuous author expounded the same views Harriet had been hearing from Shelley. It followed the stock pattern of tales of seduction, the heroine dying as her mother smoothed her pillow and promised to provide for the child. It varied from the pattern in that the child was not illegitimate, the lover was faithful until death, and the refusal to go through a marriage ceremony was Adeline's. She had fallen in love with Glenmurray through reading his anti-matrimonial book before meeting him and evoking his love. Aware of the difficulties for her, Glenmurray would have compromised with his principles and married her, but she would not. Pregnant, she suffered on seeing a small boy in a schoolyard shunned as a bastard; her vivid mind projected a scene in the future when her child would be shunned. Now she asked for marriage and Glenmurray joyfully assented, but agitation brought about a miscarriage; her resolution revived with her health, and she remained firm in refusal as Glenmurray declined in health and died.

She supported herself by a school, successful until slander closed it—to the world she had not been 'pure', but a mistress. She married a kind friend, and was for a time secure and happy; after the birth of a daughter her husband changed toward her, ill-treating her and reproaching her for her illicit connection with Glenmurray. Surreptitiously she produced moral books for children (Mary Wollstonecraft had written such tales), but the law did not protect her right to her earnings. After many vicissitudes she died, regretting

the hour when, with the hasty and immature judgment of eighteen . . . I dared to act contrary to the experience of age, and become in the eyes of the world an example of vice, when I believed myself the champion of virtue.

If Harriet did not underscore this passage she showed restraint. In his letters Hogg had answered Shelley's arguments and diatribes with stress upon the legal difficulties for an unmarried woman and her children. Mrs. Opie made clear all Adelaide's embarrassments, including the financial disadvantage of having no claim as a widow. As a widow Adeline would have been provided for; she need not have made her unfortunate marriage; she would not have been taunted; she would not have lost her means of subsistence; she would have been entitled to her earnings. Her position was pitiable, her early death inevitable. It was a question of practicality; the independence of women, civil marriage and permissible divorce were as yet theoretical.

Shelley had not asked Harriet to marry him; he had obviously talked of 'free union'. He had explained his principles, quoting from chapter vi of the eighth book of Godwin's *An Enquiry Concerning Political Justice* where marriage

is law, and the worst of all laws . . . an affair of property, and the worst of all properties. . . . So long as I seek to engross one woman to myself, and to prohibit my neighbour from proving his superior desert and reaping the fruits of it, I am guilty of the most odious of all monopolies . . .

Harriet did not object to becoming the property of the man she loved; she could not imagine any one superior to him. Unlike Shelley, she separated theory and practice; she was not alarmed at a further passage:

It is absurd to expect that the inclinations and wishes of two human beings should coincide through any long period of time. To oblige them to act and to live together, is to subject them to some inevitable portion of thwarting, bickering and unhappiness. This cannot be otherwise, so long as man has failed to reach the standard of absolute perfection. The supposition that I must have a companion for life, is the result of a complication of vices. It is the dictate of cowardice, and not of fortitude. It flows from the desire of being loved and esteemed for something that is not desert.[5]

Harriet was content to be loved beyond her deserts. It might be absurd to expect all loves to last, but theirs was different—Shelley, in verses to Harriet, was repeatedly to stress that difference. They shared more than a mutual attraction.

Harriet was sympathetic to Shelley's plans for a minor Academe, philosophers thinking, talking, working for the betterment of the world. Shelley never envisioned a rose-embowered cottage (though they were to live in two, one in Keswick, one in Lynmouth); he never intended to use the fortune he would inherit save for the benefit of others. He had already established a common purse with Hogg (Hogg's at the moment was the better filled) and he was promising to open his purse to a new friend, Elizabeth Hitchener. Eliza Westbrook would live with them, and Hogg, and Miss Hitchener, and others. It was a strange courtship intellectually, yet in other aspects an ordinary one. Like Fitzeustace in *St. Irvyne*, he was interested in the soul of his future life companion, but one cannot touch soul. For all the essential purity of Shelley's ideas, the restraints he put upon himself, he was not immune to the normal eroticism of youth. Physically and mentally he was strongly attracted to the lovely girl who respected his theories. On the other hand he was revolted at the thought of a marriage ceremony.

Discussing with Harriet the evils of marriage in contrast to the virtue of free union, Shelley, like Glenmurray in Mrs. Opie's novel, was playing with fire and fanning its flames. He enjoyed its heat. He had come to Chapel Street months ago of his own volition—his sister could have sent her gift by some other messenger. When, later, Harriet was unhappy over return to school, he need not have taken the responsibility for her happiness or her future. There was always in Shelley the element of Perseus; he would rescue from poverty, from monotony, from tyranny; he played the part of benefactor to the end of his life—his last act was to rescue Leigh Hunt and his family from a hand-to-mouth existence in London and deposit them on Byron's doorstep in Italy.

Complete credence cannot be given to his two epistolary accounts of his marriage, one running concurrently with courtship in letters to Hogg, one written in October to Miss Hitchener. Yet the reluctance he reiterated was genuine; he objected violently to the marriage ceremony, and to the compulsions of marriage. He regarded a free union as purer, more exciting, and more enduring. Seduction he regarded as abhorrent; he did not use the arts of the seducer with Harriet, but the same intoxicating persuasion of the virtuous nature of free union that had been the undoing of Adeline Mowbray.

Harriet was more circumspect than Adeline; she accepted his strictures against marriage, his encomiums on free union, but she would not guide her conduct by them. Shelley's letters to Hogg reveal the progress of his suit; Hogg's to him harped on the *legal* necessity of marriage for a woman. All this would have been waste verbiage if Shelley's attentions had not become serious. A gently reared, modest young girl in 1811 did not converse in person and in letter with a young man on the subject of marriage without cause; discussion of marriage in the abstract then, as now, was likely to turn into the concrete.

In the summer Harriet and Shelley were temporarily apart. Unless the Westbrooks were to be in Aberystwyth, Cwm Elan had little to attract Shelley who seems to have been singularly uninterested in his cousin's experiments in scientific agriculture. Like other men of wealth, Thomas Grove encouraged neighbouring farmers to improve their land and their herds of sheep by modern methods. He also beautified his estate. Shelley was in no mood to enjoy the beauties of Nature, the magnificence of the cloud-encircled rocks, the waterfalls, the woods of Cwm Elan. It was, he wrote to Hogg,

divine scenery; but all very dull, stale, flat and unprofitable; indeed this place is a very great bore. I shall see the Miss Westbrooks again soon.[6]

An interesting statement, showing the tenor of his thought. The following year, again at Cwm Elan, with Harriet, he remembered his loneliness, his discontent among those who

> . . . could not in a twilight walk
> Weave an impassioned web of talk,
> Till mysteries the spirit press
> In wild yet tender awfulness,
> Then feel within our narrow sphere
> How little yet how great we are!

Harriet could, apparently, 'weave an impassioned web of talk'.

The poem, 'The Retrospect: Cwm Elan 1812', concludes with a tribute to Harriet, the companion who had made his whole life bright. His emotional pattern was already set: here he presented a picture of himself that was constantly to recur in his poetry as one who, frozen by the lack of understanding, was revived by the warmth of a new sun. Here is the germ of *Epipsychidion*. In 1812, thinking back to his dismal state before his marriage, contrasting that with the change that made him responsive to every beauty down to the least butterfly, he burst into lyric thankfulness:

How do I feel my happiness?
I cannot tell, but they may guess
Whose every gloomy feeling gone,
Friendship and passion feel alone;
Who see mortality's dull clouds
Before affection's murmur fly,
Whilst the mild glances of her eye
Pierce the thin veil of flesh that shrouds
The spirit's inmost sanctuary.

 O thou! whose virtues, latest known,
First in this heart yet claim'st a throne;
Whose downy sceptre still shall share
The gentle sway with virtue there;
Thou fair in form, and pure in mind,
Whose ardent friendship rivets fast
The flowery band our fates that bind,
Which incorruptible shall last
When duty's hard and cold control
Has thawed around the burning soul,—
The gloomiest retrospects that bind
With crowns of thorn the bleeding mind,
The prospects of most doubtful hue
That rise on Fancy's shuddering view,—
Are gilt by the reviving ray
Which thou hast flung upon my day.

If, then, it was dull, stale, flat, and unprofitable in July 1811, it would seem to have been so because he was away from Harriet. He did not remain at Cwm Elan; early in August he went in haste to London specifically to see Harriet. On the 15th she had not yet accepted what was now a proposal of marriage; as he wrote to Hogg, she was 'undecided, not with respect to me, but herself'. She was, then, neither precipitate nor impetuous.

Since April Shelley had been increasingly preoccupied with Harriet's education as a 'scion of infidelity', his assistant in the fight against bigotry; gradually he became absorbed in her as a beautiful and desirable young girl. Ten days after Hogg had left London, he had written an excited letter:

I don't know where I am, where I will be. Future, present, past, is all a mist; it seems as if I had begun existence anew, under auspices so unfavourable. Yet no! that is stupid! My poor little friend has been ill, her sister sent for me the other night. I found her on a

couch, pale; her father is civil to me, very strangely; the sister is too
civil by half. She began talking about *l'Amour*. I philosophized, and
the youngest said she had such a headache that she could not bear
conversation. Her sister then went away, and I stayed until half-
past twelve. Her father had a large party below, he invited me; I
refused. Yes! the fiend, the wretch, shall fall! Harriet will do for one
of the crushers and the eldest . . . with some taming, will do, too.
They are both very clever, and the youngest (my friend) is amiable.
Yesterday she was better, to-day her father compelled her to go to
Clapham, whither I have conducted her, and I am now returned.[7]

He was taking every opportunity to be with Harriet who, under
his tutelage, was to become a 'crusher' of superstition—religion,
not Mr. Westbrook, was 'the fiend, the wretch'. In accompanying her to school he would have ridden with her in her father's
carriage, undeterred by the over-civility of its owner and his
elder daughter which, he would have Hogg believe, made him
wary. He was not averse to arousing Hogg's admiration and
envy: he, unwelcome at home, had been privileged to stay
alone until very late with a charming girl reclining on a couch.
He did not say that Harriet reclined; he implied it. She assuredly
was not prone; the 'couch' was probably a sofa with a back-
rest, and she may have been well-covered with shawls. He was
not alone with her all evening: 'her sister went away'; she may
have returned fairly soon. Mr. Westbrook came to greet him,
and to invite him to his masculine party 'below'. In an English
house 'below' indicates the dining-room. Harriet was, then, in
the drawing-room on the first floor above that, or in a sitting-
room adjoining. Her headache did not prohibit her from listening to Shelley's brilliant talk which may indeed have flowed on
until after midnight.

Step by step from Shelley's letters, romanticizing life in
London in contrast to the dull routine of a law office in York,
Hogg was made aware of the importance of Harriet in his
friend's emotional pattern. Harriet, had she read the letters,
would have been somewhat surprised. She did not herself write
fiction, even in letters, or highly coloured truth. From her
restraint in letters written in joy and in anguish she appears far
from impetuous. Shelley's accounts of the crisis in his life in
August could have been chapters in a novel. It is natural enough

for youth (and sometimes for age) to elevate facts into drama;
and as age knows, the element of drama—comedy or tragedy—
is often close to actuality. As early as the 3rd of August, Shelley's
excitement was at the boiling point as he wrote to Hogg:

You will perhaps see me before you can answer this; perhaps not!
Heaven knows! I shall certainly come to York, but *Harriet Westbrook*
will decide whether now or in three weeks. Her father has persecuted
her in a most horrible way, by endeavouring to compel her to go
to school. She asked my advice; resistance was the answer, at the
same time that I essayed to mollify Mr. W. in vain! And in consequence of my advice *she* has thrown herself upon *my* protection.

I set off for London on Monday. How flattering a distinction!—I
am thinking of ten million things at once.

What have I said? I declare, quite *ludicrous*. I advised her to resist.
She wrote to say that resistance was useless, but that she would fly
with me, and threw herself upon my protection. We shall have £200
a year; when we find it run short, we must live, I suppose, upon love;
Gratitude and admiration all demand that I should love her *for ever*.
We shall see you at York. I will hear your arguments for matri-
monialism, by which I am now almost convinced.

. . . . .

I am thinking at once of ten million things. I shall come to live
near you . . .[8]

'Quite ludicrous' also was this attempt to present himself as
the reluctant lover whose primary devotion was to his friend
Hogg. If this letter is read without prejudice, instead of with
the determination to regard the marriage as forced upon
Shelley by Eliza's machinations and Harriet's impetuosity, it
stands as one young man's boast to another. He had drained
Hogg of sympathy over his cousin's defection; now he was
exciting envy, and he knew it. With, however, his view of
Hogg's superiority to himself and the excessive value he placed
upon their friendship, he was in a tight spot. He had continually
belittled his feeling toward Harriet which, if not love, was something uncommonly like it. Freed from persiflage, the gist of the
letter is that Harriet had asked his advice; that like any knight
errant Shelley had tilted at once with her father who did not
yield. '*She* has thrown herself upon *my* protection', was immediately corrected by, 'What have I said? I declare, quite *ludicrous*.' Telling him that resistance to her father was vain, she

supposedly said she 'would fly' with him and 'threw herself upon my protection'. '*Would* fly', not should; the distinction between the two was still valid; she was *willing* to fly, trusting to his honour, which was what the grandiose phrase of throwing oneself upon a man's protection implied in all novels. Modern usage would make Harriet's willingness a determination; there is no evidence here that the suggestion of flight came from her rather than from him. She trusted him to treat her honourably, which to any novel reader meant marriage.

More than forty-five years later, in 1857, Charles Grove, in answer to queries from Hogg, then writing his *Life of Shelley*, 'remembered' that Shelley had in 1811 written of what he termed his summons to link his fate with another, concluding, 'Hear it not, Percy, for it is a knell, which summons thee to heaven or to hell!' This is not as ominous a pronouncement as it has been regarded; he gives himself an equal chance of heaven in marriage with Harriet. Editors of the Julian Edition of Shelley, influenced by the long years of detraction of Harriet, bracket after 'link his fate with another' an unwarranted supposition: 'in his despair, it would seem, at having lost the love of his cousin, Harriet Grove'. There is nothing to suggest that Shelley was thinking of his cousin Harriet who had rejected him and accepted the suitor presented by her father. Always with Shelley, then and in years to come, old loves whose inadequacy or inconstancy froze his heart were displaced by the new love rising like the sun to thaw the ice and reawaken spring.

Shelley's mood as he left Cwm Elan, as he arrived in London, as he raised money, and prepared for elopement, was one of high excitement: 'I am thinking of ten million things at once'. He had just passed his nineteenth birthday; he was going to 'astonish' his father; he was astonishing Hogg—and himself; he was embarking upon adult life at the head of a household that he meant to be the nucleus of his Academe. In addition he was to experience the fulfilment of love with someone as docile as she was beautiful, as appreciative of him as his family was scornful. He was far from calm at this moment, his mind filled with the image of Harriet Westbrook, soon to be Harriet Shelley.

It was on a Sunday morning, the 25th of August, that Shelley, taking Charles Grove with him and keeping a hired coach standing by, waited for Harriet. She was late, and the young men amused themselves by tossing the shells of the oysters they had eaten for breakfast across the street, 'a Shelley business!' Harriet came, and the three went off in the coach to a tavern in the City of London from which the evening coach to Edinburgh would leave. There is no account of Harriet during that day; she presumably remained in their private sitting-room; Shelley emerged at least once, as, with a plausible tale of being short of cash to pay his way home, he borrowed from a friend of his father's, casually met, ten pounds which his surprised father was ruefully to repay the next day. The presence of Charles Grove gave a slight sanction and perhaps a casual air to the elopement, and tempered the embarrassment of a young girl, unchaperoned, running away like the heroine of a novel. There was no reason for trepidation; Shelley's preference for a 'free union' did not imply disrespect; indeed the suggestion had been a compliment to her as a reasonable person; it was her reasoning power (plus that of Hogg and of Mrs. Opie) which had convinced him that the time was not propitious for such virtuous procedure. Evening came, and the long journey began, two nights and two days of continuous travel, stopping only for the coach to change horses and the passengers to refresh themselves, until Edinburgh was reached.

Two months later Shelley belatedly explained his apostasy to Elizabeth Hitchener, a schoolteacher he had met the preceding June at his uncle's in Cuckfield. She lived and taught at Hurstpierpoint, the village beyond Cuckfield, where she had the reputation of being liberal-minded and clever; she was nearly thirty, approximately the same age as Eliza Westbrook, whom he had begun to instruct. He drew Miss Hitchener into correspondence, sending her books to read and discuss with him by letter, Locke and Southey among them. Their lengthy letters to each other were mixtures of philosophic speculation and fulsome phrases of mutual admiration. Shelley fell into the rôle of intimate, protesting that he would confide fully in his new friend. Yet he had not told her about Harriet; he had not informed her of his marriage, which she learned from local gossip. To still her reproaches and salve her hurt feelings, he belatedly composed an explanatory letter, shaping his narrative even more than he had in his letters to Hogg; as an apology for his having compromised with his anti-matrimonial principles he gave her an account of his meeting, succouring, and marrying one who was too young to have reached the perfection of Miss Hitchener:

I will explain however the circumstances which caused my marriage . . . [sic] these must certainly have caused much conjecture in your mind. Some time ago when my Sister was at Mrs. Fenning's school, she contracted an intimacy with Harriet.—At that period I attentively watched over my sister, designing if possible to add her to the list of the good, the disinterested, the free.—I desired therefore to investigate Harriet's character, for which purpose I called on her, requested to correspond with her designing that her advancement should keep pace with, and possibly accelerate that of my sister.[9]

This deviates from the exact truth. Hellen was not then 'intimate' with Harriet; Mary had been her friend, and Mary did not return to school after Christmas. The ostensible motive for the January visit was to convey a present from Mary; one doubts if his interest was wholly as impersonal and educational as he makes it. He next implies that the correspondence was kept alive by Harriet; there is no indication of the length and frequency of his letters to her:

The frequency of her letters became greater during my stay in Wales. . . . They contained complaints of the irrational conduct of her relations, and the misery of living where she could *love* no one. Suicide was with her a favourite theme, her total uselessness was urged as its defence. This I admitted, supposing she could *prove* her inutility and that she was powerless. Her letters became more and more gloomy, at length one assumed a tone of such despair as induced me to quit Wales precipitately.—I arrived in London. I was shocked at observing the alteration of her looks. Little did I divine its cause; she had become violently attached to *me*, & feared that I should not return her attachment . . . [sic] prejudice made the confession painful. It was impossible to avoid being much affected, I promised to unite my fate with hers. I staid in London several days, during which she recovered her spirits. I had promised at her bidding to come again to London. They endeavoured to compel her to return to a school where malice & pride embittered every hour; she wrote to me. I came to London. I proposed marriage for the reasons which I have given you, and she complied.—Blame me if thou wilt, dearest friend, for *still* thou art dearest to me. Yet pity even this error if thou blamest me. If Harriet be not at sixteen, all that you are at a more advanced age [here one can see Miss Hitchener bridle!] assist me to mould a really noble soul into all that can make its nobleness useful and lovely. Lovely it is now, or I am the weakest slave of error.

An extremely disingenuous, carefully plotted and executed *apologia*, this, written to one who had no claim to an apology.

If this were true Harriet had given her heart away to a young man who was heartwhole (in spite of any hopes cherished by Miss Hitchener). That Harriet complained of her father's keeping her in school beyond the usual age, that she reflected on suicide is true enough. Idealists, finding the cruelties of the world unendurable, inevitably reflect upon suicide. In the winter holidays Shelley, as his letters to Hogg prove, was obsessed with suicide, carrying laudanum and pistols about with him as he walked in graveyards. Before his gloomy thoughts were dispelled as the image of his faithless cousin was displaced by that of Harriet Westbrook, he had suggested joint suicide with Hogg; 'Shall we set off? Is there a future life?' Harriet's reason was not, as his had been, disappointment in love, but that she had no one to love—which meant that at school she no longer had a bosom friend, for she did have at least her sister to whom she was deeply devoted. 'Total uselessness' was not an idle phrase; Harriet believed as Shelley did that one should use one's life for some good purpose; at school she no longer fitted in. She had no outlet for her energies and her philanthropic aspirations, a seemingly valid argument for suicide, one that weighed heavily with her in the future. Now Shelley dissuaded her, showing her that she could be useful as his aide. It was an enticing prospect. That she declared her love first may or may not be true; it does not seem in character.

The letter to Miss Hitchener made changes in the sequence of events. In early August he had written to Hogg that he was setting off to London as a *result* of his advice to Harriet; that *she* would decide whether *they* would see Hogg in York very soon or in three weeks; that she had written that she 'would fly'

with him. Now he was saying that he agreed to unite his fate
with hers after his arrival. But the glaring deviation from truth
was the statement that *still* Miss Hitchener was dearest to him;
if this were truth and not the rankest flattery, Shelley was a far
queerer young man than he has ever been pictured. There is
sufficient evidence that when he wrote this adulatory epistle
he was as happy as any bridegroom with a lovely young wife.

The elopement had occurred three weeks after Shelley's
arrival from Wales. It is hard to believe that Eliza Westbrook
was uninformed; one is inclined to think that she at least
watched Harriet around the corner, and forwarded some lug-
gage—a change of clothes. Mr. Westbrook's surprise and anger
were justifiable; he had been defied, and his beautiful daughter
had run away with a man of no immediate prospects—he also
may not have had Eliza's and Harriet's faith in Shelley's honour.

In the three weeks since he came from Cwm Elan Shelley
could have withdrawn; in the long day's waiting for the Edinburgh coach either one could have turned back, or from any
stopping-place of the coach. Neither did. At Houghton, near
Durham, Shelley penned an odd letter to his father; if Harriet
read it and approved, she must have had a firm belief that
Shelley could do no wrong. Its imperiousness and condescension could only further infuriate an irate parent :

MY DEAR FATHER,
Doubtless you will be surprised at my sudden departure; you will
be more surprised at its finish; but it is little worth the while of its
inhabitants to be affected at the occurrences of this world.

I have always considered my clothes, papers, gun, etc., as my
own property.

I cannot think altho' I confess it has been hinted to me, that you
will condescend to the pitiful revenge for the uneasiness which I may
have occasioned, of detaining these. Will you direct them to Charles
Grove, Esqr., Lincoln's Inn Fields.

At present I have little time.

You will hear from me at Holyhead more fully and particularly.—
With sincerest respect, your ever affect. son,

P. B. SHELLEY[10]

He had, of course, no intention of going to Holyhead to embark
for Ireland; he had also no intention of telling his father what

he was doing. Nor did he enlighten him when, receiving no answer, he wrote again on the 30th from Edinburgh, a most dissembling letter with no mention of his having established himself in lodgings with his wife; he directed his father to communicate with him through a friend in London. Again one wonders if he showed the letter to Harriet:

MY DEAR FATHER,

I know of no one to whom I can apply with greater certainty of success when in distress than you. I must own that I am not so frugal as could be wished, but I know you are kind to forgive youthful errors, and will perhaps be good enough to enclose me a Dft. for £50. Mr. Graham will take care to forward your letter. There is not a creature in Edinburgh, 'tis as dull as London in the dog days . . . there is, however, much worth seeing; it rains now, but a friend of mine promises if it holds up to lionize me. Holyrood, Arthur's Seat, and the Castle will, of course, be objects of my attention.

If I move I shall continue to write, but as I remain here until the receipt of your answer, in consequent of having incurred a slight debt, all letters may be forwarded by Graham.

I hope Mother, Sister, and all are well; my love to them.—With great respect,

Your aff. Son,

P. B. SHELLEY[10]

When he wrote this rude letter Shelley was already married. Two weeks later when the news had reached his father, though not from him, he wrote again, not having had any response, admitting that he had

perhaps acted with impoliteness in quitting you without previous information, yet you surely will not regard this when you well know that business of importance superseded the attention due to these considerations.

He had heard that his father was displeased; he undertook to reprove him:

. . . permit me with the utmost humility to deprecate any anger on your part, perhaps also I may succeed in pointing out its inutility and inadequacy to the happiness of any one whom it may concern. . . . To distrust your own mind (the first consideration) which the duties of legislation demands to be unruffled, which the happiness of your family requires calm, which your own peace needs to be unaffected by the base passion of anger, is certainly as wrong as it is inconsistent with the Christian forbearance and forgiveness with

E

which you are so eminently adorned. The world, too, which considers marriage as so venial a failing, would think the punishment
of a father's anger infinitely disproportioned to the offence committed.[11]

His father may be forgiven for not discerning even the slightest
humility here. His son dared to upbraid him for being a Christian . . . and to take a sly delight in pointing out that even the
church did not regard marriage as a great sin . . . venial, not
cardinal. In effect he was saying, Be a man, Father! remember
you are a member of Parliament; keep cool; don't you realize
anger is bad for you, your family, your country? Why don't you
grow up and put duty first? Intransigently he closed by referring
to the sorrow of his mother and sisters deprived of the society of
son and brother, though he did add, 'forgive the vanity'. Mr.
Shelley knew his son well enough not to put the blame for this
effusion upon Harriet.

Married the two innocents had been as fast as possible—the
28th they procured the certificate and on the 29th they were
married. Not having gone to Gretna Green, where the way for
lovers was simplified, they might have been at a loss how to
circumvent the law requiring six weeks' residence for the bride,
and the three weeks' proclamation of banns in the church. They
had been advised and aided by a fellow-traveller in the coach,
a young advocate who directed them to a complacent clergyman
who would marry them at once if they first obtained a certificate
signed by two householders and an elder of the church testifying
that

the parties are free, unmarried, of legal age, not within the forbidden
Degrees, and she has resided in Edinburgh upwards of six weeks
preceding the proclamation of Banns.

It was a nice point of ethics for Harriet—either she consented
to a fabrication or waited for weeks; the waiting under the
circumstances was highly improper; the incorrect statement of
residence seemed the lesser evil.

The Rev. Joseph Robertson, faced with the very young
couple, asked no questions. One of the witnesses was the landlord of 16 George Street whose lodgings on the ground floor
they had rented; he asked as reward (doubtless he provided the

other witnesses) the privilege of washing the bride with whisky that night, and was indignantly repulsed by the bridegroom.

Shelley was confident that neither his father nor Harriet's would, when they had swallowed their anger, let them suffer from want. His method of approach to his father did not, however, induce a shower of gold. But his uncle, Captain Pilfold, swiftly sent a sum of money which would for a short time keep the wolf from the door. Bride and groom were too happy, too busy with ambitious plans to be anxious. Those plans started with Harriet's advanced studies; she was to begin Latin at once, with Greek to follow. Shelley would train her to share in the exhilarating though difficult task of liberating mankind from inherited shibboleths, from age-long injustices. He had high hopes of persuading people to *think*, to read, to discuss, to seek truth; finding it, they would assuredly act upon it. Beyond besieging with letters clergymen, members of Parliament, and editors of free-thinking journals, and the abortive attempt to circulate *The Necessity of Atheism*, he had as yet made small progress; with Harriet's aid and sympathy he would now expand his efforts.

They adopted a serious way of life, brightened by their natural gaiety and a sense of excitement. While Shelley tirelessly wrote letters, Harriet, whose French was excellent, began translating, with a view to publication, a highly regarded novel of wearisome length and, to us today, repulsive moralizing, unaware that it had already been issued in English. Mme Cottin's *Claire d'Albe* was a tale of virtue betrayed by human weakness. The young wife of an older man and their son's youthful tutor inadvertently and innocently fell in love. Meeting after a separation during which she had fallen into a decline, they sinned, and she died, in spite of the compassionate attitude of her husband. Harriet's task was only an *ad interim* occupation, an initial step toward a wider sphere of influence when they had gathered about them a congenial circle of co-workers. They were not willing to waste even the golden days of their honeymoon.

They had not had time to view the sights of Edinburgh when Hogg arrived.

CHAPTER III

You will see Hogg

You will see Hogg.—and I cannot express
His virtues,—though I know that they are great,
Because he locks, then barricades the gate
Within which they inhabit;—of his wit
And wisdom, you'll cry out when you are bit.
He is a pearl within an oyster shell,
One of the richest of the deep.
Letter to Maria Gisborne

OVERFLOWING with enthusiasm for the purposeful life, Harriet greeted Hogg warmly, seeing him through Shelley's eyes as a paragon of wisdom and wit, as a fellow idealist. Hogg had, however, been unprepared for Harriet's sweet nature, her charm—and her beauty. In his letters Shelley had spoken of her often: as a possible disciple, as 'clever', 'amiable', a 'larger diamond' than her rather 'conceited', 'affected', but 'cultivated', and 'clever' sister; as his helper in the crusade against intolerance; as his 'poor little friend' condemned by her relentless father to 'prison' (school). Only indirectly did he suggest her loveliness.

Thomas Jefferson Hogg[1]—the name had no American association—was a self-conscious young man, more sophisticated in his thinking, more provincial in his experience than Shelley. He seemed a more profound thinker than he was, stirring other men (Shelley, and later Peacock) to depths not his. Seemingly active, he was essentially indolent; seemingly cynical, he was inclined to be sentimental; self-centred, he was equally kindhearted and generous, quickly responsive to Shelley's appeals for sympathy and for funds. With Shelley he accepted Godwin's theory of common property; it was currently Shelley's purse that was empty. Under compulsion to come at Shelley's bid-

ding, to love where he loved, Hogg had only a limited understanding of him; he neither shared nor sympathized with his
idealism; he had no belief in man's inherent goodness, or in his
future perfectibility. He found Shelley's ardour for social, political, and moral reform amusing. In discussion he egged him
on, liking to be amused.

Except for a vaguely remembered 'Mary who died', his
heart had had little experience beyond the curious Shelley-
induced passion for the unseen Elizabeth Shelley, the physical
image of her brother. Primarily Hogg's heart was captivated by
Shelley; his emotional cycle evolved around Shelley, and in his
long lifetime he lost his heart four times, each time to one loved
by Shelley: his sister, Harriet, Mary Godwin, and Jane Williams.
That he never made love to Claire Clairmont is the strongest
argument against Shelley's having done so.

This was not homosexuality. The mutual affection of Shelley
and Hogg was much like that felt by Shelley as a boy for a
school-friend, as he related in a later fragment of an essay on
friendship, the 'profound and sentimental attachment to one
of the same sex' which often 'precedes' heterosexual love, and
which is 'exempt from the smallest alloy of sensuality'. At
Oxford Hogg had built a sort of wall about himself and Shelley,
to ward off Eton friends, and make himself his sole companion.
He was eager to share Shelley's life; he listened to tales of Field
Place, but there is little evidence that Shelley learned much of
Norton House, the handsome and spacious family residence of
the Hoggs near Stockton-on-Tees. He had not made close
friends at Oxford in the months before Shelley's arrival there ;
it was as if he had been saving for Shelley his capacities for
friendship. He had not been to Eton, but to Durham Grammar
School. His father was a country gentleman of good but not
large fortune; he expected his oldest son to follow the family
profession of the law.

Hogg's devotion to Shelley, and hence to those he loved, did
not extend to his ideas; he had no realization of the genius of
Shelley, he did not respond to his aspirations. He could gleefully
share in the concrete plans, in such undergraduate pranks as
the publication of the *Posthumous Fragments of Margaret Nicholson*

and *The Necessity of Atheism*; later he, who loved to eat, became a vegetarian because Shelley and Harriet and Eliza did. His tearful mother reproached him; this was almost worse than atheism, and her clergyman put the blame squarely upon Shelley—or more probably Harriet, a 'Shelleyite' lady. The Rev. William Terrot went on to warn Hogg of 'the dangerous fascination of "women of genius"'.[2] But not even Harriet could convert Hogg into an idealist.

He was on holiday, and with Harriet and Shelley he set out industriously to see the sights. Edinburgh was a noble city with its hills, its deep gorge, the castle towering above it, the surrounding country stretching out to the Highlands, the slopes already covered with blooming heather, with the ancient university across the gorge, and, not far off, the romantic palace, Holyroodhouse, with its memories of Mary, Queen of Scots. The three set off on a strenuous programme not only as recreation but as an educational duty. Hogg was in all ways to assist in the education of Harriet, and they had none of them been in Edinburgh. It was a honeymoon *à trois*, a pattern to be repeated by Shelley, one not at the time unusual, save that this was the groom's friend instead of some female friend or relative of the bride. After the restrictions of boarding school, life for Harriet in the company of two admiring and admired young men was full of excitement and happiness.

In later years Hogg 'remembered' himself as the more attentive and constant escort while Shelley rushed to the post-office with his interminable letters; as the more attentive listener in the evenings when in sweet and clear tones she read aloud while Shelley curled up at her feet and slept. As Shelley chose for her reading solid works of moral philosophy with a view toward her enlightenment, it seems unlikely that he habitually slept; he would have wanted to make sure of the emphases. Hogg's attention was distracted to admiration of a beautiful face, exquisitely and delicately suffused with colour, of a trim figure, of the sound of a clear and soft voice. It could not have been easy for him, an inflammable nineteen-year-old, to be constantly with Shelley and Harriet who were so patently happy in their mutual love.

Edinburgh from Arthur's Seat

Long years later he recalled that he and Harriet had preceded Shelley to Arthur's Seat one day, and sat down at the
top waiting for him in vain. Hogg grew hungry, but Harriet
refused to move from the high rock until the wind abated; and so

I left her and proceeded slowly down the hill, the wind blowing
fresh. She sat for some time longer, but finding that I was in earnest,
she came running down after me. Harriet was always most unwilling
to show her ankles, or even her feet, hence her reluctance to move
in the presence of a rude, indelicate wind, which did not respect her
modest scrupulousness.

If, in that last sentence, he had said *man* instead of *wind* he would
have spoken truly; ladies did not expose their ankles to masculine eyes. What words of compliment may have been spoken
cannot be known; what glances of indiscretion can be more
safely inferred. Even in his old age Hogg resented her resistance
to his charm; at sixty-five, still piqued over his lack of success,
he could not leave her sitting there in her beauty and modesty;
some disparagement, however slight, was a sop to his vanity:

If there was not much to admire about these carefully-concealed
ankles, certainly there was nothing to blame.

Here he implied that he did see them; if so there had been
watchful waiting.

When in October it was necessary for Hogg to return to his
study of law, the three travelled expensively by post-chaise to
York where they acquired lodgings of a dismal sort at Miss
Dancer's on Coney Street, Hogg having forfeited his, presumably by not paying the rent during his absence, preferring to
lend to Shelley instead.

York had been a centre of learning under the Saxons; they
had built the first Minster in the seventh century. In the tenth
and eleventh centuries York had been a Danish capital, and
many streets still retained Danish names. The great Minster
that dominated the town, its bells tossing down the hours, dates
from the twelfth to the fifteenth century. In Edinburgh Shelley
and Hogg had gone to church services in the spirit of inquiry, to
fathom the stern doctrine preached there; at York Shelley
viewed the Minster with disapproval as an example of national

waste. To the country's maintenance of churches larger than the congregations warranted, with clergymen paid without any regard to the need for them, he had already called Harriet's attention. The interior of the Minster was none the less impressive with its high vaulted ceiling, its wide spaces, its windows— the oldest stained glass in Britain. Even an atheist could not be unmoved by the beauty of the Minster's glass, the soft afternoon sun bringing to jewelled perfection the liquid reds and greens and blues. One could fulminate against the organized church and still capitulate to the spell of that ethereal shower of colour.

Of the many ruins in York Shelley could discourse endlessly, as they walked about. Coney Street was close to both the River Ouse and the River Foss; close, too, to the ruins of St. Mary's Abbey with its lawn on which peacocks flaunt their medieval colours and swans flutter their wings. Harriet had not yet read Volney's *Ruins of Empires*; York gave occasion for Shelley's quoting it; ruins, picturesque in themselves, were more than romantic reminders of past grandeur: they were the symbols of democracy. In ruins there was evidence not only of the vanity of power, the inevitability of death, there was also a promise for the future. As flowers bloomed in the crumbling stone, so would democracy and justice and freedom blossom in the crumbling ruins of tyranny, injustice, and oppression.

The gardens and lawns of the ruins contrasted with the narrow sunless streets—the butchers' street, the Shambles, so narrow that overhanging windows of the upper stories all but touch those across the way. On the one hand was the wealth of the church; on the other the poverty of the populace. Their lodgings were in no way comparable to their light and airy quarters in Edinburgh's gracious George Street; they were a makeshift, the best that could be found in their penurious state. If they were to be replaced with anything better, money had to be procured. Hogg's father, incensed at hearing in a roundabout way of his son's having joined the Shelleys in Edinburgh and their joining him in York, closed his purse, allowing a scant sufficiency for one person. Timothy Shelley sent nothing at all; his son's allowance was rescinded.

Exchanging heartbroken letters over their sons, the two

fathers bolstered each other's resolve. Shelley's outdid Hogg's in the vehemence of his denunciations; he had no faith in his son's stability—he had married the girl, would he stay with her, or would he deposit her on Hogg's hands? A horrid thought this; but two weeks after their arrival in York Shelley did leave Harriet there, with Hogg lodging in the same house. Momentarily it looked as if Shelley's father had been astute. Yet to Shelley it seemed natural and proper; he had to have money to live; his father did not answer his letters of appeal; he hoped to accomplish a reconciliation with a personal interview, aided by his uncle, Captain Pilfold. He could rely upon his mother's private sympathy, though she would never go counter to his father.

The Romney portrait of Mrs. Shelley, now in New York, shows her to have been a pretty woman, complaisant and kindly, but not intellectual. The Romney portrait of Timothy Shelley shows him to have been a handsome man with ruddy colouring, fine features, an obstinate mouth, a hint of merriment in his eye. His correspondence preserved in the Horsham Museum indicates a genial man interested in his neighbours, a good dinner companion; a sufferer from gout, yet ready to go on exhausting political junketings, though he often wondered why he went to all this 'parliamentary bother', taking consolation in a wry bit of philosophy:

Upon Earth we have much to go through—what the next world may be, is for our own look-out. The well known Mystery of Human Nature is well explained—Man came into the world Naked and Bare, His progress through the World is trouble and care, His exit out of the world is the Lord knows where.[3]

This sententious statement comes at the end of a letter to a local clergyman for whom he had gone to a great deal of trouble involving Recognizances sent to the Secretary of State in behalf of a minor; 'I shall hope, a most faithful discharge of Duty . . . will repay your goodness to her'. His own goodness extended to prescribing in detail for the Rev. Mr. Marshall's flatulence: purges, emetics, light diet, gruels, and patience. In spite of his temper he was a man whom Harriet would have pleased; her merry laughter would have chimed with his; her sense of duty as a wife would not have gone counter to his. He would not have encouraged her to express opinions on serious matters, private or public. He was never part of the Whig society in which a man's mistress, and his wife who might be another powerful man's mistress, were consulted on public affairs. That group was politically illiberal, having a low opinion of human nature: reform, if it came, would do little good and much harm.

Timothy Shelley within his lights was a liberal; he supported a number of political reforms which did not, however, include free-thinking, or a free press. The tie between religion and politics was close; with state and church united, infidelity was a political offence. Men went to jail for publishing and/or selling Paine's *Age of Reason* because atheistical ideas attacked the very foundation of the state. The law of blasphemous libel— which he feared might be invoked against his son—existed to prevent the spread of such ideas among the people. The government was deeply concerned over the rising tide of disbelief, lest it uproot morality. There were those who believed that Napoleon's meteoric career was a terrible warning to men to pay heed lest they feel the vengeance of the Lord; Napoleon was to them 'the appointed instrument of Divine Justice' to awaken men to the danger of the 'usurpation of Reason over Revelation'. Societies were formed to fight the spread of 'Infidelity and Insubordination', a fight fully as important as that against the actual armies of Napoleon.[4] Even if Mr. Shelley had been moved by his son's arguments, if he had been converted to his views, as Harriet had been, he would still have shuddered at the prospect of his son's imprisonment. To be proud of a son or a daughter who risks martyrdom for a principle of belief, religious, political, or philosophical, takes stamina. Though Harriet feared Shelley's incarceration she could face the risk; his father could not. Within a few months Shelley was in danger—had he not been the son of a Member of Parliament, close to the Duke of Norfolk, he might not have gone free; his activities were watched, his writings scanned; though she did not know it, one letter of Harriet's was intercepted and held with her husband's pamphlets among state department papers.

In October, 1811 their only fear was lack of funds. There

was not enough money for Harriet to accompany her husband to Field Place. Had she appeared at the door with Shelley, his parents *might* have been touched by her youth and beauty and her sweet nature, and have attempted to enlist her as an ally. That she stayed in York in the same house with Hogg caused offence. To them and to Hogg's parents the impropriety was shocking. Mr. Hogg's letter to Mr. Shelley has survived:

DEAR SIR,

I return you my most grateful thanks for your very kind letter of to-day, and I think it proper to inform you that I received a letter from York, stating that your son left that place (it is supposed for London) about the 18th, leaving his lady to the protection of my son, saying he would return in about a week or ten days. Mrs. Hogg and I were greatly alarmed at this information, thinking it highly improper that they should be left together, and remembering what you said in a former letter, that you should not be surprised at your son's leaving his lady on my son's hands.

Mrs. Hogg thought it proper to write to her, telling her how very imprudent it was for her to be left with our son, and also informing her that he had no money to support her in Mr. Shelley's absence, that she hoped she would by no means continue with him, and pitying her situation, offer'd to write to her friends. To this she wrote a very civil answer, much in the stile of a Gentlewoman, thanking Mrs. H. for her kindness, but declining her service for the present. I am sorry to say I had a letter from your son about a week since declaring that it was his firm resolution never to part from my son—and my son declares he will not give up your son's friendship on any account. How this business is to end God only knows. I really know not how to act. I find they are in debt at York.

I did all I could to get them once separated, and was happy in succeeding, and was at much expense in placing my son at York with a Barrister for a year, hoping that absence would dissolve our son's unfortunate friendship before I entered him of Lincoln's Inn. I have been disappointed, and all my hopes are banished!!! Oh, my dear Sir! I am almost heartbroken, and so is my wife! We flattered ourselves that one day we should have seen him an ornament to his profession, and no expense from my moderate fortune should have been spared to have made him so—he was well and religiously brought up I can assure you; every person here and in the neighbourhood loved and esteemed him! I can add no more! I shall say with the Psalmist: 'It is good for me that I have been in trouble, that I may learn thy Statutes!'

Mrs. Hogg begs to unite with me in wishing every consolation to you and yours.

I am, dear Sir,
your obliged humble st.,
JOHN HOGG[5]

Mr. Hogg's anguish is the cry of all fathers whose faith in their sons is wrecked. Relief that Harriet was a 'Gentlewoman', not an adventuress, did not quiet his alarm that her support might devolve on him as his son's only source of income. He knew the peculiar economic views of Hogg and Shelley, their purse-sharing which up to now had meant that the bulk of their funds had been supplied by his son, not Mr. Shelley's. He had sources of information in Edinburgh and York, and kept account of his son's expenditures—and his associates. One wishes for Mrs. Hogg's letter to Harriet; Mrs. Hogg was in a quandary, knowing nothing of Harriet before she received her civil answer: was she a lady or a person of easy morals? were her relations with young Hogg innocent or improper? If innocent, would they continue so in the absence of her husband? Had her husband, as his father had written fearfully, abandoned her? Was there time to ward off disaster by warning her? Neither of his parents was as sure of Hogg's purity as Harriet and Shelley were. Mrs. Hogg's letter with its mixture of moral and economic prudence was an odd communication for a sixteen-year-old bride to receive. Harriet might have laughed off the warning as parental prudery, or the older generation's lack of understanding of the new morality, had Hogg's attitude been that of a brother. Instead she answered politely, inferring that she was capable of handling the situation herself.

She resolutely kept Hogg at arm's length. By day he was in the law office; in the evenings she picked up a book, one of solid worth, 'staid and instructive', and read to him relentlessly. She kept conversation within bounds, wondering about the precise whereabouts of her husband, and talking 'in the style of an inspired prophetess of a glorious advent . . . the . . . return of the golden age'. If this is any more accurate than the statement that Eliza was 'old enough to be her mother', it shows that Harriet was trying to impress the cynical Hogg with the validity

Thomas Jefferson Hogg, aged Eighteen

of Shelley's utopian ideals; one suspects, in view of Hogg's disposition, that he teased her. At some point he broke through her
wall of impersonality. It would have been hard under the circumstances not to have been moved by a plainer bride. Harriet
was on the contrary radiantly lovely; and they were alone in
the evenings. No propriety on her part could prevent some
expression of the love that overwhelmed him.

Hogg was not a seducer. He was a shy, clever young man with
no girl of his own. His youth made amatory thoughts and long-
ings press upon him, and he was held at bay by Harriet's
determination to improve her mind; she read Robertson's his-
tories which he could not divert into anything personal. At
some point he finally spoke to her not of history or philosophy
or Shelley, but of love, his love for her. Before this, in Edinburgh, he had indicated to her the warmth of his feelings; now
he went further. He was not, in his own eyes, suggesting anything morally wrong, or anything traitorous to his best friend,
or anything injurious to Harriet. Even at this moment his
ardour of friendship for Shelley was greater than Shelley's for
him, and he paid the greater price: he had been his father's heir
but the estate was not entailed—his father could, and did, divert
the greater part of his fortune to his second son. Hogg was not
unaware of the risks he took for Shelley's friendship; he neither
would nor could give him up. And since he could not hold that
elusive spirit as tightly to him as he was himself bound, he
compulsively turned his love to Shelley's women, as if it were
the most natural and proper thing in the world. As he shared
his slender purse with Shelley, he sought to share Shelley's
wealth of love.

He tried to convince Harriet by quoting Godwin as Shelley
did. And there was *Love, an Allegory*, the Chevalier Lawrence's
long poem which enchanted Shelley, a poem in three parts,
Paradise, Paradise Lost, and Paradise Regained; in which Love,
driven from Paradise by Superstition, found refuge among the
Vices until, with Love recalled, the Virtues again flourished and
the Golden Age was restored. The Jailer of Love was, of course,
Hymen. Godwin's strictures against chained love were more
specific; Godwin asserted that no one had the right to prevent

any one from loving a superior person; Shelley regarded Hogg as his superior; why, then, should Harriet not love Hogg? How specific his proposals to her were cannot be definitely established; Hogg's biographers err in reducing the matter to a mild flirtation. There is ample evidence in the Shelley-Hogg correspondence of this period that Hogg had fallen violently in love with Harriet whom Shelley designated as the personification of 'beauty and excellence'—he did not think it safe for Hogg to be exposed to her presence.

In the light of Hogg's future relationship to Mary Godwin and Jane Williams, it is difficult not to believe that his intentions, however 'reasonable' to him and, he thought, to Shelley, were what the world called dishonourable. Shelley was not a conventional husband; he did not 'own' his wife; love was free. Had Harriet been moved by Hogg's love and reciprocated it, Shelley would have been bound to respect that love and permit it. It was as much a matter of honour as the ordinary husband's prevention of such an eventuality. Harriet had accepted most of Shelley's ideas—in theory; in practice she was conservative. Besides, she did *not* love Hogg; she loved Shelley with every fibre of her being. There was a vein of obstinacy in Harriet that Hogg had not expected to find.

Harriet summoned Eliza who was to have waited to accompany Shelley on his return. Recalling her hostility to him, Hogg, decades later, took revenge by immortalizing Eliza in a deliberately spiteful portrait. She built a wall about her young sister, keeping Hogg well outside its perimeter. Because she 'barely deigned to notice' him, he maliciously slandered her, calling her 'a barmaid by origin, or at best the daughter of the house'. Shelley had long since been dead, and could not point out that Eliza had, on the contrary, been a woman of cultivation, and that her father's coffee-house had been one of excellent standing, neither a tavern nor a public house. Eliza had been brought up in a solid middle-class home of wealth; in her old age she lived grandly at Tunbridge Wells, a dignified, handsome old lady riding about in her carriage with a lady companion and a manservant.

Shelley had arrived a day after Eliza who quickly found new

lodgings to which the three removed themselves, leaving Hogg alone in the dingy Coney Street quarters. That neither she nor Shelley overestimated Hogg's susceptibility is revealed by his own memory of his days alone in York:

There was no end of pretty girls of all ranks to be found in the streets, for the ancient city was always celebrated as the abode of beauty. It was at once pleasing and painful to meet them; delightful and dangerous.[6]

'Painful' and 'dangerous' to view pretty girls on York streets, before he met Harriet; how much more dangerous to be in close contact with her when he was longing for success in love. It was thoughtlessly cruel to have left him alone with her. He was not a villain; if there were a villain, it was Shelley who exposed to temptation a normally erotic lad of nineteen. There was no virtue in Harriet's resistance—she was not tempted. Had it not been for Eliza's promptings she might never have told her husband; Hogg would presumably have recovered his balance, and a plethora of turgid letters would never have been written.

Shelley was told. His violent reaction was a surprise to Hogg; re-reading his letters in old age Hogg could not bear either to publish them accurately or to scrap them. Unwilling to cry *peccavi*, he ingeniously wove them into his biography of Shelley under the pretence that they were the 'fragment of a novel'. Such letters as he published in their proper place he tampered with so that they expressed the ardour of Shelley's attachment to him rather than the great perturbation of spirit under which Shelley laboured. Shelley wrote to Hogg; Hogg wrote to Shelley; Hogg wrote to Harriet; Harriet wrote to Hogg. The two men took long walks, talking vehemently; Hogg suggested that they clear the atmosphere with a duel. Shelley refused; he did not believe in physical violence; besides he was the better shot.

Suddenly Hogg found the Shelleys and Eliza gone, leaving no clue to their whereabouts. From Keswick he soon received a letter telling him that Eliza and Harriet had chosen this spot, but it is more likely that Shelley was drawn to the Lake District because Southey lived in Keswick, Wordsworth and Coleridge near by; moreover, the Duke of Norfolk at this time of year was likely to be at Greystoke, his estate in Cumberland. The Duke had already tried to reconcile father and son, and Shelley still placed faith in his intercession. As yet Shelley had no income except for the gifts of his uncle and whatever Mr. Westbrook may have provided for Eliza. He could and doubtless did send Eliza an allowance without breaking his promise to Mr. Shelley. Eliza would scarcely have arrived with an empty purse; she would not have expected to live on the nothing a year of her brother-in-law, or to be a burden upon him. Her father would have continued whatever allowance he had been in the habit of giving her. Shelley spoke of her managing their 'common purse', which suggests that its contents were partly hers. The discomforts to which she submitted herself speak volumes for Eliza's devotion to Shelley, and to Harriet.

Between Keswick and York ink flowed; Hogg was most eager not to lose Shelley; Shelley was most eager not to lose Hogg—he was also eager to understand and if possible exculpate Hogg as well as to vindicate himself from the charge of inconsistency, from the vice of possessive love. He wanted to be a Godwinian, firm in belief that love unrestricted was purest; he did not believe that marriage was necessarily permanent, for when love flew out of the window, physical love was abhorrent. It happened that between Harriet and himself love had not ceased. He assured Hogg (and himself) that he would not be so narrow as to refuse to share with Hogg, if she were willing. What made it wrong was her positive rejection of the idea, and her lack of love for Hogg. Under these circumstances their close association must for the present cease entirely.

Yet Shelley reiterated his affection for Hogg, still first in his heart (a phrase too readily on Shelley's tongue to be taken at face value). He over-protested until finally he terminated the correspondence. It was more than a year before communication was resumed, not then or ever quite on the same level. Currently he was reporting a highly coloured and distorted account of the affair, a blow by blow tabulation, exposing the secret recesses of Hogg's heart to his 'dearest' friend Elizabeth Hitchener, the Hurstpierpoint school-teacher whom he intended to include in his household. As yet Harriet had not met her.

To tear apart Hogg's letters and enlarge upon his 'perfidy', at the same time dilating upon his own emotional reactions, was hardly discreet. His need for an audience for his disillusionment could have found satisfaction with Harriet and Eliza who were at hand; they would, however, have toned down some of his wilder expressions. In writing intimately to one whom he knew so little he was, in a way, talking to himself; he did not visualize Miss Hitchener as a person avidly reading this gossipy romance, and asking for more. He had confided to her other matters which, if they had been true, as they were not, should especially have been concealed from her. She lived not far from Field Place, he had no guarantee of her discretion, and was later to have evidence that she was not discreet. He wrote absurd and fantastic nonsense, an accusation of his mother's having been the mistress of a family friend, Edward Fergus Graham. He wasted high emotions over this imaginary impropriety. The only excuse for his imparting such matters was that he believed the rumours to be widespread, and that his highly emotional reaction needed the relief of vocalization. It is more likely that his agitations were calmed by new scenes, new friends, new activities, than by the perfervid outpourings to Miss Hitchener.

The removal to Keswick was to bring a period of calm delight and expanding interests. First in lodgings and then in a rose-embowered cottage the three settled into a life in which intellectual effort and joy in beauty were equally satisfying. Across the lake were the soft-coloured hills, blended greens, soft browns, pearly greys touched with rose and gold in the autumn light. Skiddaw and Helvellyn lifted their heights into the clouds. Wrapt in faint mists in the frequent rains the village, sliding downhill to the lake, was the country of their dreams. Like a hero-worshipping schoolboy, Shelley had upon arrival hastened to gaze upon Greta Hall where Robert Southey lived. From Southey's exotic poems, *Thalaba* and *Curse of Kehama*, Shelley had quoted long passages to Harriet, including the blood-curdling curse. Shelley did not yet know that he was himself a poet, or suspect that he would bring to greater perfection and

F

magnificence of expression the new rhythms and the thoughts
he praised in Southey, who had written:

> Oh what a glorious animal were Man
> Knew he but his own powers, and knowing, gave them
> Room for their growth and spread.

For Southey 'The virtuous heart and resolute mind, are free',
words which lingered in Shelley's mind and reappeared in his
own verse. And Southey understood love:

> They sin who tell us Love can die,
> With life all other passions fly,
> All others are but vanity.

Shelley could tell Harriet about Southey, the man, in advance
of their meeting. Mistakenly thinking Southey was away, he did
not call upon him at once. At Oxford Southey had met Coleridge (then at Cambridge) and with him and his friend Lovell
had made plans for a utopian community across the ocean in
America, on the banks of the Susquehanna River. Twelve
young gentlemen were to marry twelve young ladies; twelve
couples would increase to twelve families; twelve families would
increase to twelve communities. Lovell had already found his
future wife, who obligingly had sisters for Coleridge and Southey
to espouse. The community had never been founded; Lovell was
dead, Coleridge was lecturing in London, Southey, the great
poet, was living and writing in Keswick.

Time for Shelley, Harriet, and Eliza fled in study, writing,
and the pleasures of the countryside. Harriet studied Latin;
Eliza was reading Paine, with the intention of publishing a
volume of selections; Shelley worked on a novel, *Hubert Cauvin*—
neither his project nor Eliza's was ever completed, but Harriet's
advance in Latin was rapid. They took long walks; Shelley and
Harriet went boating, and were upset; Shelley sailed paper
boats, a favourite diversion. There was joy in escape from the
narrow streets of York into the region of lake and hill. It was a
tranquil life, full of happy plans for the future. The cottage was
so small compared to what any of them had known that housekeeping, taken over by Eliza, was not onerous. Necessary service
was easily obtained. Chestnut Cottage was on the Penrith Road,

on the slope of the hill, with a garden behind, which, though not theirs, was open to them. It was not a long walk to the lake or to the post-office. Though they were charmed by the scenery and the prospect of meeting Southey they did not intend to remain long; Shelley felt drawn to the lovely country around Field Place in Sussex.

To have a settled residence they needed a settled income. Shelley appealed to the Duke of Norfolk to intercede for him. The Duke responded with an invitation to Greystoke, which included Harriet and Eliza. Harriet would have been less than a normal sixteen-year-old had she not been excited when she saw the ducal crest, when she read the invitation. They were in financial difficulties, the future was uncertain, but they were going to visit a duke.

Shelley wrote to Medwin, the Horsham lawyer, to ask if there were any way to borrow money at anything like reasonable interest while he was under age. He pictured them as 'now so poor as to be actually in danger of . . . being deprived of the necessaries of life'; a danger averted for

Mr. Westbrook has sent a small sum, with an intimation that we are to expect no more; this suffices for the immediate discharge of a few debts; and it is nearly with our very last guinea that we visit the Duke of N. at Greystoke tomorrow.

Mr. Westbrook was trying to keep his promise to Mr. Shelley, yet he was obviously unwilling to have his daughters suffer hunger—or lose the chance to visit a duke. His remittance made it possible to hire a carriage for the fourteen-mile journey, and they swept through the gates and along the wide drive if not with style, at least with propriety. To Harriet it was like stepping into the pages of a novel. Their host was the Duke of Norfolk, hereditary Marshal, an intimate of the Prince of Wales, a politician of power, who was prepared to promote a Parliamentary career for Shelley. Greystoke was only one of his many estates, a rather modest one compared to the magnificence of Arundel in Sussex; the house was not much larger than Field Place, and no farther from the entrance gates. To Shelley the wonder felt by his wife and sister-in-law was gratifying; it was he who conferred the pleasure of this visit; he was bringing them into his circle. The Duke was democratic, and somewhat impatient of the elegances of polite living, but he maintained a proper household with liveried servants. As a skilled politician he was used to putting people at their ease, and with ladies his manners were courtly. At this time he was a corpulent man in the sixties, not an impressive figure, plainly dressed in a purplish blue coat. Often loud-mouthed and coarse in the company of men, talking his opponents down if he could—yet he granted their right to their own opinions—he was restrained, though frank and easy in manner, in mixed company. He was a warm-hearted man, a charming host and dinner companion; he had wit and a sense of fun.

He was truly concerned over the breach between Shelley and his father. He himself commanded the young man's respect because of the liberality of his political views, his interest in reform. He had never concealed his liberalism even when it was politically inexpedient. Shelley had been only a small boy when the duke had flaunted his interest in democracy before the king. At a political dinner he had risen to propose the toast to King George III; looking at the king he proposed: 'Our Sovereign's Health: the Majesty of the People!' That had been long ago, in 1798. The Duke had paid dearly for his daring. A few days later while the Prince of Wales was dining with him he had received a royal dispatch; silently he read it, then turning to the Prince read it aloud with a laugh. It deprived him of two honours, a Lord-Lieutenancy, and the command of his regiment. Nevertheless he continued to support the cause of reform.

Charles Howard, 11th Duke of Norfolk,[7] born in 1746, had inherited the dukedom at the age of forty. In determined contrast to his frustrated father, he had abjured Catholicism and as a member of the Church of England entered upon a political career, a field closed to him as a Catholic. His father, bitter over exclusion from public life, had become a hermit, a scholar of unimportant trifles; the son became a man of varied and lusty tastes. He was not at all what Harriet might have imagined a duke to be; he was not a slim graceful figure in elegant silks, speaking easy compliments. He was a red-blooded hearty man, not very different from some of her father's friends. That he

HIS GRACE
CHARLES DUKE OF NORFOLK, F.R & A.S.
as President of the Society for
The ENCOURAGEMENT of ARTS, MANUFACTURES & COMMERCE,
from the original Picture by W.C. ROSS,
in the possession of D.R TAYLOE.
Engraved by Thomas Williamson.

LONDON PUBLISHED JULY 24th 1813 FOR THE PROPRIETOR, BY ROBERT CRIBB & SON Nº 788 HOLBORN.

Charles Howard, Eleventh Duke of Norfolk, 1811

Engraving by Thomas Williamson, 1813, after a drawing
by W. C. Ross exhibited at the Royal Academy, 1811

found nothing amiss in her or in her sister is attested by the fact that their visit was extended from four days to slightly over a week, and that the duke wrote effectively to Timothy Shelley. Two of the guests, Mr. and Mrs. Calvert of Keswick, became firm friends; their kind offices were many; and it is a credit to Harriet that when, almost two years later, the Shelleys were on their way from London to Edinburgh, with a baby, a nurse, a friend, and Eliza, they were made welcome by the Calverts.

At Greystoke there was ample opportunity to get acquainted. It was usual at house-parties to take long walks through gardens and shrubberies, drives and rides to admire the estate. In the fashion of the times, excessive wealth had been expended upon 'Follies', those decorative absurdities which supplied picturesque effects. The desired effect of antiquity and decay was often obtained, as at the Greystoke farms, by adding to existing buildings castellated walls, or portions of them, and incongruous towers. Greystoke, however, had no church in ruins to symbolize the hope for the 'decay of superstition'; the Duke was interested in Catholic emancipation, not in the cause of free-thinking. His democratic principles were responsible for the names of his three farms: Bunkers Hill, Fort Putnam, and Jefferson, two commemorating British defeats in the American Revolution, the other honouring a rebel American leader. Like many another English liberal, the Duke had been sympathetic to the revolt of the American colonies, a revolt in the finest British spirit, deriving from the same impulses that had obtained Magna Carta. The 1812 war with America had not yet broken out to disturb the amusement of the guests or distract their admiration from the farms with their absurd façades, their castellated walls, their Gothic arches, stone coronets, cones, and balls, and their hexagonal watch-towers. Greystoke's Spire House, with three sides of its octagonal tower supplied with Gothic windows, was an innocuous bit of pseudo-inspirational architecture. Harriet had not previously known any one who could indulge in such conspicuous waste.[8]

To her it was a new world; she could now better understand Shelley's natural environment. The scantiness of ceremonial brought the level of living almost down to that of Field Place, still much above that of Chapel Street, London. However impressed by Greystoke, Harriet did not pine to remain in its orbit, or make an issue of her husband's return to Field Place as a repentant son, thereby securing for her a place in society and, more important, in his family. Even before she had met Shelley she had held a sober view of life, censorious of the social butterfly who ignored the starvation and beggary at her door. Command of wealth, as Shelley reiterated, brought the responsibility to use it wisely to end want and injustice, to bring about an egalitarian and just world.

More impressive than anything else were the discussions at the dinner-table and around the drawing-room fire, to which Harriet was an attentive listener. Much discussion was, of course, out of earshot when the ladies withdrew after dinner, but there was good talk much of the time. Shelley had missed this aspect of his life for months. From boyhood he had been called down to the dining-room when his father entertained, and he was early accustomed to lively discussion. One reason for his tremendously long letters—hours of quill pushing—was the need to converse. Expelled from Oxford, he had lost companionship with voluble men; this was what he missed from his life at Field Place where, if all else failed, he had had his sister Elizabeth whom he had himself trained as an intellectual companion. He missed Hogg who, like him, could talk endlessly. At the moment he was in need of direction for his iconoclastic, benevolent, and utopian ideas, a concrete outlet; Greystoke opened the way. As one who had obtained political prominence only by changing his religion, the Duke was a strong believer in the abolition of religious qualification for public life. He worked to bring about Catholic Emancipation. That by itself was regarded as only a half-way measure by many who would include all forms of dissent, even atheism and Unitarianism. Unitarians were in the eyes of the law little different from atheists, children of the same Devil. Shelley took a wide view; he argued for free speech, a free press, free thought, and political rights independent of church affiliation.

He was in his element, a good talker among good talkers. It was a pleasure for Harriet to watch him, to listen; her schooling stood her in good stead, and Eliza could feel gratified to see her take her place in the society to which her husband belonged. The immediate results of the Greystoke visit were threefold: they now had friends at Keswick who, pleasant in themselves, would introduce them to Southey; the Duke, pleased with his youthful guests, interceded for them, inducing Shelley's father to restore the allowance of £200 a year; Mr. Westbrook, thereby absolved from the promise to withhold funds, added another £200; and Shelley had found a Cause to abet. Four hundred a year was a modest income considering their upbringing, even if augmented by Mr. Westbrook's allowance to Eliza. It was possible to live within their income, not that Shelley ever in his life sufficiently felt the necessity to reduce his expenditures. For all his egalitarianism, his social sympathies, he felt no more compunction than other gentlemen over delays, or failure to pay his debts. His love of giving, of being a benefactor, made insolvency inevitable.

At Greystoke he heard of a movement which could profit by his support; he learned of the Irish patriots who were holding meetings to agitate for the repeal of the Act of Union with Great Britain, and for Catholic emancipation. Returning to Keswick at the end of the first week of December, he began to map out his possible part in this campaign. The Calverts, though not in sympathy with his project, willingly discussed it with him and Harriet and Eliza, and were consistently helpful. They appeased the landlord when he asked the Shelleys to move, their neighbours alarmed by the flames Shelley set leaping in the air in his chemical demonstrations for the instruction of Harriet. Mr. Calvert was himself an amateur chemist; in 1801 Coleridge had appealed to Humphry Davy for advice on the setting up of a proper laboratory, something more professional than the 'nick-nacks' already possessed by Calvert.[9]

Introduced to the Southeys, the Shelleys quickly became friends with them. Southey was the first writer of distinction Harriet had met; she was prepared to be more impressed by a poet than by a duke; dukes were born to their distinction, poets earned theirs, which was the distinction of mind, higher than that of rank or wealth. Southey had been in his youth a rebel aflame with belief in the perfectibility of man who was innately good. Like Shelley, he had been expelled (from school) and had married without the consent of his guardians. Shelley expected to find in him a kindred spirit.

Before they met, Shelley had read to Harriet and Eliza poems of Southey, Wordsworth, and Coleridge, the three Lake poets who had freed poetry from neo-classic rules, given it new form, substance, and diction, and proved the power of natural language for the expression of natural feelings. For Southey Shelley had had the greatest enthusiasm because of the Gothic expansiveness of his longer poems, and their vivid realization of the supernatural. Admiring Wordsworth—he was later to convert Byron from scorn to admiration and imitation—and sensitive to the magic and the Godwinian philosophy of Coleridge's *Ancient Mariner*, he gave preference to Southey's *Thalaba* and *Curse of Kehama*. These poems were peopled with men and women of larger stature than life, their adventures ranging through earth and hell. With Coleridge, love overcame loneliness; with Wordsworth, the pangs of poverty and grief; with Southey, the black power of hate and the spell of black magic. There was turbulence in Southey's lines, a violence like that of a rushing stream, intoxicating to Shelley; Harriet caught his excitement and was prepared to be awed by the great poet.

They found Southey a handsome man in his late thirties, friendly to a young writer, seeing in Shelley the ghost of his young self, ardent, impatient with wrong, eager to see justice established on earth. Quieted by literary success, by the approach of middle age, and by domestic cares, Southey was more concerned with the problem of making a livelihood for his many dependants than with that of revolutionizing the world. His dreams of Utopia had withered; Lovell had died, leaving him to cope with the widow and child; Coleridge was in London, lecturing on literature, leaving his wife and children for Southey to care for. Lovells, Coleridges, and Southeys made a large group to feed; Southey's immediate interest was to publish enough to provide for all. To Shelley's horror the radical had softened into a conservative. Yet his intellectual interests remained; he was a good talker with a well-stored

mind; he gladly entered into religious, political, and philosophic polemics with the ardent young man so reminiscent of
his own fiery youth. Time, he asserted, would soften Shelley's
views; he was suffering from intellectual growing-pains; he
would recover balance and emerge on a plateau more comfortable than the immense heights toward which he now strove.
Shelley failed to convince Southey of the need for Parliamentary
reform, for Catholic emancipation, for freedom for Ireland. A
radical turned conservative is a sorry sight; to a young radical
using his whole force in plans for righting wrongs, it was bitter
to find the revered liberal a stodgy conformist.

He tried to shake Southey's complacency. Both enjoyed mental sparring with a worthy opponent. And Southey enjoyed the
incense that was burned generously for him. He felt confident
that Shelley's radicalism, like his own, was a disease like measles
from which one recovered. He wrote to a friend of Timothy
Shelley, John Rickman, that if Mr. Shelley would have patience,
his son would return to his family, having overcome his 'eccen-
tricity' while retaining 'his morals, his integrity, and his
genius'; he felt safe in predicting that Shelley would 'become
an *honour* to his name and his country'. Having watched and
listened to the pretty Harriet, he voiced his approval:

As for the early marriage I consider that rather a good than an evil,
seeing—as far as I have yet seen—that he has chosen well.[10]

To Harriet it was amazing that Southey held out against
Shelley, that he could offer his conservative views as the proper
ones, and call Shelley's the aberration of youth. Shelley was
quick to point out to Harriet the dangers of becoming like Mrs.
Southey, Mrs. Lovell, and Mrs. Coleridge, domesticated women
who thought Harriet should learn how to make the tea-biscuits
her husband devoured at their house; Mrs. Southey obligingly
gave her the recipe. Shelley deplored the lack of intellectuality
of these women: Mrs. Southey he found 'very stupid; Mrs.
Coleridge is worse. Mrs. Lovell who was once an actress is the
best of them.' He would not have Harriet take them for models;
he had no desire for a housekeeper-wife. He forgave Southey
more easily than these dull women who never used their minds;

Southey's apostasy sprang from the stern necessity of writing what would sell; upholding the government, complimenting the royal family was obligatory for him. Still it irked him:

Mark this disgusting abominable flattery. . . . I can't contain myself . . . 'the best Monarch that ever adorned a throne'.

Such truckling, such separation of politics and ethics was anathema to Shelley in the poet of his quondam hero-worship:

He to whom Bigotry, Tyranny, Law was hateful, has become the votary of these idols in a form the most disgusting—the Church of England, its Hell and all, has become the subject of his panegyric, the war in Spain, the prodigal waste of human blood to aggrandize the fame of statesmen, is his delight. The Constitution of England— with its Wellesley, its Paget, and its Prince—are inflated with the prostituted exertions of his Pen. I feel a sickening distrust when I see all that I had considered good, great, and inimitable, fall around me into the gulph of error.

Shelley's disillusionment did not lessen his respect for what Southey had been, what he still might be, if he would listen to Shelley and rejuvenate his ageing soul. He had not objected to being told that he was not an atheist but a pantheist or animist; he had been outraged when Southey ended arguments with the smug 'When you are as old as I am, you will think as I do'. Shelley would never become a conformist, a flatterer, an upholder of the *status quo*, averting his eyes from suffering. For Keswick had not proved to be an idyllic retreat. Industry had intruded into this lovely region, and where factories had sprung up country girls had come to grief:

Children are frequently found in the River, which the unfortunate women employed at the manufactory destroy.

Harriet and Eliza accepted Shelley's disillusionment as they had accepted his enthusiasm. He turned away from Southey, writing on 3rd January 1812 a letter to William Godwin, seeking acquaintance; Godwin, his lodestar, would not, he was sure, have aged in mind. He represented himself as young, but already persecuted for his principles.

Study of the history and sorrows of Ireland occupied the household. Shelley began an appeal to the Irish people proclaiming an Englishman's sympathy with their aims and suggesting a peaceful, non-violent solution of their difficulties. Eliza began a study of Irish history, at Shelley's instigation, keeping in mind the possibility of publishing a volume of historical extracts. Eliza, enduring cheerfully the rigours of a cottage, living on a scale more simple and less orderly than her father's home, struggling with finances as well as the history of Ireland and the writings of Thomas Paine, fails to fit the picture given by Hogg, that of a watchful dragon, keeping her sister in check. Her compliance with the Irish scheme, her undertaking projects of study and writing, indicate an amiable disposition, and an admiration of Shelley as yet uncritical.

Shelley now planned a life no longer wholly contemplative but filled with action which might lead to his imprisonment. He was fairly confident of his safety: he was under age, he was the son of a member of Parliament, and, as he observed, more flamboyant liberals than he had gone free, or had been soon released: 'Thomas Paine died a natural death', 'Godwin yet lives', and Sir Francis Burdett had been released in spite of the hatred of the Prime Minister. Harriet, however, was not free from worry; she feared his imprisonment, and she was further worried about his health. Shelley was subject to violent headaches and to nervous tensions, relieved, he recorded, by Harriet's love, and by laudanum, the usual sedative of an aspirinless age.

He was in want of money for the trip to Ireland. He appealed to his uncle who obliged with fifty pounds; the Duke of Norfolk was asked to help with one hundred pounds as a loan. It was hoped that money would be raised by publications; Shelley would publish two volumes in an expensive format, one of 'minor poems', the other of metaphysical essays; these sold at a high price should net enough profit to defray the cost of printing the *Address to the Irish People* which they would distribute free. If he completed his novel, *Hubert Cauvin*, that would sell in a cheap edition. These schemes entailed heavy work. After composition all manuscripts had to be copied in a 'fair hand' legible enough for the printers. In the end the novel was put aside. The *Address* was completed, and a poem modelled upon some satiric verses of Southey and Coleridge, a 'Devil's Walk', was composed.

In the midst of the toil of composition and copying and study-ing, and the preparations for departure, there was an untoward occurrence, the first of the mysterious assaults upon Shelley for which there have never been completely satisfactory explana-tions. Opening the door of the Keswick cottage upon hearing a suspicious noise, Shelley was attacked, his assailant fleeing at the arrival of the landlord who lived next door. Shelley had been knocked senseless as by a blow. Neighbours who had been alarmed at his chemical experiments, and who were suspicious of his views, declared it an hallucination. But there had been robbers about, and Southey had armed himself against possible attack, as had other local residents. Shelley was receiving £100 quarterly, besides which he had had money from his uncle and possibly from the duke. He was gathering the cost of a trip to Ireland for three people, and rumours may have exaggerated the amount of cash he had in the cottage.

In any case Shelley and his household had had a bad fright. The Calverts quickly offered hospitality, gratefully accepted. Preparations were concluded, and not without trepidation Shelley, Harriet, and Eliza set out; they had none of them ever been to sea before. On the 2nd of February they left Keswick, a place that had at first been 'heavenly' in their eyes, and then much 'like a London suburb', where the rich fattened on the wretchedness of the poor. They stopped overnight at White-haven, 'a miserable manufacturing sea-port Town', from which at midnight of the 3rd they sailed for the Isle of Man on the first stage of a voyage that was persistently rough. Their storm-tossed ship, blown to the North of Ireland, put them on shore, to make their way by coach to Dublin where they finally arrived on the 12th; the journey had taken in all twelve days. Harriet and Eliza were exhausted. Shelley had apparently been sustained by excitement. He had infected Harriet and Eliza with his enthusiasm for Irish freedom, a cause worthy of their efforts, Eliza as well as Harriet being enlisted in the crusade against oppression. He had read aloud to them in Keswick Coleridge's *Ancient Mariner* in which the dead albatross around

the mariner's neck symbolized the sin of self-centred isolationism, that loneliest of seas.

Harriet and Eliza quickly recovered and were ready to explore Dublin and assist Shelley's labours. The Liffey River—all
waters fascinated Shelley—was not far from their lodgings in
Sackville Street (No. 7), running through the centre of the city.
Though they were not sightseers but people with a mission, they
enjoyed the beauties of Dublin and felt its charm. Having
engaged a printer for fifteen hundred copies of the *Address to the
Irish People* they had a slight breathing spell; by the 24th of
February it was off the press, and was advertised on the 25th;
and now they were busy addressing copies to be sent to all the
leading Irish patriots, to various liberals in England, to Harriet's
father, to Shelley's father and his Horsham lawyer. A man was
hired to place copies in Dublin's sixty taverns, and to sell them
throughout the city. With a pile of pamphlets Harriet and
Shelley walked the streets, bestowing them; Harriet, though she
understood the gravity of its import, could not restrain her
merriment:

I am sure you would laugh were you to see us give the pamphlets,
We throw them out of Window, and give them to Men that we pass
in the Streets. For myself I am ready to die of laughter when it is done
and Percy looks so grave; yesterday he put one into a woman's hood
of a cloak. She knew nothing of it, and we passed her. I could hardly
get on, my muscles were so irritated.[11]

The distribution took on the likeness of a prank, but in this way
almost the entire printing was exhausted in three weeks.

Shelley tried to meet and consult with prominent Irish
patriots. From Godwin, with whom he was in close correspondence, Shelley had brought a note of introduction to the great
liberal leader, John Philpot Curran. Years ago Godwin and
Curran had been good friends, and Shelley had expected to be
welcomed at once. It was, however, some time before he met
Curran—not for want of trying—and though Curran then
invited him to dinner, there was no cordiality. Shelley did not
know that Curran had been pressed for a loan; he would not
have believed, had he been told, that Godwin was a notorious
beggar of 'loans'. A letter of introduction from Godwin made

the recipient wary. Moreover, Shelley, though engaging in politically dangerous activities, was only nineteen and a half, and
looked younger. Hamilton Rowan, formerly a friend of Mary
Wollstonecraft, and Roger O'Connor, a friend of Sir Francis
Burdett to whom Shelley had written often and sent pamphlets,
were recipients of letters. More friendly was a journalist, John
Lawless, with whom Shelley entered into a scheme for founding
a radical newspaper as a 'powerful engine of amelioration'.
Lawless checked visionary ideas, but was ready to accept financial backing—if so young a man could really provide it. Harriet
and Eliza visited his wife.

At some gathering they met Catherine Nugent, a cultivated
woman of forty who had been involved in the revolution of 1798
so deeply that, she said, only the reluctance to execute a woman
had saved her life. She was the first 'heroine', as well as the
first working-woman, they had met socially. Mrs. Nugent (she
was unmarried, but like many older women assumed the title),
often dined with them and was soon a beloved friend. Harriet
continued in correspondence with her in the following years.
Mrs. Nugent sewed furs at the shop of John Newman in Grafton
Street, straining her eyesight making luxurious garments for
the rich. It was a lesson for Harriet in social injustice. Everywhere in Dublin she saw evidences of cruelty and evil. Keswick
had revealed the hard lot of the country poor, drawn into the
factories; Dublin was a city where vice, luxury, and poverty
crowded one another on the streets. Harriet rubbed elbows with
the sodden, the sick, the undernourished; she did not recoil, but
tried to understand:

Poor Irish People, how much I feel for them. Do you know, such is
their ignorance, that when there is a drawing-room held, they go
from some distance to see the people who keep them starving to get
their luxuries; they will crowd round the state carriages in great glee
to see those within who have stripped them of their rights, and who
wantonly revel in a profusion of ill-gotten luxury, whilst so many of
those harmless people are wanting Bread for their wives and children. What a spectacle! People talk of the fiery spirit of these distressed creatures, but that spirit is very much broken and ground
down by the oppressors of this poor country. I may with truth say
there are more Beggars in this city than any other in the world. They

College Green, Dublin

are so poor they have hardly a rag to cover their naked limbs, and such is their passion for drink, that when you relieve them one day you see them in the same deplorable situation the next. Poor creatures, they live more on whiskey than anything, for meat is so dear they cannot afford to purchase any. If they had the means I do not know that they would, whiskey being so much cheaper, and to their palates so much more desirable. Yet how often do we hear people say that poverty is no evil. I think if they had experienced it they would soon alter their tone. To my idea it is the worst of all evils, as the miseries that flow from it are certainly very great; the many crimes we hear of daily are the consequences of Poverty and that to a very great degree; I think the Laws are very unjust—they condemn a person to Death for stealing 13 shillings and 4 pence.[12]

In London as a schoolgirl Harriet had noted the contrast between the luxury of the rich and the misery of the beggars, but she had seen nothing comparable to the contrasts of Dublin, nor had she come in close contact with drunken wretches or seen them arrested for stealing a roll.

Shelley ferreted out case after case of hardship; starving children, widows whose sons were snatched for the army, men who drank because they had nothing to eat; he tried to feed the hungry, protect the weak, teach the ignorant. It was a task too great for an individual. He convinced Harriet that something could ultimately be done. The first step was to end English exploitation of the Irish. He was not so naïve as to believe that a mere restoration of her Parliament would cure Ireland's ills; it was, however, a step in the right direction. The Irish people needed to be guided, to be educated.

It was with high hope that Harriet and Shelley looked forward to the delivery of his address. The occasion was the Aggregate Meeting of the Catholics on 28th February in the theatre in Fishamble Street. Such meetings, attended by Catholics and enlightened Protestants, were not forbidden but were carefully watched, with government spies sprinkled among the audience. It was a brilliant gathering Shelley addressed; the leading Catholics were men of rank and wealth; their richly dressed ladies occupied the boxes as if this were the opening night of the opera. For Harriet it was thrilling; unlike Shelley she had not seen such a spectacle in London. There were journalists;

there were notables on the platform and in the audience, some
of whom she already knew by sight, some of whom she had
actually met. She could feel herself a part of the scene, a participant. A year ago she had not known even the terms, 'Repeal
of the Union', and 'Catholic Emancipation'. The independence of Ireland (not to be achieved for more than a century)
was now dear to her heart; and she began to identify herself
with the Irish.

For her the highlight was her husband's speech, every word
of which was already as familiar as his voice. Much has been
said of the shrill quality of that voice. In excitement it jarred on
the ears, at other times it was more or less ordinary; in poetry
readings it was well-pitched and melodious. Harriet was a prejudiced listener to his address; she was not disappointed. For
more than an hour he held his audience's attention.[13] Two
government spies failed to find him dangerous, one getting him
slightly confused with another young man who made a different
speech, the other noting only that Mr. Shelley 'stated himself
to be a native of England'. The former commented on the
elegances of his language, the length of his speech, and his disrespectful reference to the Prince Regent. It was favourably
reported in the newspapers, and these Harriet sent to impress
her father along with the pamphlets and broadsides; similarly
Shelley tried to impress his father, who would also read the
account of the address in the Sussex newspaper to which he
subscribed. Shelley said there was hissing when he spoke of
religion, but the newspapers did not report this, only the
applause and the shouts of 'Hear! Hear!' Too young and too
earnest to compromise, Shelley had uttered strictures against
organized religion and the Catholic Church, pointing out that
Catholics, persecuted by Protestants, had persecuted them. He
referred to the cruelties of the Inquisition, and the misdeeds of
the clergy in private and in public life, corrupted by power:

This power made them bad men; for although rational people are
very good in their natural state, there are now, and ever have been,
very few whose good dispositions despotic power does not destroy.

To soften his criticisms of Catholicism he dilated upon the sins
of Protestantism in power, urging the audience to realize that

virtue and wisdom, not sect, were of primary importance; that Mohammedans, Quakers, and Heathen were as worthy of Heaven as Protestants (who would send them to Hell) and Catholics (who would send them to Purgatory).

In pursuit of his idea that power corrupted, he presented kings as tyrants because

they think everything in the world is made for them . . . they have no other right of being kings but in virtue of the good they do. The benefit of the governed is the origin and meaning of government.

In viewing rulers as the servants of the people Shelley was presenting a concept of the future, a lofty idea applauded but not digested by Irishmen who wanted to hear concrete plans for disunion and the restoration of an Irish Parliament. The Irish peers, as Shelley was aware, put their faith in the Whig party and in the Prince of Wales; he warned them that their faith was misplaced—neither the Whigs nor the Prince believed in Irish independence or in political rights for Catholics. If the Irish were to be free they had to act for themselves. Eloquently Shelley deprecated violence and pictured the long, arduous path to freedom not only for the Irish but for all men. 'Think, read, talk' he advised them; by discussion they would arrive at truth and in action practice it. The working-men he urged to labour faithfully, take care of their families, do good to others, avoid quarrels and drink. Virtuous living would lead to the decay of government, no longer needed when men were no longer evil. Poverty and wealth would both disappear; 'riches have generally the effect of hardening and vitiating the heart'. Poverty, however, was a great evil; 'people in moderate circumstances are always most wise and good'.

Built upon a philosophy of social betterment through the improvement of human nature, the address came down to earth, to the subject of Catholic emancipation, and the right to assemble and discuss their cause. He roused his audience with stirring words:

Are you slaves or are you men? If slaves, then crouch to the rod and lick the feet of your oppressors; glory in your shame: it will become you, if brutes, to act according to your nature. But you are men: a real man is free. . . . Then firmly yet quietly resist. When one cheek

G

is struck, turn the other to the insulting coward. You will be truly brave: you will resist and conquer. The discussion of any subject is a right that you have brought into the world with your heart and tongue. Resign your heart's blood before you part with the inestimable privilege of man. . . . Is war necessary to your happiness and safety? The interests of the poor gain nothing from glory, a word that has often served as a cloak to the ambition or avarice of statesmen. . . . The poor purchase this glory and this wealth at the expense of their blood. . . . It is horrible that the poor must give in taxes what would save them and their families from hunger and cold.

Hope and patience, peace and harmony, needed some basis in actuality; for this he proposed an association of philanthropists to work first for the freedom of Ireland, and then for the freedom of the world. This suggestion came only in the 'Postscript' to the eloquent address, impressive as that of a non-Catholic Englishman. Had Shelley looked less like a schoolboy it would have carried more weight; but Harriet and Shelley could both be gratified by its reception.

Shelley was most serious about his *Proposals for an Association of Philanthropists*. He believed that Ireland could lead the way toward the melioration of the world when, the well-being and the happiness of the governed attained, governments would disappear. The immediate aim of the Association would be to restore Ireland

to the prosperity which she possessed before the Union Act; and the religious freedom, which the involuntariness of faith, ought to have taught all monopolists of Heaven, long, long ago, that everyone had a right to possess.

The mistakes of the French Revolution were to be avoided, its aims retained and fulfilled. The grim pessimism of Malthus, seeing war and pestilence as necessary checks to over-population, was like one who, 'when he walked in the freshness of the spring, beheld the fields enamelled with flowers' and could only express discontent over the approach of winter.

Formulating thirty-one apophthegms based upon the 1789 and 1793 declarations in France, upon Thomas Paine and William Godwin, Shelley printed them as a broadside, *Declaration of Rights*. In succinct paragraphs he set forth the fundamental rights of man as opposed to those of government. No man was superior to another because of birth, wealth, or religion; virtue alone—and talents—conferred superiority. No man, even in uniform, had a right to kill. The right to free discussion, and to work for change, did not confer the right to disobey the law; until repeal, laws must be obeyed in the interest of peace. No man should own more than he needs or have less than he needs. Today when income and inheritance taxes limit wealth, and assistance to the needy and the aged has been widely established, some of Shelley's reforms, then regarded as indecently radical, have either come about or appear innocuous. Then advocacy of free speech, a free press, religious freedom, political equality as well as the abolition of war, was dangerous doctrine.

Harriet was well aware of the nature of her husband's proposals. On the 18th of March she started a long letter with a sentence that electrified the government official into whose hands it came:

As Percy has sent you such a large Box so full of inflammatory matter, I think I may be allowed to send a little, but not such a nature as his. I sent you two letters in a newspaper, which I hope you received safe from the intrusion of Post-masters.

Shelley had packed this letter in a deal box together with copies of the *Address to the Irish People*, the *Proposal for an Association*, and the *Declaration of Rights*, addressed to Miss Hitchener, Hurstpierpoint, Sussex, pre-paying the cost of carriage as far as Holyhead; from there it would normally have been forwarded to her at her expense. At Holyhead, however, it was inspected for possible dutiable items. Pierce Thomas, surveyor of customs, alarmed by Harriet's 'inflammatory', was not mollified when he had read her letter through, and examined the printed matter. He forwarded everything to his superior, and he to his. They posed a problem for the Secretary of the Post Office; he referred it to the Secretary of State. Harriet would have been astonished had she known that copies of her letter were sent to various high officials including the Earl of Chichester, the Postmaster-General. The earl identified these dangerous characters. He wrote to Francis Freeling (later Sir Francis) a mixture of truth and gossip, misnaming the district which Mr. Shelley represented in Parliament, and slandering Harriet:

DEAR FREELING,—I return the Pamphlet and Declaration, the writer of the first is son of Mr. Shelley, member for the Rape of Bramber, and is by all accounts a most extraordinary man. I hear that he has married a Servant, or some person of very low birth; he has been in Ireland for some time, and I heard of his speaking at the Catholic Convention.

Miss Hichener, of Hurstperpoint, keeps a school there, and is well spoken of; her Father keeps a Publick House in the neighbourhood, he was originally a smugler [sic], and changed his name from Yorke to Hichener, before he took the Public House.

I shall have a watch upon the Daughter, and discover whether there is any connexion between her and Shelley.[14]

Freeling retained Harriet's letter together with some copies of the pamphlets and broadside as long as he lived (1870). There were only a few copies of the *Address*, which had been freely distributed; there were many of the *Declaration* for Miss Hit-chener to disperse among the farmers of Sussex who were, Harriet quoted Shelley as saying, fond of posting such things on their walls. The seizure deprived them of this pleasure. Neither Harriet nor Shelley was questioned. Presumably Miss Hitchener was unaware that her relationship with Shelley was a matter of governmental concern; she might have been flattered had she known.

After two busy months in Dublin the Shelleys were ready to leave. Shelley had neither money nor an established reputation, either of which would have made him a person of consequence, and time did not rush fast enough to increase his age or his fortune. Moreover, to his chagrin he learned that his mentor, William Godwin, with whom he was in steady correspondence, decidedly disapproved of his plan for an association; Godwin disapproved of *all* associations. Obstinate in opposition to his father, Shelley was submissive to Godwin whom he had not yet met; he had introduced himself by letter as a young man whose principles had been moulded by *An Enquiry Concerning Political Justice*, whose wife shared his sentiments and would help him implement them. Godwin was not impressed by Shelley's philanthropic plans for Ireland and, by extension, for the

world; he *was* impressed by Shelley's statement that he was heir
to six thousand pounds a year. At Godwin's bidding Shelley
sadly relinquished his plan of small associations which, starting
in Ireland, would eventually merge into a union of nations.

Though he promised Godwin to take no further steps toward
forming an association—Harriet told Miss Hitchener that the
scheme was 'impracticable now'—he would not abandon his
experiment in multiple living, the first modest step in that
direction. He had charmed Harriet and Eliza with his picture
of life in the centre of a group of serious thinkers. Though the
inclusion of Hogg had ended unhappily, they would start anew
with 'Portia', as Miss Hitchener was now to be called. That
Harriet should accept his appraisal of her is not surprising; that
Eliza should, indicates not only Shelley's persuasive powers but
her devotion to and faith in him.

They were all now firmly on the 'Pythagorean diet', earnest
vegetarians, assuring themselves that they had never felt better.
Harriet lamented the lack of variety in the market, hopefully
looking forward to spring's greater profusion of natural foods.
Man, she cheerfully agreed, is not naturally a carnivore; to
make harmless animals die to provide food, the ingestion of
which causes indigestion and liver trouble, is foolish and cruel.
Shelley pointed out that the legend of Prometheus could be
viewed as a warning against meat-eating. Water and tea were
the only healthful drinks, but the water needed to be distilled
to eliminate impurities and mineral content. Fortunately the
food of the mind remained rich and satisfying. Harriet at boarding school had been used to simple food, but one wonders about
Eliza.

Shelley expanded in the congenial atmosphere of his own
home, even under temporary roofs; no one contradicted him;
no one tried to coerce him; no one held his views up to scorn.
Eliza as well as Harriet recognized his rationality and his right-
ness of purpose; *they* conformed to *him*. Had this conformity not
come from conviction, he would not have valued it. Neither
Harriet nor Eliza could argue with him on equal terms, neither
could stimulate his thinking as Hogg and Southey could,
but time and instruction would develop them into worthy

disputants. As a trained school-teacher Miss Hitchener would
be of great help.

It was less a desire, or need, for the presence of Miss Hitchener than a desire to create his Academe that provoked his
rhapsodic letters to her, perfervid in expressions of affection. He
was not in love with the spinster nearly ten years his senior; he
was in love with the idea of a household that would be a beehive
of intellectual activity directed toward the task of awakening a
wide public to the necessity of reform. First England and then
the world would become an egalitarian Arcadia with Love 'the
only moral law of this so lovely world'. Reading his letters to
Miss Hitchener, one has to remember that he was very young,
and that he was still addicted to writing fiction, emotionally
high-pitched.

The voyage from Ireland was again rough. The twelve-hour
sail to Holyhead took thirty-six hours. They landed in the
middle of the night, and walked above a mile

over rock and stone in a pouring rain before we could get to the
Inn; the night was dark and stormy, but the Sailors had lanterns or
else I think it would have been better to have remained on board—
as soon as we could get supper we did. We did not eat anything for
36 hours, all the time we were aboard, and immediately began *upon
meat*; . . . Percy and my sister suffered so much by the voyage and
were so weakened by the vegetable system, that had they still continued it would have been seeking a premature grave. I fared the
best of any as I slept most part of the way.[15]

Harriet seems not to have been wholly uncritical of the 'Pythagorean diet'. Fortified by their lapse into carnivorous food, they
set out to explore Wales for a suitably large house. Shelley
hoped eventually to settle in beautiful Sussex near Field Place,
assuming that his current modest allowance would, on his
twenty-first birthday (more than a year hence), be augmented
by a shower of gold, as in all proper fairy-tales. Wales with its
wild beauty and its presumed lack of dire poverty seemed a
desirable location; the Westbrooks and the Groves had summer
homes there, and Godwin had placed his novel *Fleetwood* in
Wales.

From place to place, from inn to inn they travelled, making
inquiries. From Barmouth they went by open boat the thirty

miles to Aberystwyth—Shelley had apparently no objection to
settling near Harriet's parents. And then in Radnorshire, near
Rhayader, only a mile from Cwm Elan, they came upon a
house so close to their needs and desires that it was always to
remain in memory as a corner of Paradise; Shelley called it 'a
perfect Heaven'; Harriet, less effusive, called it 'our beloved
Nantgwillt'. It was not large, but its two hundred acres offered
variety of scenery, and sufficient farming area to support them.
The bankrupt owner was willing to come to terms: ninety-eight
pounds a year until at his majority Shelley obtained funds for
its purchase. It was necessary, however, to pay at once five
hundred pounds for the farm equipment and the furnishings.
The house was large, pleasant, and comfortable; it approxi-
mated Field Place in commodiousness and in retired position,
and would renew for Shelley something of his childhood life.
There were trees and brooks and hills and rivers about; there
would be fresh fruits and vegetables for their table; and the
farms, orchards, and meadows would provide an income. There
was space and privacy for chemical experiments with no alarmed
neighbours complaining that he set the air on fire. At Nantgwillt they could live with dignity, and invite others to join
them.

They moved in, Shelley, Harriet, Eliza, and Dan Hill (or
Healey) their Irish manservant, and the requisite house-servants.
It was April and life, too, was at its spring-time. But the strain
of the voyage and the long days of house-hunting left Harriet
exhausted; she fell ill of a slow, persistent fever. By the first of
May Shelley, thoroughly alarmed, sent for the nearest doctor,
forty miles away. Not for another week did the fever begin to
subside. As Harriet recovered from her three-week illness,
Shelley succumbed to an 'inflammatory fever', which lasted a
fortnight. Harriet was deeply concerned over his health, and
they considered going to Italy for sunshine and warmth.

They had had hopes of help from Mr. Shelley, to whom
Shelley had written a request for the down-payment which
would secure Nantgwillt for them. He had written persuasively:

You have now an opportunity of settling the heir to your property
where he may quietly and gentlemanly pursue those avocations

which are calculated hereafter to render him no disgrace to your family on a more extended theatre of action.

The reply, an unequivocal refusal, was penned by Mr. Shelley's ungracious lawyer, Whitton. Mr. Shelley had had cause to resent his son's earlier impolitic letters, and to be alarmed at his activities in Ireland; that anger coloured his judgment. No doubt he was also suspicious of the 'avocations' planned. Yet his help in settling his son at Nantgwillt might have led him back to Field Place. It is, however, probable that he had heard of the quixotic scheme to include Miss Hitchener in the household; in her letters to Shelley and to Harriet there is more than a hint of her having boasted of Shelley's friendship; she wrote of gossip about herself and Shelley which she said emanated from the Pilfolds (his uncle and aunt), and from the Duke of Norfolk. She may have helped start gossip by talking of Shelley's interest in her. She lived near enough to Cuckfield to be within gossip range, and Field Place was only a few miles off. She may also have talked of Shelley's corresponding with Godwin of which he gave her a running summary. Mr. Shelley's disapproval and distress would have been genuine, and understandable.

The plans for Nantgwillt miscarried. Without his father's help Shelley could neither pay for the furniture and equipment nor give a satisfactory guarantee of his ability to pay the purchase price at his majority. Though they had both been ill there, Shelley and Harriet were deeply grieved; Nantgwillt was to persist in their memories as the Happy Valley, its hills and rocks shutting out the tumult of the world. They continued to cherish hopes of return. Meanwhile they took refuge at Cwm Elan where Harriet found John Grove, Shelley's cousin, 'a very proud man', and his wife 'a very pleasant woman, tho' too formal to be sociable'.[16] Mrs. Grove expressed approval of Harriet as a guest and as a pretty young wife. She was not as warmhearted a hostess as Mrs. Calvert, perhaps on her guard lest Shelley borrow from her husband.

The summer was advancing and they had found no substitute for Nantgwillt. Godwin wrote suggesting Chepstow, where a friend of his was building some cottages; Godwin had in mind their youth and their scanty funds. Obediently Shelley with

Harriet and Eliza set out for Chepstow, a charming old town, with part of its wall still standing and the ruins of an old castle. Close by is Tintern Abbey which had inspired one of Wordsworth's finest poems. The cottage was in sharp contrast to Nantgwillt; it was quite unsuitably small. Shelley was not thinking of his present restricted means as dictating his way of life; he would be twenty-one in a little more than a year and, surely, in better circumstances. He could not wait until then to start his multiple household. He wanted under his roof not only Elizabeth Hitchener but all the Godwins—Godwin, his wife, and a miscellany of children. With themselves and Elizabeth Hitchener this added up to eleven people. Even if all the Godwins did not come at first, he hoped for some of them; and there would be others. The Chepstow cottage would not do even for one guest.

Reluctantly Shelley postponed plans for the coming of the Godwins and concentrated on securing Miss Hitchener; he arranged for her to spend a night in London at Mr. Westbrook's on her way to join them, and to dine with the Godwins, thereby meeting the great man face to face before Shelley did himself. The Shelleys had found a cottage in Devon for a temporary haven, not large enough, but with several bedrooms; Harriet called the smaller bedrooms 'servants' rooms', regarding them as inappropriate for important guests like the Godwins, though perhaps possible if the oldest daughter visited them. At Lynmouth, the small seaside village nestling under the hill below Lynton, they eagerly awaited the arrival of their friend 'Portia', a name (selected by herself) that reflected their mental image of Elizabeth Hitchener.

Occupied with house-hunting, they had not ignored what was happening in the world. Cobbett's *Political Register* and Leigh Hunt's *Examiner* kept them informed about matters that stirred their wrath. Before they had left Ireland, at the end of February, they had learned of the introduction in the House of Lords of the iniquitous Frame Work Bill, which made it a capital offence to destroy the mechanical looms which desperate weavers were smashing. The young Lord Byron, not yet personally known to Shelley, had risen in the House of

Lords in indignation, to make his maiden speech, a defence of
the weavers for whom industrialization of their craft spelt
starvation.

Cobbett was no favourite of Shelley's, and hence was freely
criticized by Harriet, but they both read his *Political Register*
faithfully. By April Cobbett was urging the workers to seek
political power, and the government was anticipating riots. In
May the Prime Minister, Spencer Perceval, was shot in the
lobby of the House of Commons. Harriet, commenting on this
act of violence, expressed sympathy for Mr. Perceval, 'a very
good private character', surprise at the calm behaviour of the
assassin, and a wish that the victim had been Lord Castlereagh
—'he really deserved it'. Riots, assassinations, executions in the
great world emphasized the need for reform. Here was work
for Shelley's pen; Lynmouth provided the right atmosphere.
Harriet described it to their Irish friend:

It combines all the beauties of our late residence with the addition
of a fine bold sea. We have taken the only Cottage there was—which
is most beautifully situated, commanding a fine view of the sea with
mountains at the side & behind us. Vegetation is more luxuriant
here than in any part of England. We have roses & myrtle creeping
up the sides of the house, which is thatched at the top—it is such a
little place that it seems more like a fairy scene than anything in
reality. All the houses are built in the cottage style. I suppose there
are not more than 30 in all. We send to Barnstaple for every thing.
. . . We have an immense precipice to descend into this Valley about
2 miles in length which no carriage can come down—It seems as if
Nature had intended that this place should be so romantic and shut
out from all other intercourse with the neighbouring Villages &
Towns.

One detects a wistful note here, a sense of being shut in, with
the eighteen miles on horseback to Barnstaple not a journey for
every day. For the summer months it was perfect; 'we think of
going to London for the Winter'.

For Shelley and his writing projects it offered undisturbed
quiet, and the joys of the sea. Below high hills Lynmouth rests
on the shore of an exquisite bay, blue as the Mediterranean.
Ten years hence Shelley was to spend his last summer in a
startlingly similar situation in Italy, so much does the Bay of

Lerici resemble that of Lynmouth. Today to fly between Italy and England and see in close point of time the two bays scooped out of the hills is to have the curious sensation of having stayed in one place. Shelley's determined choice of Lerici would seem to have been dictated by this resemblance, by a desire, whether or not fully conscious, to recapture the sunny earlier days of Lynmouth.

Devon was only an interlude, a retreat after the Irish involvement, a pause to prepare new polemics in the campaign for reform. Here their first co-worker joined them. Elizabeth Hitchener was received by the three of them with open arms and closed minds, with the highest regard for her as a superior person. With her arrival their life was to enter another new phase.

CHAPTER IV

The Thirst for Action

The thirst for action, and the impassioned thought
Prolong my being; if I were no more,
My life more actual living will contain
Than some gray veteran's of the world's cold school,
Whose listless hours unprofitably roll
By one enthusiast feeling unredeemed.

To Harriet.

HARRIET accepted Elizabeth Hitchener on Shelley's terms. At his uncle's dinner-table she had made something of a parade of her liberal views; instead of inquiring closely into them Shelley had embarked upon a disquisition of his own; and she had asked questions, listening intently to his answers, the assured method of gaining a reputation as a brilliant conversationalist. She had risen in her little world. Hurstpierpoint had been a centre for smuggling. Even the more respectable inhabitants sometimes engaged in it, receiving goods from France and Holland—liquor, laces, tea, and tobacco—under cover of darkness, and disposing of them without paying import duty. Similarly they exported woollens. There were those, too, who engaged in piracy, seizing French vessels with their cargoes; for this the penalty was death. Mr. Hitchener's change of name and the determined respectability of his new enterprise suggest that he may have been suspected of the more risky trade; his ultra-moral stance in opposing his daughter's friendship with Shelley strengthens this suspicion.

Mr. Hitchener was not an egalitarian; and he never met Shelley personally. His daughter can be excused for having been dazzled by Shelley and his proffer of friendship. When in his letters he stressed the fact that he would in time have command of a grand fortune, she assumed that he was already wealthy—by her standards he was not poor even now. She had deprecated the idea that she wanted any financial assistance herself, but soon suggested that he subsidize her impoverished old school-mistress. He had voluntarily offered to share all he would have with Miss Hitchener; she did not know how wide the scope of his benevolence was to be. In her letters to him, exhaustingly long as were his to her, she posed as one of Nature's noblewomen, humbly born, altruistically devoted to the good of others, and eager to improve her mind and her capabilities (which she did not rate low). She credited Shelley with putting her chaotic ideas in order, and let him believe that he had converted her to all his views. Rather cleverly she presented herself as perplexed, in need of guidance, and deeply indebted to him for his 'precious' friendship. Her vanity misconstrued the nature of her attraction for him, and the warmth of his letters did nothing to disillusion her. She hinted at the impropriety of their friendship, an insinuation he promptly labelled 'absurd'. But no woman likes to feel that her proximity offers no temptation to a man, even one ten years her junior. When Shelley called her the sister of his soul he meant precisely that; for him their warm relationship was that of their minds. Her physical presence was desired, when he had a home in which to receive her, partly because thus he could relieve her of the necessity of earning her living, and confer benefits upon her. He was not aware of his enjoyment in practical condescension, and he believed that she would be a help to him, to Harriet, to Eliza. His marriage had been a blow to her pride, and possibly to her hopes, but she swallowed her chagrin and fawned upon Harriet who was immediately 'precious' to her.

Harriet thought of her before they met as another Eliza; the highest compliment she could pay her:

When you see her you will form your judgment of her. I did think before I was acquainted with you, that she was the best and most superior woman in the world. I do not say that I have changed my opinion: no, that remains fixed. I have only so far changed it as to think there are some like her; but as to being better, that I cannot think.[1]

Harriet, then, expected to find Miss Hitchener another sister,
who would take an interest in their projects and, by her superior
attainments, advance them. She had not been critical of Miss
Hitchener's effusions, though she had herself written with her
usual good sense and clarity rather than in the rhapsodic style
of her husband and Miss Hitchener. When Harriet was suffering
from fever at Nantgwillt the most effusive letters arrived; Harriet's existence, Miss Hitchener protested, was necessary to *her*
happiness; Harriet must live for the sake of her sister-friend. She
called Harriet an 'exalted soul', a 'treasure', a 'blessing', a
'rare' woman free from vulgar prejudice (i.e. she was not jealous of her husband's interest in another woman). Winding up
an apostrophe to Harriet at the end of a letter to Shelley, she
breathed devotion, ostensibly to Harriet but obviously to Shelley:

My dearest friend, believe me immovably and unalterably thine
whilst time shall last thro' all changes of being still for ever thine.[2]

'Dearest friend' was her appellation for Shelley; her letters to
Harriet began 'Dear Madam'. Such gushing should have forewarned the Shelleys; it did not. She, too, should have been wary
of Shelley's protestations of affection.

   More creditable than her letters are her two published
volumes of verse, one in 1818, one in 1822. *The Fireside Bagatelle*
was a collection of verse enigmas on the chief towns of England
and Wales; *The Weald of Sussex* verses on her home country.
She showed ingenuity in presenting within the comprehension
of young school-children both the enigmas and the local legends.
Liberty, Benevolence, Universal Sympathy, Peace, Reason,
Truth the Sun of Light, Mercy, and Brotherhood are all celebrated in the re-telling of old tales of Sussex. She wrote fairly
well of the beauty and history of the county, and displayed
competence in the composition of simple verse. Neither book
has distinction or shows any great maturity of thought; both
exhibit moral earnestness.

   If the Shelleys expected of her an intellectuality she did not
possess, she expected of them a deference she did not receive.
Harriet, shrewder in judgment than her husband, wrote an
artless letter to Mrs. Nugent which reveals more than it says:

Our friend Miss Hitchener is come to us. She is very busy writing for the good of mankind. She is very dark in Complexion with a great quantity of long black hair. She talks a great deal, if you like great talkers she will suit you. She is taller than me or my Sister & as thin as it is possible to be. I hope you will see her some day. I should think that next summer you might take a peep at us. . . . Miss Hitchener has read your Letter & loves you in good earnest, her own expression. I know you would love her did you know her. Her age is 30 & she looks like as if she was only 24 & her Spirits are excellent. She laughs and talks and writes all day. She has seen the Godwins & thinks Godwin different to what he seems, he lives so much from his family only seeing them at stated hours— . . . He would not let one of his Children come to us just because he had not seen our faces. Just as if writing to a person in which we express all our thoughts was not a sufficient knowledge *of them*. I knew our friend whom we call *Bessy*, just as well when we corresponded as I do now.[3]

Harriet was making a valiant attempt to keep her illusions but it was obvious that their long-awaited guest had been over-estimated. Her 'writing for the good of mankind' was not on Shelley's level. He was writing a pamphlet in a stirring style beside which her efforts were feeble; it was ready for the Barnstaple printers in July; on the 29th twenty-nine copies were sent to London to the bookseller Hookham, with fifty copies following on the 18th of August.

In the form of a letter to the judge Shelley voiced his protest, and his defence of a free press, occasioned by the trial the preceding March of an elderly bookseller, Daniel Isaac Eaton, for publishing and offering for sale the third part of Thomas Paine's *Age of Reason*. In May Lord Ellenborough, the presiding judge, had sentenced Eaton to eighteen months in Newgate prison, and to stand in the pillory for two hours every month. Shelley and Harriet had followed the accounts of the trial and sentence with indignation; they had, Harriet said, been gratified to read that one clergyman defended Eaton, and that the crowds, instead of pelting him with rotten eggs and tomatoes, had cheered the old man; his punishment on the pillory had become a triumphant reception of sympathizers. Protests had already appeared in such journals as Cobbett's *Political Register* and Leigh Hunt's *Examiner*. Shelley believed his would be the first separate publication. Cobbett, himself a staunch member of the Established Church, challenged ministers, if they could, to answer Paine's anti-religious arguments in the pages of his *Political Register*. Refutation, not prosecution, he advocated—in vain. Harriet could not but be deeply moved by Shelley's powerful prose:

The time is rapidly approaching, I hope that you, my Lord, may live to behold its arrival, when the Mohametan, the Jew, the Christian, the Deist, and the Atheist, will live together in one community, equally sharing the benefits which arise from its association, and united in the bonds of charity and brotherly love. My Lord, you have condemned an innocent man—no crime was imputed to him —and you have sentenced him to torture and imprisonment. I have not addressed this letter to you with the hope of convincing you that you have acted wrong. The most unprincipled and barbarous of men are not unprepared with sophisms to prove that they could have acted in no other manner, and to show that vice is virtue. But I raise my solitary voice to express my disapprobation, so far as it goes, of the cruel and unjust sentence you passed upon Mr. Eaton; to assert, so far as I am capable of influencing, those rights of humanity which you have wantonly and unlawfully infringed.

These were brave words. Harriet feared that he would be arrested; they were not idle fears. At Lynmouth Shelley was launching pamphlets and broadsides in sealed, carefully-constructed boxes, and in bottles, to the consternation of the authorities who feared they would in drifting from the bay reach the 'sea-faring sort of people' among whom 'incalculable mischief' might be done. The Town Clerk of Barnstaple felt it his duty to report to the Home Secretary, Lord Sidmouth, that two of the bottles picked up by revenue cutters contained a seditious paper, 'Declaration of Rights'. The Postmaster, Richard Jones, reported his suspicions to Francis Freeling who at once reported the matter to the Earl of Chichester. The Earl reported the distressful news to the Secretary of State, urging that it be kept as secret as possible:

It will have no effect to speak to Mr. Shelley's family, they suffer enough already for his conduct.

Fortunately, though Harriet's fears had a basis, there was respect for rank and wealth to save Shelley from prosecution;

but he was watched. He had taken the precaution of omitting his name from the title-page of the pamphlet he now printed (it was not published); he removed the name of the printer; and this pamphlet was not, like the *Declaration of Rights*, suitable for dispatch by sea to all and sundry.

The Town Clerk informed Lord Sidmouth that he had been watchful:

Mr. Shelley has been regarded with a suspicious eye since he has been at Lynmouth, from the Circumstances of his very extensive Correspondence, and many of his Packages and Letters being addressed to Sir Francis Burdett—and it is also said that Mr. Shelley has sent off so many as 16 Letters by the same Post.[4]

He had been observed wading out into the bay to set afloat a bottle which was recovered and taken to the Mayor who had not yet been able to decipher the contents. Shelley was assisted, Lord Sidmouth was informed, by 'a female servant (supposedly a foreigner)'—poor Miss Hitchener, dark of complexion, and poorly dressed!

The occasion of these reports was the arrest of the Irish man-servant, Daniel Hill, on the 19th of August as he distributed and posted in Barnstaple the broadside, *Declaration of Rights*. He told a cock-and-bull story of having been given five shillings by a 'Gentleman dressed in black' encountered between Lynton and Barnstaple. He cheerfully admitted that he worked for a Mr. Shelley, whose home was somewhere in London; he had worked for him previously in Dublin. Mr. Shelley was the son of a Member of Parliament, his wife formerly a Miss Westbrook, whose father lived in Chapel Street, Grosvenor Square; two of her sisters were now with the Shelleys in Lynmouth. He was no doubt confused by the Shelleys' calling Miss Hitchener their sister.

For dispersing printed papers without the printer's name affixed Dan was fined two hundred pounds and sentenced in lieu of payment to the common gaol for six months. It was noted that Shelley visited him the next day. Lacking the funds for the fine, he could only by paying fifteen shillings a week provide comforts for Dan's period of confinement. In June they had wished to send him back to Ireland as no longer of use to them;

H

he had stayed on, and they had found a way to use him, with this result.

There was no more joy for Shelley and Harriet in their rose-embowered cottage. The arrest of Dan had increased Harriet's fears for Shelley's safety, and he did not himself enjoy being under official observation. They departed abruptly, borrowing from their kind landlady enough to take them to Ilfracombe (she was repaid). No one remembered that they were to have the honour of a visit from Godwin; unnotified of their change of residence he arrived three weeks later, and found consolation in listening to the landlady's praise of the young couple. In time he learned that they had gone to North Wales.

Tremadoc where they came to rest was, like Lynmouth, on the sea encircled by mountains, and there they had the finest possible view of Snowdon. They had been drawn to Tremadoc partly because the town was the creation of a liberal member of Parliament, the friend of a man Shelley admired greatly, Sir Francis Burdett. William Madocks, M.P. for Boston, had three years earlier attempted to impeach the Prime Minister, Perceval, and the Foreign Secretary, Castlereagh, accusing them of corrupt practices. (Harriet sometimes amused her husband by drawing caricatures of Castlereagh.)

The immediate purpose that drew Shelley to Tremadoc was, however, to help with the Embankment which Madocks had begun in 1800. He had redeemed from the sea thousands of acres, and in so doing had provided work for many; but bad storms and heavy seas had not long since caused great damage. Large sums of money were needed if it was to be repaired so that the sea could be held back and the land saved; only completed in 1811, in 1812 it was in danger of ruin—Madocks himself could not raise enough to save it. Here was a concrete need in which they, Shelley, Harriet, and the two Elizas, could help. Madocks's agent, John Williams, was sending out appeals for money to pay the workers; horses, carts, and men had been sent by many, but the outlook began to look bleak. Shelley's enthusiasm was a catalytic force, and his efforts were untiring as he threw himself heart and soul and purse into the project.

He established himself and his *entourage* in the local inn

while they looked for a residence. There were only three gentle-men's residences in the small town, two of which had been built by Madocks, the third that of the Attorney-General of the County, Mr. Nanney. One of Madocks's houses, Morfa Lodge, was occupied by the Hon. Robert Leeson, son of the Anglo-Irish Earl of Milltown. The other, a mile from the centre, he had used himself when he was at Tremadoc, often bringing with him a number of guests. Because of financial stringency he decided to rent Tanyrallt, and Shelley was quick to hire it. Madocks's agents protested against his rental to Shelley who was a minor at odds with his father, and with no personal fortune. Madocks countered with his confidence in Shelley's father, a fellow M.P. and a highly responsible person; moreover, Shelley would contract for the furniture in the house, and would have more made; that would reimburse Madocks if the rent were not fully paid.[5]

Tanyrallt, described by Shelley as a small Italian villa, is a wide two-storied white house facing the sea; it nestles in the side of a hill, three-quarters of the way to the top. The driveway curves up from the gate-keeper's lodge. A spring tumbles down offering clear cold water almost at the door of the house. It is a delightful estate, its grounds giving the effect of thick woods and dells. There is an unsubstantiated legend at Tremadoc that Shelley, befuddled with wine, duelled with a tree close to the house, and the heavily hacked tree was offered as proof for over a century.

Within, there were spacious living-rooms; a large study where Shelley was to write his first long poem, and ample bedrooms, not like those at Lynmouth, but large and elegant enough for guests. Though the first attempt at multiple living was coming to an inglorious close, the Shelleys still planned to gather a group about them. Miss Hitchener was not destined to share their life at Tanyrallt; before they moved in there was to be a trip to London, and when they returned she would not be with them. Neither as 'Portia', as she wished to be, nor as 'Bessy', as she had become, did she fit into the family. She had had her misgivings, being uncertain about giving up her independence; she had asked how could she support herself? and been told by both Shelley and Harriet that she had no needs they would not satisfy—was she not their sister? She would not be dependent, as by her literary efforts she would contribute to their work for reform; and the purse would be in common. When she had written that her father thought it improper for her to come to them, Shelley wrote Hitchener indignant letters. By what right did Mr. Hitchener refuse the invitation to his daughter? was he her 'governor'? Neither the laws of Nature nor those of England, he admonished him, made children private property:

You may cause your daughter much anxiety . . . you may stretch her on a bed of sickness, you may destroy her body, but you are defied to shake her mind . . . her mind is free.

Shelley apparently saw nothing absurd in this contest over a thirty-year-old woman between her father and a youth of nineteen. Mr. Hitchener prudently wished his daughter to stay in her school; he thought better of the bird in the hand; his daughter after much persuasion chose the bird in the bush.

Miss Hitchener overestimated from the warmth of his language Shelley's affection for her, her attraction for him. He had reiterated that she was dearest to him, and she did not know that he used the same words to Hogg. That she should even momentarily have believed that she was dearer to him than his lovely young wife betrays her vanity. He wanted co-workers; she wanted attention; and certainly her letters showed an interest in the wealth he generously offered to share (but he did not have it). Her letters to him and to Harriet were never critically examined by either of them; they should have lessened their ardour for her presence. When Harriet was ill Miss Hitchener's letters breathlessly expressed wild anxiety in anticipation of Harriet's demise. She implored Shelley to write her by every post, a device to keep herself in his mind. She made much of the great sadness about to fall upon Shelley, Eliza, and herself when

all of happiness would be in the sympathy of mourning the loss of her who was to each their richest treasure.

This could hardly have been comforting to Shelley who, even prejudiced in her favour, could not have accepted her calling Harriet *her* 'richest treasure'; she had not as yet met Harriet.

In his anxious attendance at Harriet's bedside he may not have had full leisure to read her protestations and perceive the drift of her thoughts which were digging the grave. She went on to compose a sort of elegy for Harriet:

a more exalted soul never was confin'd in a human frame, ah me, my Harriet, bear for our sakes still longer that confinement. I am older than thee many years; cheat me not then of my claim to explore for thee those unknown scenes which human footsteps ne'er have trod; surely the right is mine to welcome rather than be welcomed by thee there. . . .[6]

The fulsome lament thinly concealed a wish.

Harriet, however, recovered, and at Lynmouth they met at last. Miss Hitchener was warmly received. By the time the four of them came to Tremadoc her tinsel was tarnished; she had not been an inspiration or a help. She could not easily doff her schoolroom manner; she spoke with authority and expected the attention she had received from her very young pupils and their parents. Harriet she treated as a schoolgirl whose mind was not trained to understand the abstruse discussions between Shelley and herself. And Eliza, it is to be feared, she treated as a housekeeper.

Tremadoc was not like Lynmouth, where they had known no one; the gentlefolk here called upon the Shelleys, and her position was anomalous; Harriet's courtesy and deference would still not explain her position in the family. In Mrs. Nanney, wife of the Attorney-General, Harriet found a friend. Shelley was more and more away from home, spending long hours in the office of John Williams, trying to understand the entangled affairs of the Embankment, and writing countless letters to obtain contributions. Elizabeth Hitchener found herself thrust into the background. She felt the need of asserting herself. Not maliciously but from a natural desire for self-aggrandisement, she caused mischief. To show Williams how much she was in Shelley's confidence, and how important a person he was, she told him of Shelley's having entered into public life in Ireland, and gave him Shelley's Irish pamphlets. Of this neither Shelley nor Harriet had an inkling. Poor Miss Hitchener! her plans had gone awry; in her little world in Sussex she had been of

importance. To be secondary to an Embankment, to be sub-
ordinate to a seventeen-year-old wife was a disillusionment. In
her bitter moments it was Shelley, not Harriet or Eliza, whom
she blamed; for it was Shelley who was to have been her close
companion, and it was Shelley who had withdrawn from her.

They would all journey to London together, and there she
would remain with them until their plans and hers were completed. Shelley was to seek sponsors for the Embankment re-
pairs: he hoped (in vain) to interest the Duke of Norfolk in so
worthy a cause. On their way they stopped for a dinner meeting
of North Wales gentry, its object to arouse active interest in the
Tremadoc Embankment's necessities; Shelley had been asked
to address the company. There were rumours afloat that
Madocks was on the verge of bankruptcy which discouraged
many from associating themselves with his project. John
Williams, Madocks's agent, shrewdly made use of Shelley to
bolster confidence; Shelley was young, but he was enthusiastic;
he was also well connected, son of a Member of Parliament
(which suggested that he and/or his father knew Madocks
personally.) At the dinner Shelley was the guest of honour, and
the company drank his health. His belief in the value of the
Embankment was heartening, reinforced, as it was, by a pledge
to devote his entire energies to its repair, and by the gift of a
substantial sum of money—variously reported as one hundred
pounds and five hundred (he had recently resorted to London
money-lenders with Tremadoc connections). The creditors and
the enemies of Madocks could not fail to be impressed by such
practical support.

The dinner on the 28th of September 1812 was at Beaumaris,
at the home of the Lord Lieutenant of Wales, Lord Bulkeley.
It was a triumph for Shelley, whose efforts in Ireland had had
no concrete results; here he was taking part in a public service
that would be permanent. The Embankment was finally repaired, and still stands, the reclaimed land saved.[7] In the
garden of Tanyrallt there is quite properly a memorial to
Shelley.

The triumph at Beaumaris belittled the recent distress when
Shelley had been arrested for debt at Caernarvon. He had been

quickly released on bail provided by a Dr. William Roberts.
Money-lenders had provided the cash needed—probably for the
expenses of Shelley, Harriet, and the two Elizas at the Tremadoc
inn; the loan may have been large enough to pay the pledge to
the Embankment Fund.

The *North Wales Gazette* reported his speech, quoting his
praise of the 'glorious work' which would

give no less than three thousand souls the means of competence.
How can anyone look upon that work and hesitate to join me when
I here publicly pledge myself to spend the last shilling of my fortune,
and devote the last breath of my life, to this great, this glorious cause.

This was a large promise, and Williams had cause to be grateful
for its help in building up confidence in the project. Both
Shelley and Harriet could feel that he had taken his place in
the world and was making his weight felt. The long journey to
London was lightened by pleasant memories of Beaumaris.

They arrived at Lewis's Hotel, St. James's Street, on the 5th
of October, remaining in London until nearly the middle of
November. These weeks did much to shape their future. They
also ended their connection with Miss Hitchener who during
this time took her departure. Harriet, who had suffered the
annoyance of her attempts to monopolize Shelley's time and
attention at Lynmouth, and her resentment of his neglect of
her at Tremadoc, recorded her leaving in less harsh terms than
Shelley did. To Mrs. Nugent, Harriet on the 14th of November
wrote:

We were entirely deceived in her character as to her republicanism
and in short every thing else which she pretended to be. We were not
long in finding out our great disappointment in her. As to any noble
disinterested views, it is utterly impossible for a selfish character to
feel them. She built all her hopes upon being able to separate me
from my dearly loved Percy & had the artfulness to say that Percy
was really in love with her, & 'twas only his being married that
could keep her within bounds. Now Percy had seen her twice[8] before
his marriage. He thought her sensible [i.e. sensitive] but nothing
more. She wrote continually, & at last I wrote to her & was very
much charmed with her Letters. We thought it a thousand pities
such a mind as hers appeared to be should be left in a place like that
she inhabited. We therefore were very urgent for her to come & live

with us, which was no sooner done than we found out our mistake. It was a long time ere we could possibly get her away till at last Percy said that he would give her £100 per ann. & now, thank God, she has left us never more to return. We are happier now than all the time she was with us.

Harriet's normal truthfulness records factually; no doubt Miss Hitchener had in a moment of irritation referred to Shelley's written expressions of love; he had indeed signed letters 'unalterably' hers; he had written after his marriage that 'still' she was 'dearest'. Harriet, secure in his love, could put such extravagances into correct perspective; Miss Hitchener had taken them at face value.

Harriet, never having felt so ardently for her, had a less violent revulsion from her than Shelley's. Earlier than he, she had begun to suspect her of insincerity, though she was not prepared for her misapprehension of his sentiments. Miss Hitchener thought of herself as Shelley's intellectual equal, his love for her on a higher plane than that for Harriet. She was not sufficiently modest in self-appraisal to discount his epistolary superlatives. They had been mutually deceived. Shelley swung from his overevaluation of her to harsh devaluation when he wrote to Hogg:

The Brown Demon, as we call our late tormentor . . . must receive her stipend. I pay it with a heavy heart and an unwilling hand; but it must be so. She was deprived by our misjudging haste . . . of a situation where she was going on smoothly: and now she says that her reputation is gone, her health ruined, her peace of mind destroyed by my barbarity; a complete victim to all the woes mental and bodily, that heroine ever suffered. This is not all fact, but certainly she is embarrassed and poor, and we being in some degree the cause, ought to obviate it. She is an artful, superficial, ugly hermaphroditical beast of a woman, and my astonishment at my fatuity, inconsistency, and bad taste was never so great as after living four months with her as an inmate. What would Hell be, were such a woman in Heaven?

It was Shelley Miss Hitchener blamed: he had been 'barbarous' to her. Though he mocked her woes, he recognized obligation, his and Harriet's, for he says 'we' were 'in some degree' to blame for her loss of her livelihood. Whether or not the annuity was regularly paid has never been clear. She died in the same year as Shelley, leaving an estate of four hundred pounds, a not inconsiderable sum for a country school-teacher to have saved.

However artful she had been in prompting the invitation to join them, they had pressed it upon her. Having lived largely among intellectually inferior people she believed hers to be an original mind. She had never come in contact before with any-one like Shelley whose mind outsoared the highest reaches of hers. The vegetable diet played its part in the mutual disillusionments: physical emptiness must have augmented asperities. Miss Hitchener had not entered fairyland or even a house of easy wealth; she had been welcomed in the thin air of idealistic endeavour such as she had never before breathed. Her failure makes the success of Eliza Westbrook's adjustment the more remarkable: vegetarianism, restless journeyings, difficulties and dangers, lack of funds, lack of a settled domicile, the months of Miss Hitchener, all these Eliza had taken in her stride, and was still high in her brother-in-law's regard.

New friends cancelled the loss of 'Portia', friends who were what they had hoped she would be, intellectually stimulating. Through the bookseller and publisher, Hookham, Shelley met Thomas Love Peacock, a sound classical scholar, and a poet— Peacock had not yet discovered his talent for prose satire. The acquaintance begun in the autumn of 1812 ripened the next year into a lasting friendship. And finally, after knowing him through letters, they met Godwin in the flesh. They came to burn incense at his shrine and found him all they had expected him to be. Godwin, Shelley averred, had formed his mind; and he had educated Harriet in Godwinian principles. He dated his own adult thinking from his first acquaintance with Godwin's great and influential book, *An Enquiry Concerning Political Justice*; having read that, he put away childish things, and became inspired with a 'passion for reforming the world'.

Harriet, sharing his hero-worshipping, wrote the news to Mrs. Nugent:

We have seen the Godwins. Need I tell you that I love them all? You have read his works, therefore you know how you feel towards the Author. His manners are so soft and pleasing that I defy even

an enemy to be displeased with him. We have the pleasure of seeing
him daily, & upon his account we determine to settle near London
for long Journeys do not agree with him, having never been in the
habit of travelling when a young Man. There is one of the Daughters
of that dear Mary Wollstonecraft living with him. She is 19 years of
Age, very plain, but very sensible. The beauty of her mind fully
overbalances the plainness of her countenance. There is an other
Daughter of hers, who is now in Scotland. She is very much like her
mother, whose picture hangs up on his Study. She must have been
a most lovely woman, her countenance speaks her a woman who
would dare to think & act for herself. I wish you could share the
pleasure we enjoy in his company. He is quite a Family Man. He
has one Son by his present wife, a little boy of 9 years old. He is
extremely clever, and will, I have no doubt, follow the same enlightened path that Godwin has before him. Godwin is particularly
fond of Curran & I am to be introduced to Miss Curran on Sunday. . . . You know that Mrs. Godwin keeps a Shop, she conducts
the whole herself. . . . They are sometimes very much pressed for a
little ready money. They require such an immense Capital, but
taking every thing as it goes, I think they will succeed. The many
trials Mrs. Godwin has had to encounter makes me very much inclined to believe her a woman of great fortitude & unyielding temper
of mind. There is a very great sweetness marked in her countenance.
In many instances she has shown herself a woman of very great
magnanimity & independence of character. Oh if you could see
them all. Tomorrow I am going to stay all day with them. G— is
very much taken with Percy. . . . He has given up everything for the
sake of our society. It gives me so much pleasure to sit and look at
him. Have you ever seen a bust of Socrates? for his head is very
much like that.

Obviously Godwin had boasted of his daughter Mary, Mrs.
Godwin of her endurance of hardships, and her business acu-
men; and young William had been encouraged to show off.
Both had emphasized the need of capital in the business; and
had disclosed their strength under adversity—adversity for them
being perpetually in their purse. Shelley seemed sent to rescue
them from drowning in a sea of debts. Overburdened with
Tremadoc commitments, he could do little at the moment.

Though the Shelleys did not realize it, Godwin was a failure,
a meteor come to earth; a hack writer, an insolvent publisher;
yet his plan for a juvenile library was a brilliant one: to give
children in abbreviated form the best of literature, and old tales

William Godwin, 1816

Signed G. H. H. (George Henry Harlow)

retold by skilled writers. Wordsworth and Coleridge, both of whom had been influenced by him, declined—he had asked Wordsworth to versify Bluebeard—but Charles Lamb and his sister produced their *Tales from Shakespeare* (which is still in print). Godwin himself under the pen-name Baldwin wrote various volumes, his re-telling of Greek legends retaining popularity for more than a century. Instead of providing moral tales for children, Godwin believed in exposing them to good and great literature carrying its moral indirectly. An efficient business manager might have made the *Juvenile Library* a well-deserved success; Mrs. Godwin struggled vainly to make it support them. Sensitive to loss of caste in tending shop, with a husband whose ways would have tried a wife upon whom he did not put the burden of earning money, she was a much harassed woman whose charm had been eroded by incessant worries; her temper earned for her vituperative epithets from Godwin's friends, even the kindest of them finding that her deviations from the truth made wariness obligatory. At first overawed, the Shelleys could not shut their eyes to the fact that the Godwin household was disorganized and needy; that did not alter their allegiance to the great thinker.

In his reverence for *Political Justice* Shelley was at one with the successful lawyer, Crabb Robinson, who, coming upon it at its publication in 1792 when he was a young man, found the whole shape of his life altered. From it he learned the evil of 'living to oneself', the virtue, the necessity, of using one's life for the good of others. Wordsworth and Coleridge had felt its influence; 'The Ancient Mariner' is built upon the theme of evil and virtue, the utter loneliness of isolationism and the saving grace of love for fellow-creatures. Shelley had been prompt to introduce Harriet to Godwin's book, and his beliefs. Moral character was not innate, but the result of the incidents of life:
. . . if these incidents could be divested of every improper tendency, vice would be extirpated from the world.

At the moment environment was not favourable for the Godwins, but in spite of adversity their virtues shone bright.

The Godwin household was a mixed one, with five children of whom only two were actually Godwin's, a fifteen-year-old

daughter, Mary Wollstonecraft Godwin, who returned from
Scotland in time to meet the Shelleys before they left London,
and a precocious nine-year-old son by his second marriage,
given to declaiming in the manner of Coleridge (a frequent
visitor) standing on a little pulpit. The two Clairmont children
of Mrs. Godwin, Charles about nineteen and Mary Jane Clara
(who chose soon to be 'Claire'), eight months younger than
Mary, were away. The young William was at home, and Fanny
Godwin, not yet nineteen. Fanny's history Shelley and Harriet
knew, though she did not herself; she believed herself the
daughter of Godwin and Mary Wollstonecraft. Often referred
to as Fanny Imlay she was more accurately Fanny Wollstonecraft. From the memoir Godwin had published of his first wife
the Shelleys learned the story of Mary Wollstonecraft; how she
had for a year been a governess in Ireland, and had then come
to London, earning her living as Godwin himself did, in literary
work for the bookseller Johnson. Through Johnson Godwin had
met her. They were not mutually attracted until later after she
had gone to France, captivated by the slogan of liberty, equality, and fraternity. She had already published *A Vindication of
the Rights of Woman*, advocating equal educational opportunities
so that women might become men's *companions*—and reasonable
creatures.

In France she had formed a free union with Gilbert Imlay, an
American writer, architect, and adventurer. In May 1794 their
daughter was born. Imlay left them in France when he moved
to London, but after a few months she joined him; and undertook with her child and the nurse a business trip for him to
Norway. Returning to London and failing to recapture the love
of the faithless Imlay, she twice attempted suicide, once as a
device to awaken his pity, once in grave earnest, throwing herself into the Thames. Not long after her rescue she again met
Godwin and briefly knew happiness. Fanny had been a bond
between them, both feeling pride in her beauty and her clever-
ness. Ten days after the birth of their daughter Mary, Mary
Wollstonecraft Godwin had died. For the sake of the child she
and Godwin had before its birth gone through the distasteful
marriage ceremony. Though Godwin was partial to his own

daughter, he had never let Fanny suspect that she was not equally his, and dear to him.

Godwin, who had never been domesticated—he had remained in his bachelor quarters in the same street as Mary Wollstonecraft's—had at her death been forced to move in with the two little girls. His search for a wife to mother them was unsuccessful until he met another of Johnson's literary hacks, a translator and writer of minor items. Mrs. Clairmont lived next door; the story goes that from her balcony she addressed him with charming naïveté: was it truly the great Mr. Godwin she had the pleasure of seeing? Eight months after this flattery, in 1801, when Fanny was seven and Mary four, they were married. She said that her first husband had been Swiss; gossips, looking at the dark complexion of her children, hinted Portuguese; others, still more unkind, said that she had never had a husband, and had been deserted.

Though he often chided her, Godwin was and remained fond of her. She left him again and again; always he begged her to return; he would write to her that he knew his way of life was difficult for her, that she had not been accustomed to debt—she would get used to it. She had, he admitted, had an easier life before marrying him, with holidays by the sea, and in France; she had ruined her health in their first years together, overworking with heavy consignments of translation, to help support the family. She was still overworked, and her disposition had soured.[9] Over the years Godwin complimented her when she was in good spirits, and deprecated her bad moods.

However poor the dinner at the Godwins', there was always a feast for the intellect; for a time Harriet was awed. At their first meeting Godwin noted in his diary that the conversation had ranged over a variety of subjects: matter and spirit, utility and truth, German thought and literature, the clergy and church government, and atheism. Godwin had withdrawn into his study with Shelley, a habit that was continued. Harriet later learned that it was not abstract philosophy that he wished to discuss but his concrete financial needs. Both Harriet and Shelley had been shocked when Godwin suggested that Shelley ought to make peace with his father, join the Whigs, and proceed with his career. Southey had prophesied that Shelley would outgrow his radicalism; Godwin could not wait, he needed money now. Shelley's promises were pleasant, but he had no money to give; if he were reconciled to his father he would have an ample allowance, and be in a position to advance money to Godwin. This was not as coldly mercenary as it sounds; Godwin believed in the sharing of property and, when he had funds, readily shared with those in need. Shelley professed to believe in the Godwinian theories; let him act upon them.[10]

By the end of their stay in London Harriet had become rather disillusioned, more so than Shelley who none the less resisted pressure and refused to make peace with his father or join the Whig party. Harriet felt that Godwin had lost his enthusiasms. Shelley could and did reject Godwin's advice as he had Southey's; and this may have been the reason for his abrupt departure from London with Harriet and Eliza. The Godwins, who had been invited to dine with them at their hotel, arrived to find them gone. Godwin's necessities did not permit him to take umbrage. Shelley's letter to Fanny offered a lame excuse:

It must indeed, I confess it, have appeared insensible and unfeeling . . . an ill return for all the kind greetings we had received at your house, to leave in haste and coldness . . . to bid not one adieu to one of you. But had you been placed in a situation where you might justly have balanced all our embarrassments, qualms, and fluctuations; had seen the opposite motives combating in our minds for mastery, had felt . . . the pain with which . . . we submitted to a galling yet unappealable necessity, you would have sympathized . . . pitied rather than criminated us unheard.

In reproaching gentle Fanny for having reproached him Shelley was evasive; it is more than probable that both he and Harriet had taken alarm at Godwin's mundane advice.

The return to Wales was through beautiful scenery; they took delight in the grandeur of the mountains. Moving into Tany-rallt, they turned their attention again to the Embankment affairs, Shelley spending hours a day at John Williams's office. Mrs. Nanney may have elicited Harriet's help as she drove about the countryside seeking contributions. Harriet and Mrs. Nanney became close friends, exchanging books and music, singing old songs, playing Mozart, dining together with their husbands. Harriet's Latin lessons advanced and a letter in Latin to Hogg was planned; friendship with him had been renewed in London.

By mid-January there was again disillusionment. Coming from Ireland's misery, remembering that of Keswick, the Shelleys had rejoiced to find in Wales a beautiful spot where justice and virtue reigned. They learned that there were, alas, unemployment, underpayment, exploitation, and want here too. Madocks was not the philanthropic citizen they had believed him to be. Gossip enlarged upon the house-parties he had held at Tanyrallt. Worse still, he had not met his obligations and was in debt to his employees. In the letter to Mrs. Nugent in which she referred to Godwin as old and unenthusiastic, forgetful of the principles for which he had once suffered gloriously, Harriet also found Madocks wanting:

All the good I wrote of Mr. Madocks I recant. I find I have been dreadfully deceived respecting that man. We are now living in his house, where formerly nothing but folly & extravagance reigned. Here they held their midnight revels insulting the Spirit of Nature's sublime scenery. The sea which used to dash against the most beautiful grand rocks, for grand indeed they are, & the mind is lost in the contemplation of them, towering above one another, & on the opposite side the most jagged mountains, whose peaks are generally covered in Clouds, was, to please his stupid vanity & to celebrate his name, turned from its course, & now we have for a fine, bold sea, which there used to be, nothing but a sandy marsh, uncultivated & ugly to the view. How poor does this work of man seem when standing on one of the mountains, we see them all rising one behind the other looking as tho' they had stood the iron grasp of time many centuries, then to look down on this embankment which, viewed from the heights, looks as if a puff of wind from the mountains would send it to oblivion like its founder's Name. The harm that Man has done thro' his extravagance is incalculable. Here he built the town of Tremadoc, and then almost ruined its Shopkeepers by never paying their just debts. We have been the means of saving the Bank from utter destruction, for which I am extremely glad, as that Person who purchases it will reap very great benefit from it.

Harriet and Shelley did not regret the time, effort, or money poured into the Embankment's repair, but the enterprise was crumbling in their hands. Four months ago, in September, Shelley had pledged a life interest in it; he had thought of Madocks as an enlightened employer, a far-sighted citizen. He had seen Wales through rose-coloured glasses unaware of the rigid attitude of its gentry banding together to resist the working-class; unaware of the misery and poverty in the district. As in Keswick and Dublin he, and Harriet, too, found the contrast of the beauty of the country and the misery of the poor unbearable. They had entered fairyland and found in it the gate to hell.

The annoyances and discomfitures of Embankment affairs turned Shelley's attention more and more to the poem he had begun in August and which he was now eager to complete, his first long poem which became the primary interest of Harriet, too. They might have remained at Tanyrallt until it was ready for the printer had there not been an occurrence even more dramatic than the attack at Keswick. Harriet wrote a full account to Thomas Hookham, which has been both accepted and discounted. The attack has been variously called a figment of Shelley's imagination, a drama staged to expedite departure, a self-attack under a delusion. The soundest conclusion would seem to be that there was a genuine attack upon Shelley, foiled; the second attack the same night *may* have been an hysterical delusion. On the 12th of March, two weeks after the attack, Harriet wrote to Thomas Hookham:

35 Cuffe Street, Stephens Green, Dublin

March 12

My dear Sir,

We arrived here last Tuesday after a most tedious passage of forty hours, during the whole of which time we were dreadfully ill. I'm afraid no diet will prevent us from the common lot of suffering when obliged to take a sea voyage.

Mr. S. promised you a recital of the horrible events that caused us to leave Wales. I have undertaken the task, as I wish to spare him, in the present nervous state of his health, every thing that can recall to his mind the horrors of that night, which I will relate.

On Friday night, the 26th of February, we retired to bed between ten and eleven o'clock. We had been in bed about half an hour, when Mr. S. heard a noise proceeding from one of the parlours. He immediately went downstairs with two pistols, which he had loaded that night, expecting to have occasion for them. He went into the billiard room, where he heard footsteps retreating. He followed into an other little room, which was called an office. He there saw a man in the act of quitting the room through a glass window which opens into the shrubbery. The man fired at Mr. S., which he avoided. Bysshe then fired, but it flashed in the pan. The man then knocked Bysshe down, and they struggled on the ground. Bysshe then fired his second pistol, which he thought wounded him in the shoulder, as he uttered a shriek and got up, when he said these words: By God, I will be revenged! I will murder your wife. I will ravish your sister. By God, I will be revenged. He then fled—as we hoped for the night. Our servants were not gone to bed, but were just going, when this horrible affair happened. This was about eleven o'clock. We all assembled in the parlour, where we remained for two hours. Mr. S. then advised us to retire, thinking it impossible he would make a second attack. We left Bysshe and our man-servant, who had only arrived that day, and who knew nothing of the house, to sit up. I had been in bed three hours when I heard a pistol go off. I immediately ran down the stairs, when I perceived that Bysshe's flannel gown had been shot through, and the window curtain. Bysshe had sent Daniel to see what hour it was, when he heard a noise at the window. He went there, and a man thrust his arm through the glass and fired at him. Thank Heaven! the ball went through his gown and he remained unhurt. Mr. S. happened to stand sideways; had he stood fronting, the ball must have killed him. Bysshe fired his pistol, but it would not go off. He then aimed a blow at him with an old sword which we found in the house. The assassin attempted to get the sword from him, and just as he was pulling it away Dan rushed into the room, when he made his escape.

This was at four in the morning. It had been a most dreadful night, the wind was as loud as thunder, and the rain descended in torrents. Nothing has been heard of him; and we have every reason to believe it was no stranger, as there is a man of the name of Leeson, who the next morning that it happened went and told the shop-keepers of Tremadoc that it was a tale of Mr. Shelley's to impose upon them, that he might leave the country without paying his bills. This they believed, and none of them attempted to do anything towards his discovery.

We left Tanyrallt on Saturday, and staid till everything was ready for our leaving the place, at the Sol General of the county's house, who lived seven miles from us. This Mr. Leeson had been heard to say that he was determined to drive us out of the country. He once happened to get hold of a little pamphlet which Mr. S. had printed in Dublin; this he sent up to Government. In fact he was forever

I

THE HUNT LIBRARY
CARNEGIE INSTITUTE OF TECHNOLOGY

saying something against us, and that because we were determined
not to admit him to our house, because we had heard his character
and from many acts of his we found that he was malignant and cruel
to the greatest degree.

The pleasure we experienced at reading your letter you may conceive, at the time when every one seemed to be plotting against us
. . . pardon me if I wound your feelings by dwelling on this subject.
Your conduct has made a deep impression on our minds, which no
length of time can erase. Would that all mankind were like thee.

Mr. Shelley and my sister unite with me in kind regards; whilst
I remain,

Yours truly,

H. Shelley.[11]

It should be noted that the night was stormy, with pelting
rain and wild wind, the sort of night to arouse apprehension,
and to cover up foot-tracks; and a wind that sounded like
thunder might sound also like a pistol shot. For some unex-
plained reason Shelley had been expecting trouble and had
loaded his pistols. Preparation for defence does not, however,
preclude the actuality of the attack. There was labour unrest in
the neighbourhood, and active enmity on Leeson's part. His
precipitate spreading of the story in the morning before Shelley
himself could tell it, his using it to create prejudice and disbelief, are indications of his involvement. He had been more
than unfriendly, and they had been hostile to him because of his
treatment of the labourers; he was a harsh employer, boasting
that he could get more work out of his men than others. The
Shelleys did not like what they heard about him, and did not
receive him socially. He did not like what he heard about them;
the Irish pamphlet reinforced his dislike. A member of a prominent Protestant family of Dublin, he was hostile to the movement for Catholic emancipation. Moreover, he was displeased
by, and possibly jealous of, the attention focused upon Shelley's
efforts for the Embankment with the corresponding belittlement
of his own more arduous, less spectacular labours. His time,
men, and horses had given help that was constant and considerable; Shelley, not Leeson, had been the guest of honour at
Beaumaris.

Leeson had come to Tremadoc, interested in Madocks's proposal to develop the area by diverting the direct route to Dublin from Holyhead to Tremadoc. He had been the main organizer of the repair work on the Embankment since its damage in February 1812, only to have his efforts now overshadowed by the promises of a stripling. The social snubs of a young couple should not have greatly perturbed the son of an earl, but the opinions of Shelley were of genuine concern; he tended to align himself on the side of the workmen, betraying his own class. There was trouble enough with the poor without the presence of a gentleman agitator. Leeson was also suspicious of his sincerity; promises did not repair a broken seawall. He had apparently been outspoken in his desire for the departure of this over-active young man who showed no respect for his substantial aid to the welfare and safety of Tremadoc.

Leeson had, then, sufficient motive for directing a seemingly murderous but actually harmless attack. It was not inconsistent with his character, nor were such hoaxes inconsistent with Welsh character—Leeson would have employed a Welshman. Shelley afterwards drew a picture of his assailant, as a Devil with horns and a tail. This may have been a distortion, but it is possible that the assailant was dressed to resemble the Devil; it is also possible that the servants had been bribed to interfere with Shelley's pistols so that they would misfire. There were three maids; and there was Dan, recently released from Barnstaple gaol. More than anything else the threats of the intruder are suspect; such melodramatic utterance is barely credible; had Shelley invented it he would have made it more plausible. It is inconsequential nonsense, lacking completely the sound of actual speech, the mouthings of a hireling acting a part, and seeking to arouse terror. Revenge, murder, ravishment—but saying this he fled with no attempt to find Harriet and Eliza. Murderers and ravishers do not succinctly announce their intention nor do they incontinently flee. The preposterousness of the utterance validates it.

The second attack *may* have been a delusion arising out of nervous apprehension; the first was real enough, with much evidence pointing to Leeson as its instigator. He used his prestige to persuade shopkeepers that it was a device of Shelley's to

expedite his departure without paying his debts; they either believed him or feared to go counter to him. They may have been
ready enough to believe the worst of a young man who had
leapt into prominence, and had run up large bills. Servants may
have gossiped about the strange household; it was not natural
to forgo meat and live on vegetables; and Shelley was odd,
forgetting meals, writing poetry, turning night into day. That
it was all Shelley's hallucination Peacock heard when he came
there the next year. Long years later a shepherd boasted that
he had been the assailant in revenge for Shelley's having in pity
shot his scabby and suffering sheep; but when he boasted,
Shelley was famous, and no one noticed that he was altogether
too young—he had been about four in 1812. Yet in essence he
was right—it was Shelley's sympathies which led to the attack;
had he not been the friend of the poor, had he not been an
agitator for Irish freedom, had he held Leeson's harsh views
of the working-man, and been moderately friendly with him,
Leeson would not have hated him and undertaken to drive him
away.[12]

Though in later years, when Shelley's fame was rising, Mr.
Madocks, who had not been in Wales during Shelley's months
as his tenant, was to claim a non-existent personal acquaintance
with him to give weight to the theory that the attack was an
hallucination, he had at the time believed it as fact, writing to
his agent, Williams:

How could Shelley mind such a contemptible trick as has been
played off to get him *out of the Country*, on account of his liberal principles. Whoever the hoxters are it is a transportable offence if discovered.[13]

His use of the terms 'trick' and 'hoxters' suggests that such
practices were not unknown. Shelley's demand for an investigation had been undermined by Leeson; by spreading his version
impugning Shelley's veracity he deprived Shelley of credence
when he impugned Leeson's. Moreover, Shelley was leaving
Tremadoc; Leeson remained. Harriet's interpretation of his
character and suspicions of his involvement gain credence from
a deliberately insulting letter written to Shelley shortly after
they had left:

Sir,—Having heard from several quarters that you lie under a mistake relative to the manner in which I was put in possession of a pamphlet signed "P. B. Shelley", I think it is a pity that you should not be undeceived. I beg to tell you it was not given to me by Mr. Ashtone, nor taken by him from Mr. John Williams' house,—*but* was handed to me by *John Williams* with a remark that you had been in the practice of haranguing 500 people at a time in Ireland. So much for your friend.

Sir I remain your
Robert Leeson.[14]

Only momentarily did Shelley distrust Williams. Williams in all probability had repeated what he had been told by Miss Hitchener, his aim, like hers, being to prove the importance of Shelley.

From Tremadoc the Shelleys with Eliza turned to Ireland with three objects in mind: to leave Tremadoc far behind; to find leisure to get the long poem, complete with its notes, ready for publication; and to obtain from a negligent printer in Dublin certain manuscripts that had been left with him, including short poems to be included in the volume with *Queen Mab*. By the time they reached Ireland they were sufficiently relaxed to extract amusement from the resentments and feeble attempts at revenge made by Miss Hitchener. Reading her letter threatening to inform against Shelley, he commented gaily to Williams:

I laughed heartily at her day of retribution, and at her idea of bringing you, me and herself before a Being whom a few months ago she was the most active to deny. If you write to her you may tell her (but not from me) that her threats of confiscation and death savour so little of vengeance or intimidation that my heart is quite subdued by the bewitching benevolence of her intentions but that I fear the government (tho' perhaps the weakest in the world) is not so miserably silly or wicked as to help the wiles of a scornful and disappointed woman.

Having dismissed her from his mind as 'a woman of desperate views and dreadful passions but of cool and undeviating revenge', he had worked off his spleen and was ready to forget her. In a postscript he suggested that Williams send this letter to her, adding

I am above all secrecy and her threats are surely calculated rather to amuse than alarm any but little boys and girls.

Harriet, reading as he wrote, saw no point in deliberately angering Miss Hitchener; with her usual good sense she cancelled her husband's instructions, writing a final postscript herself:

> Do not send this letter to Miss H. and do not answer hers.

Miss Hitchener had needed to soothe her pride and to find excuses for her separation from the Shelleys. It was Shelley against whom she spoke, not Harriet. She did tell one tale reflecting against Harriet and Eliza: that they had insulted John Williams; she added that Shelley had embarrassed Williams's brother seriously by not repaying a large sum of money. Much later Captain Pilfold, to whom she said all this, wrote to Williams expressing his relief at learning that her tales were not true. Eliza Westbrook's letter to John Williams, written as they were leaving Tremadoc permanently (a decision soon reinforced by Shelley), is both courteous and friendly:

MY DEAR MR. WILLIAMS

As Mrs. Shelly [*sic*] & myself have determined against ever residing again at Tan-y-rallt we shall be obliged if you will send the Boxes remaining there to my Fathers with proper directions, 23 Chapel Street, Grosvenor Sqr.

My good Friend, though disappointed you cannot be surprised at our not returning, the unpleasant scenes which occurred there would ever make that situation disagreeable; lovely as is the spot by nature, the neighbourhood is too corrupt for us ever to take delight in Tan-y-rallt again, particularly as a fixed residence—We are going a tour through the South of Ireland. The Carriage is now at the door waiting, all are engaged writing necessary letters. Mr. Shelley will write himself soon. They unite in kindest remembrance with

Yours very truly

E. W.

I forgot to mention the boxes must be forwarded to London immediately as there are Library Books in them which is of consequence to have returned as soon as possible.

Direct your letters as usual to 35 Great Cuffe St.[15]

On the 21st of March Shelley wrote to Williams to ask if he had secured for him from the money-lender the £400 needed to discharge his debts in Tremadoc for

> if he will not, I must be content that Leeson's lies should gain credit, and never return again.

Leeson's lies did gain credit. Tanyrallt and the Embankment became memories. The furniture made for them was sold, some of it being today still in Caernarvon with the descendant of the purchaser. The concrete interests of Catholic Emancipation and the Embankment were to be supplanted by the broader aspects of social betterment.

The 'happiest of the happy', Shelley had called himself at home with Harriet, instructing her in Latin, reading to her from the books he devoured, instilling in her mind the ideas which were crystallizing for him in the poem he was writing. The dissemination of ideas, of truths, was of utmost importance, a more lasting benefit to society than concrete schemes. Harriet's quick sympathy for the families of the poor men hanged for breaking the mechanical looms had prompted her to ask Hookham to give five pounds each for Shelley, her sister, and herself. When immediately afterwards Shelley had heard of the imprisonment of Leigh Hunt and his brother, editors of the liberal journal *The Examiner*, for their published scorn of the Prince Regent, he wrote to Hookham subscribing twenty pounds for them; he did not cancel Harriet's pledge, but, he added, it was 'an affair of more consequence' to help pay the Hunts' fine (£1000) than to succour 'the widows and children of the poor men at York'. The fight for a free press, free speech, the promulgation of liberalism, was essential to the cause of liberty.

Shelley's efforts had been put into concrete works; his previous visit to Ireland had been for a specific purpose. Now, though Harriet proclaimed herself still at heart Irish, he would not engage in polemics, but complete his poem. With *Queen Mab* he was to appeal to a wider public. It would bring together all the strands of his thinking, and give them the power of poetry that would linger in readers' minds. Harriet and Eliza served as testing ground. Begun the preceding August, *Queen Mab* had been finished and transcribed by the middle of February—in spite of pressures, frights, and journeyings.

In Dublin they stopped with their friend Lawless at 35 Great Cuffe Street long enough to deal with Stockdale and obtain the manuscripts of the poems he had refused either to publish without pre-payment (which was not customary), or to return to Shelley, or to release to Mrs. Nugent. Leaving Dublin they travelled to the lakes of Killarney, hiring a cottage where Shelley could complete the notes to *Queen Mab* and arrange a selection of the recovered poems to include in the volume. He was always to remember the beauty of 'the arbutus lakes of Killarney'; when he first saw Lake Como he found it lovelier than anything he had yet seen save Killarney. Like Nantgwillt and Lynmouth, places where he had been with Harriet, Killarney stayed fresh in his mind. But their stay was fleeting; in a few days Shelley and Harriet journeyed two days and nights, without stopping, to Dublin, in the hope of seeing Hogg. He had gone when they arrived, not having found them there. Leaving Eliza stranded with Dan and their books, they followed Hogg to London.

At first in Chapel Street at Mr. Westbrook's and then at a hotel near by, they settled down where Shelley could be in contact with Hookham, who was to publish the poem in which their interest centred. Harriet could not foresee that no poem that Shelley would write in the future would have so great an influence. She gave ready credence to its hopeful picture of the perfect world of the future, so perfect had her own little world become in less than two years. Through Shelley she had been released from the boredom of school, from the repressions of her father's home, from the narrowness of Methodism; she had been lifted into the world of the intellect and the imagination, and the world of love. With Shelley study and life itself had become a gay lark. She felt the intoxication of his ideas; in developing her mind she pleased her exciting and excitable teacher; living joyously herself, she would have all the world happy. *Queen Mab* was a guide-book to happiness; Shelley meant it to be this for her and for all who would read it. Holding the handsome little volume in her hand in late spring of the year 1813, Harriet's pride in poem and poet kept her from probing beneath the surface where lurked the threats to her very existence.

CHAPTER V

The Happiest Years

Harriet! let death all mortal ties dissolve,
But ours shall not be mortal! The cold hand
Of time may chill the love of earthly minds

    .   .   .   .   .

It dies, where it arose, upon this earth.
But ours! oh, 'tis the stretch of Fancy's hope
To portray its continuance as now,
Warm, tranquil, spirit-healing.
To Harriet: 1812

To Mrs. Nugent on 21st May Harriet wrote that Shelley's health was at last restored and that his 'poem of Queen Mab' was now printing, though

it must not be published under pain of death, because it is too much against every existing establishment. It is to be privately distributed to his friends, some Copies sent over to America. Do you [know] of any one that would wish for so dangerous a Gift?

Harriet, not yet eighteen, was expecting her first child in a month, but of her health or her coming confinement she wrote nothing; the household properly revolved around her husband, now almost twenty-one, engaged in his first major literary production. There was also to report the possibility of Shelley's reconciliation with his father; her next letter might be from Field Place. Her hope proved abortive. Both father and son were stubborn; though both desired the family united, neither would yield.

A month later Harriet forgot to be respectful, and referred to Mr. Shelley as an 'old Dotard' for demanding that Shelley write to the Oxford authorities that he would return to the Christian Church. Though his sisters continued to write to Harriet, and she to them, she ceased to expect an invitation to Field Place.

They had the more time to devote to *Queen Mab*. From Lynmouth months earlier Shelley had sent the opening cantos to
his friendly publisher, Hookham, assuring him that though
imbued with his 'constitutional enthusiasm', it could safely be
published; the Attorney-General would overlook in a poem
what he would not permit in prose. Harriet was less sure; she
feared her husband's arrest and trial for blasphemous libel. He
allayed her fears—and his own—by deciding not to issue an
inexpensive edition to be widely distributed. In March he wrote
to Hookham:

If you do not dread the arm of the law, or any exasperation of public
opinion against yourself, I wish that it should be printed and published immediately.

.   .   .   .   .

I expect no success. Let only 250 copies be printed, a small neat
Quarto, on fine paper, and so as to catch the aristocrats; they will
not read it, but their sons and daughters may.

Shelley underestimated *Queen Mab*. Though it was printed,
not 'published', though only seventy copies were distributed
in his lifetime, the poem survived, and was attentively read.
Within two years long excerpts were published in a monthly
journal; in six more years a pirated edition appeared (its publisher was sentenced to gaol). It did not have to wait a generation for audience. Though often wrongly placed among the
Juvenilia, it is a mature poem, the serious work of a developing
genius. In poetic expression it falls far short of *Prometheus
Unbound*, but it foreshadows it; the same excoriation of evil and
violence and the same joyous proclamation of Utopia are clearly
voiced. With Harriet at his side Shelley had in less than two
years grown from the schoolboy setting off verbal fireworks
under the seats of the Oxford authorities, from the adolescent
innocently urging the Irish to stop drinking and to be wary of
organized religion, from the prankster launching pamphlets in
cunningly contrived receptacles, from the enthusiast offering
his life's efforts to the preservation of the Tremadoc Embankment, into a writer of powerful prose (*Letter to Lord Ellenborough*)
and of powerful verse (*Queen Mab*). Later poems are more
splendid and more often quoted; none has more deeply in-

fluenced men's minds. One may quote the 'Ode to the West Wind' ignoring its plea for the dissemination of liberal ideas, and 'To a Skylark' without realizing that in it Shelley longed for the lark's compelling song to fill the air with reforming ideas; but no one could read *Queen Mab* without becoming aware that it is a plea for a 'life of resolute good', for an anti-materialistic, egalitarian society from which injustice, greed, and superstition (formal religion, the organized church) had been abolished. It was fitting that the final battle for a free press in England (in 1841) was fought over the publication of *Queen Mab*.

This 'long philosophical poem' was modelled on Lucretius (98(?)-55 B.C.) who in his *De Rerum Natura* attempted to free men from superstition and inherited beliefs by making them understand the nature of the universe. So Shelley proceeded to show that man could be made free by use of his *mind*; it is therefore a high tribute that he paid Harriet in calling her his 'purer mind', and as such his inspiration.

The completed poem was in nine cantos, largely, except I and II, in blank verse with lyrical passages in the stanzas popularized by Southey in *Thalaba*. Its radical subject matter is presented in a conventional framework, such as Volney used in his *Ruins of Empires*[1] and Sir William Jones in his *Palace of Fortune*,[2] both favourites of Shelley and Harriet: a frame in which the narrator (as in Volney) or a maiden (as in Jones) is magically lifted above the earth and shown visions. In *Queen Mab* the soul of the sleeping Ianthe is unbodied by the spirit of Nature and carried high in space whence she views the ant-hill earth in its place in the mighty universe, the harmony of the spheres contrasting with the discord on earth. Ianthe is both an idealization of Harriet and the ideal toward which she should strive. Ianthe accepts instruction from Queen Mab as Harriet accepted it from Shelley, her eager mind grasping the truths of astronomy, physics, history, and ethics. Ianthe, beautiful in soul as in body, is sincere, of resolute mind, free from pride and meanness, fitted to wage war against falsehood and tyranny, to conquer violence with the calm of virtue. Ianthe shudders as she sees tyranny and war, the burning of Moscow by Napoleon, and other scenes of violence and evil; yet she is assured that man is not irretrievably evil, only corrupted by environmental influences:

> Man is of soul and body, formed for deeds
> Of high resolve.

Ideas of death and rebirth are recurrent in the poem, which opens with death, the concomitant putrefaction promising renewal of life:

> Thus do the generations of the earth
> Go to the grave and issue from the womb,
> Surviving still the imperishable change
> That renovates the world; even as the leaves .
> Which the keen frost-wind of the waning year
> Has scattered on the forest soil and heaped
> For many seasons there—though long they choke,
> Loading with loathsome rottenness the land,
> All germs of promise, yet when the tall trees
> From which they fell, shorn of their lovely shapes,
> Lie level with the earth to moulder there,
> They fertilize the land they long deformed;
> Till from the breathing lawn a forest springs
> Of youth, integrity, and loveliness.

Parallel to this cycle in nature have been the cycles in history, ruins testifying to the fruits of tyranny and war, the decay of man's once triumphant vanity, mute testimony to man's hope, for in death all are equal. Ianthe views the present as the past, glaring with cruelty, virtue and love smothered by greed and superstition:

> But hoary-headed selfishness has felt
> Its death-blow, and is tottering to the grave;
> A brighter morn awaits the human day,
>
> .   .   .   .   .
>
> When poverty and wealth, the thirst for fame,
> The fear of infamy, disease and woe,
> War with its million horrors, and fierce hell,
> Shall live but in the memory of Time. . . .

Meteors, the speed of light, the great chain of Nature, and

> . . . this interminable wilderness
> Of worlds, at whose immensity
> Even soaring fancy staggers . . .

were all made clear to Ianthe. By understanding 'the nature of
things' the virtuous could lead human society gradually along
the path of love to final perfection; 'O happy Earth, reality of
Heaven!' The tyrannies of state and church overthrown, the
oppressions of wealth, commerce, and carnality outmoded, men
and women would live serenely, with no fear of death, for only
the body dies; reality lies beyond.

Shelley was already seeking expression for life as the veil
obscuring reality. Before their marriage both Harriet and
Shelley, in the mode of their generation, had thought and
talked of suicide; Shelley's letters to Hogg had been full of
poison, pistols, graveyards; Harriet's thoughts those of any
novel-reading schoolgirl. As Ianthe in *Queen Mab*, she is fearful
of death, and in need of reassurance that it would be only a
gentle ceasing of temporal life; in the happy future it would not
be preceded by the disabilities of age and disease. As her soul is
returned to her sleeping body, Ianthe is praised as

> . . . sincere and good; of resolute mind,
> Free from heart-withering custom's cold control,
>
>   .   .   .   .   .
>
> . . . worthy of the boon
> Which thou hast now received; virtue shall keep
> Thy footsteps in the path that thou hast trod,
> And many days of beaming hope shall bless
> Thy spotless life of sweet and sacred love.
> Go, happy one, and give that bosom joy
> Whose sleepless spirit waits to catch
> Light, life, and rapture from thy smile.

When she wakes she sees

> Henry, who kneeled in silence by her couch,
> Watching her sleep with looks of speechless love.

It was an exciting poem. It is a tribute to Harriet and to the
housekeeping of Eliza that Shelley had had the time to read so
many books, to compose so many thousand lines, arrange and
write so many notes, notes supporting the poetic argument by
quotations from or reference to Spinoza, the French philosophers, Cuvier, Condorcet, Cabanis, Pliny, Lucretius, Hume,
Locke, Godwin, the Koran. With one note Harriet had long
been familiar, the *Necessity of Atheism*, here slightly modified;

these were the arguments Shelley had used early in 1811 to convert her. The economic theory did not disturb her—she accepted the view that they themselves would never be the owners of wealth but its custodians, using it for social betterment, sharing it with others. With no foreboding she took calmly the note on love and marriage, its force negated for her by the glowing tributes to her in the poem itself and in the dedication to her as one who had warded off from Shelley the world's scorn, who had revived his soul, who had increased his love for mankind. The note was dealing with a hypothetical marriage, not theirs:

Not even the intercourse of the sexes is exempt from the despotism of positive institution. Law pretends even to govern the indisciplinable wanderings of passion, to put fetters on the clearest deductions of reason, and, by appeals to the will, to subdue the involuntary affections of our nature. Love is inevitably consequent upon the perception of loveliness.

Shelley had often told her that she was lovely. 'Love withers under restraint', but there was no constraint.

A husband and wife ought to continue so long united as they love each other; any law which should bind them to cohabitation for one moment after the decay of their affection would be a most intolerable tyranny. . . . There is nothing immoral in . . . separation. Constancy has nothing virtuous in itself. . . . Love is free; . . . Persons of delicacy and virtue, unhappily united to those whom they find it impossible to love, spend the loveliest season of their life in unproductive efforts to appear otherwise than they are, for the sake of the feelings of their partner or the welfare of their mutual offspring. . . . Had they been suffered to part at the moment when indifference rendered their union irksome, they would have been spared many years of misery; they would have connected themselves more suitably and would have found that happiness in the society of congenial partners which is forever denied them by the despotism of marriage.

But Harriet knew that she and Shelley *were* suitably connected; it was inconceivable that either could find in another the love and companionship they had found in each other. Shelley had already looked forward to their future years:

> . . . nor when age
> Has tempered these wild extasies, and given
> A soberer tinge to the luxurious glow

Which blazing on devotion's pinnacle
Makes virtuous passion supersede the power
Of reason; nor when life's aestival sun
To deeper manhood shall have ripened me;
Nor when some years have added judgment's store
To all thy woman sweetness, all the fire
Which throbs in thine enthusiast heart; not then
Shall holy friendship (for what other name
May love like ours assume?) not even then
Shall custom so corrupt, or the cold forms
Of this desolate world so harden us,
As when we think of the dear love that binds
Our souls in soft communion, while we know
Each other's thoughts and feelings, can we say
Unblushingly a heartless compliment,
Praise, hate, or love with the unthinking world,
Or dare to cut the unrelaxing nerve
That knits our love to virtue. Can those eyes
Beaming with mildest radiance on my heart
To purify its purity, e'er bend
To soothe its vice or consecrate its fears?
Never, thou second self![3]

Written the previous year this verse has little to recommend it as poetry, but much as an expression of conjugal devotion that its writer fully expected to continue indefinitely; it is an explicit statement of their congenial interests and of her beneficent effect upon him. The divorce which he believed the law should grant freely was for other people. Even then he advocated restrictions, continuing his note:

I by no means assert that the intercourse should be promiscuous; on the contrary it appears, from the relation of parent to child, that this union is generally of long duration, and marked above all others with generosity and self-devotion.

Harriet awaited with confidence the birth of their first child. Their love had survived many hazards: the threat from Hogg's lovemaking, the threat from Miss Hitchener, discomforts and disappointments. Meanwhile they were happy to be back in London, for which Harriet had often longed wistfully. Shelley could personally see his writings through the press with Hookham, with whom they were very friendly, as they were with Peacock. Peacock provided the intellectual companionship essential to Shelley's well-being. Hogg was in London, ready to accept friendship on their terms; whatever his sentiments, he did not again seek Harriet's love. He was no longer a completely satisfactory companion, for he made no pretence of sharing their wide sympathies and radical views. Though welcome, he no longer was a dominant influence.

Frank Newton, who, with his wife and five children, lived not far from Cooke's Hotel, was an ardent vegetarian and nudist. Though Harriet ate meat during pregnancy she still was, together with Shelley and Eliza, a professed vegetarian. Mrs. Newton shared Harriet's interest in music; both were singers, but neither moved Shelley to lyrical appreciation of her singing voice. The Shelleys became even more intimate with Mrs. Newton's sister, Mrs. Boinville, who, though she had a daughter of Harriet's age, was still a comparatively young woman; Shelley called her 'Maimuna' after Southey's sorceress in *Thalaba* whose

> . . . face was as a damsel's face,
> And yet her hair was white.

Mrs. Boinville was beautiful, charming, romantic; she was all that he would have Harriet become in character and in cultivation. The recent loss of her father and her husband in close succession had turned her hair white overnight. She had eloped with a French émigré met at the home of her liberal father; later, with her husband, a friend of Lafayette, she had gone to France where he had hoped to reclaim his estates. For years her life had been full of excitement, and she had suffered imprisonment and shipwreck. Her husband had died in Poland of exposure to cold on the disastrous retreat from Moscow. She had settled in a pleasant house with ample gardens in Bracknell, not far from Windsor and Eton, in country which Shelley had long known and loved. About her she gathered a group of people interested in the arts and in the art of conversation: French émigrés, poets, artists, writers, all earnestly cultivating the life of the mind by simple living and vegetarianism, the current interest being the study of Italian literature—Petrarch, Tasso, Ariosto.

The Shelleys did not move to Bracknell until after the birth of the baby at Cooke's Hotel in London on the 23rd of June. This date is that given in the baptismal registry of St. George's Church, Hanover Square, and on the tombstone of Ianthe Eliza Shelley Esdaile in Cothelstone churchyard, Somerset. It is also indicated by the dates of Shelley's letters written before and after the birth; and the presence of Harriet at the hotel at the time of his writing indicates that the child was born there. Eliza had returned from Killarney and was near by at Chapel Street. On the 21st of June Shelley had written to the Horsham lawyer, Thomas Medwin, that he could not come to confer with him as he could not leave Mrs. Shelley, who might be confined at any moment, or not for six weeks; on the 28th he wrote him of her rapid recovery from the birth of her daughter. On the 27th he had written to John Williams, then in London, inviting him to call that same day:

. . . at any time before two o'clock, I shall be at home, if afterwards, Mrs. S. will be very happy to see you.

The baby's name was that of the heroine of *Queen Mab* added to Eliza which had multiple reference: it was the name of Harriet's well-loved sister, of Shelley's favourite sister, and of his mother. Hogg, who never saw the child, asserted that Shelley paid it little attention; Peacock, who saw it often, affirmed that Shelley was very fond of it, lulling it in his arms with a chant: Yáhmani, Yáhmani. Like many another young person he had long talked of the proper way to raise children; he had definite ideas, many culled from George Ensor's book on education. Ensor stressed the importance of the early months and the importance of a mother's nursing her own infant, which was not the custom. For the first time Harriet opposed her husband's wishes; she hired a wet-nurse to whom he took an instant dislike. Eliza may or may not have instigated her refusal; she would have wanted Harriet to follow the normal procedure of the well-to-do and the upper classes. (In a little over two years Lord Byron's wife, following the new fashion, nursed her infant.) Harriet was none the less extremely fond of her daughter; she wrote to Mrs. Nugent:

I wish you could see my sweet Babe. She is so fair, with such blue eyes, that the more I see of her the more beautiful she looks.

K

Hogg's charge of coldness toward the child was a fabrication. If his story is true that she insisted upon being present when the doctor performed some slight operation upon Ianthe's eye, her presence bespeaks not coldness but the warm love that would soothe the child, and an interest in her welfare that would make it essential to be present. Her refusal to nurse the infant was caused not by a lack of love but by a sense of propriety. Apparently she did not comprehend how deeply disturbed Shelley was to have his child suckled by a stranger.

In all else Harriet remained acquiescent. She willingly moved to Bracknell to be near Mrs. Boinville and Cornelia Turner, her young married daughter who spent much of her time with her mother. The Shelleys' house, High Elms, named for the trees which together with a yew hedge separated its grounds from the road, was a house of solid size and charm, its long windows and high-ceilinged rooms giving it spaciousness. Here they could entertain all the Newtons; here Peacock could often join them, walking from Marlow. In anticipation of financial solvency as his twenty-first birthday approached, Shelley had a carriage made; not a luxury, but a necessity in the country where they were settling down as a family. Neither Shelley nor Harriet—nor for that matter Eliza—had, previous to recent times, known life without such amenities as horses and carriages. Travel by coach had been as much of an austerity as their cottages in Keswick and Lynmouth, romantic because out of line with their upbringing. They still hoped to acquire Nantgwillt; meanwhile High Elms was a pleasant temporary residence.

There is nothing to substantiate Hogg's statement, years later, that Harriet dropped her studies after the baby's birth, turning her attention to frocks and hats. Bracknell was not a metropolis; and Harriet's tastes had always been toward quiet elegance. Obviously, like any mother, she needed new clothes after pregnancy. She showed no diminution of interest in discussion; and Peacock found her an agreeable companion. Peacock did not share Shelley's high opinion of the Boinville set; he tolerated them but was not fully sympathetic. Indeed he found their intensity comic; they found his lack of intensity deplorable. Peacock was a more serious scholar than any of them except

Shelley, whom he was guiding in the study of the Greek classics. Harriet had progressed well in Latin; she had read some of the *Odes* of Horace and some Ovid, but she was not yet ready for Greek, reading it only in translation. She did not take life as lightly as Peacock who deprecated over-seriousness:

The world is a stage, and life is a farce, and he that laughs most has most profit in the performance.

This was a different cynicism from Hogg's. Peacock had a better-informed mind, and a more active one. His understanding of Shelley was deeper than Hogg's, his wit more penetrating, his mind richer. Harriet's naturally merry nature responded to his gaiety; he turned to her to share his amusement over the Boinville group of earnest thinkers, and Harriet was sometimes caught smiling or laughing with him. She admired Mrs. Boinville, and always remained friendly with her, but she did not romanticize her.

Shelley began Italian lessons at this time, learning the musical language from the pretty lips of Cornelia. He needed relaxation from the gruelling labour of the notes to *Queen Mab*, a labour in which Harriet had helped; in his verses to her he praised her sharing of his 'thoughts and feelings'; the writing of the poem, the preparing of the notes, had not separated them but drawn them closer together. She did not join him in Italian lessons; probably because she was occupied with Ianthe, possibly because she did not wish to turn from her Latin. The summer slipped by pleasantly, though creditors were growing insistent, especially as Shelley, now of age, was responsible for his debts. His father's intransigence postponed a settlement or an enlarged allowance. Rumours spread; they feared disinheritance; they heard that the Duke of Norfolk was advising Mr. Shelley to divert property to his younger son; they feared Shelley's arrest for debt. Idle rumours, all; Harriet had letters from Shelley's sisters telling her that their father was still interested in his older son; that he was cognizant of his difficulties and would try to prevent his arrest. There was the debt for the carriage; the debts contracted at Tremadoc; and a host of bills contracted at Oxford, including the cost of publishing *St. Irvyne*. Shelley had rashly at that time underwritten the books of others. Since

marriage he had helped various writers and countless poor
people; he had pledged a heavy sum for the repair of the Embankment; £100 a year to Miss Hitchener; and he was planning
to settle a similar annuity upon Peacock (who in return was to
be a sort of literary agent for him).

Though they had lived simply, they could not keep within the
modest allowances given by her father and his. Mr. Shelley had
never increased the sum originally granted Shelley as a bachelor
of eighteen. Their income was not sufficient for them to live in
the manner of their upbringing, or to live at all well. With a
growing family Shelley showed no disposition to alter his benevolent ways. He was also becoming more and more concerned
with the financial stringency of Godwin. Harriet, pregnant, had
avoided Mrs. Godwin's temper and ill-nature; Shelley's reverence for Godwin had not abated.

To evade their creditors, the Shelleys, taking Peacock with
them, suddenly left Bracknell in the autumn, heading for the
Lake country. As Peacock was not one to subject himself to
strain, his readiness to accompany Harriet and Shelley speaks
well for them; indeed for all of them; and for Eliza's good
management—that four adults of disparate dispositions and
abilities should travel for many days by carriage, with a small
infant who at three and a half months would have required a
wet-nurse, without obvious strain. No doubt the long philosophical discussions, though interrupted, went on; Harriet had,
on the 10th of September, written to Miss Nugent of what they
had been talking about with Peacock:

Of late we have had many arguments concerning the respect that all
men pay to property. Now what do you think of this affair? I wish
much to know if your ideas on this subject correspond with ours!

Obviously she and Shelley were in accord; and there was nothing acrimonious in these 'arguments', even though Peacock's
views, notably on the subject of commerce, differed from
Shelley's; Shelley called commerce a 'blighting bane', a selfishness, unable to see its virtues as Peacock expounded them.

Peacock fitted well into the family. He had a deep love of
waters, and was happy idling along stream or lake, launching
paper boats with Shelley. He had not been to a university but,

well grounded in the habits of study at school, he had continued his education by spending over three years reading in the British Museum. It was not lack of feeling that gave him the aspect of coldness, but its control. This was one of the bonds with Harriet who, unlike the Boinvilles, did not give rein to her enthusiasms. Peacock, who seemed heart-free, was in reality susceptible; at twenty-two (he was now twenty-eight, seven years older than Shelley, ten than Harriet) he had fallen in love with an eighteen-year-old girl, holding romantic meetings with her in the ruins of Newark Abbey, not far from Chertsey where he was brought up. When her family interfered and she married someone else, he did not, so far as is known, peek and pine and rave about suicide as Shelley had over his cousin's defection, but he cherished her memory all his life (she had died a year after her marriage) and always wore a locket with her hair in it.

The sentimentality of cherishing an early frustration was a habit of the period. Though he did not talk of it, he was in love again with a Welsh girl he had met in the spring of 1811. He was to have other adventures in love in the next few years; but in the end he proposed to and married the Welsh lass whom he had not seen for eight years. Harriet may have reminded him of her whom he recalled as 'the most innocent, the most amiable, the most beautiful girl in existence'; meanwhile he kept outwardly a cool non-committal attitude toward love and life.

It was, of course, Shelley who financed the journey begun early in October, receiving from money-lenders the sum of £500 in return for a post-obit bond of four times that amount, payable when he should come into his inheritance. The cash was enough to provide for living expenses but not enough to pay debts; therefore as Harriet wrote, 'We do not wish anyone to know where we are', and Hookham was instructed to address Shelley under cover to Peacock. Shelley pinned his hopes on November when he was to see his father, but Harriet wrote Mrs. Nugent:

I do not expect they will settle anything, for Mr. S. will never give way to his son in the least!

Loyally she upheld her husband and did not expect him to accept his father's terms.

After an overnight stop at Warwick they had gone to Low Wood Inn, Ambleside, Westmorland, 'close to the Lake of Winandermere'; Harriet's letter to Mrs. Nugent reflected their joy at being 'again among our dear mountains', as well as much pleasure in her 'sweet babe'. At this point the servant Dan was sent back to Ireland, discharged for some unspecified conduct Harriet called 'unprincipled'. They had come to Low Wood because it was the scene of Godwin's novel *Fleetwood*; at this inn the hero had lived when he wooed his wife. Shelley was still hero-worshipping, eager to breathe the air that had inspired Godwin. But they found no house here, nor in Keswick near the Calverts, toward whose home they now turned, assured of a hospitable welcome for their party.

Such a cottage as that in which they had been happy before was now inadequate. Until they could afford to buy Nantgwillt, still their dearest hope, they needed other quarters large enough for a growing family. They continued northwards, and came once more to Edinburgh. On the 20th of October Harriet expressed her joy in being there:

MY DEAR MRS. NUGENT

My last Letter was written from the Lakes of Cumberland where we intended to stay till next spring but not finding any House that would suit us we came on to this far famed City. A little more than two years has passed since I made my first visit here to be united to Mr. Shelley; to me they have been the happiest and the longest years of my life. The rapid succession of events since that time make the two years appear unusually long. I think the regular method of measuring Time is by the number of different ideas which a rapid succession of events naturally give rise to. When I look back to the time before I was married I seem to feel I have lived a long time; tho' my age is but eighteen yet I feel as if I was much older.

Why are you so silent, my dear Friend? I earnestly hope you are not ill; I am afraid it is nearly a month since I heard from you. I know well you would write oftener if you could. What is your employment on a Sunday? I think on those days you might snatch a few minutes to gratify my wishes. Do not direct your letter to me at Mrs. Calvert's but to the Post Office in this City. We think of remaining here all this Winter. Tho' by no means fond of cities yet I wished to come here, for when we went to the Lakes we found such a set of human beings living there that it took off all our desire of remaining among the mountains. This City is, I think, much the best. The people here are not so intolerant as they are in London. Literature stands on a higher footing here than any where else. My darling Babe is quite well & very much improved. Pray let me hear from you to tell me if I can do any thing for you. Mr. Shelley joins me and Eliza in kind regards to you whilst I remain

Your affectionate friend

H. S.

Do not tell anyone where we are.

As with today's air-letters, all was crowded in the single sheet. It is a revealing letter, showing that all was well within the family. Shelley, who in September had seen his father with no good results, would sooner or later go to London to talk with him again; but, as Mr. Shelley was laid up with gout, the meeting was postponed. The judgment of cities, of Edinburgh as a cultural centre, that Harriet expressed was undoubtedly Shelley's reflection; that on the measurement of time other than chronologically, her own.

Settled in pleasant lodgings in Frederick Street, not far from those of two years ago in George Street, Harriet felt her happiness keenly. Then she had gone on foot with Shelley and Hogg; now she could go further in her carriage, and now she had her blue-eyed Ianthe. Instead of Hogg, there was with them Peacock, whose conversation was more stimulating, his laughter less wild. With him Shelley was deep in discussion as he worked on a prose dialogue, *A Refutation of Deism*. And there was a new friend who sat admiringly at Shelley's feet, a Brazilian medical student, Joachim Baptista Pereira; as he worked upon a translation into Portuguese of *Queen Mab*, prefacing it with a sonnet to 'Sublime Shelley', he caught their enthusiasm for vegetarianism—which Peacock never shared. Because it had not been feasible to publish *Queen Mab*, its audience was restricted; the translation to be published abroad was therefore gratifying; its ideas would be spread. Though he had acquiesced when Godwin objected to his Irish pamphlets, especially the plan for an association, he had been saddened at discontinuing their distribution. He had then written to Godwin:

But I submit; I shall address myself no more to the illiterate. I will look to events in which it will be impossible that I can share, and make myself the cause of an effect which will take place ages after

I have mouldered in the dust; I need not observe that this resolve requires stoicism. To return to the heartless bustle of ordinary life, to take interest in its uninteresting details, I cannot. Wholly to abstract our views from self undoubtedly requires unparalleled disinterestedness. There is not a completer abstraction than labouring for distant ages.[4]

He had faced the situation; it was necessary to avoid the suspicion of inciting to violence. The title-page of the *Refutation* omitted the author's name; and it was 'Printed', not published; its public was narrowed by its expensive format, and by the warning: ΣΥΝΕΤΟΙΣΙΝ. [For the Intelligent.] It was an exercise in irony too subtle to invite prosecution, too intellectual to be within the comprehension of the man in the street for whose protection the laws of libel were designed. Harriet's fears were further lulled by the wording of the preface:

The mode of printing this little work may appear too expensive, either for its merits or its length. However inimical this practice confessedly is, to the general diffusion of knowledge, yet it may be adopted in this instance with a view of excluding the multitude from the abuse of a mode of reasoning, liable to misconstruction on account of its novelty.

Yet he had not scrupled to declare his purpose in the first paragraph of the preface:

The object of the following Dialogue is to prove that the system of Deism is untenable. It is attempted to prove that there is no alternative between Atheism and Christianity; that the evidences of the Being of a God are to be deduced from no other principles than those of Divine Revelation.

The Author endeavours to show how much the cause of natural and revealed Religion has suffered from the mode of defence adopted by Theosophistical Christians.

The casual reader might assume that the author meant to establish the truth of Christianity by demolishing Deism; the true meaning was not immediately obvious and might have to wait for recognition; in the end it would be believed. It was all clear enough to Harriet as explained by Shelley, discussed with her and with Peacock; modern readers have been baffled or misled. With skilful irony and thinly veiled glee, Shelley presented conventional believers as ignoramuses or self-deluded simpletons; proving that few men really think:

It is among men of genius and science that Atheism alone is found, but among these alone is cherished an hostility to those errors with which the illiterate and vulgar are infected.

The conclusion thus attaches obloquy to believers rather than to atheists for 'men of powerful intellect and spotless virtue' in every age have protested against credulity. Shelley was tripping readers into the net of disbelief by leading them along the plank of belief until in midstream it broke beneath them. Normal self-respecting readers, Shelley thought, would reject alliance with the ignorant, and would be beguiled into assent point by point until their inconsistency overcame them. He made the absurd depend upon the obvious, the dangerous conclusion derive from the commonplace; certainties proved at best only probabilities.

His pleasure in its writing was enhanced by the pleasure of his audience, Harriet and Peacock, in his wit, his artfulness. Any attempt to prosecute would be met by the explicit warning in the Preface against misconstruction of its mode of reasoning. The unwary, then as today, could take it to be a defence of conventional Christianity. The risk of being misunderstood was less dangerous than the risk of prosecution for blasphemous libel. Shelley never, after his experience with the *Necessity of Atheism* at Oxford, courted martyrdom; and Harriet had a dread of his imprisonment.

In the dialogue, Eusebes, a Christian, and Theosophus, a Deist, attempt each to convert the other. If Deism is proved untenable 'there is no alternative between Atheism and Christianity'; and the Deist finally agrees to 'endeavour to adopt as much of the Christian scheme as is consistent with my persuasion of the goodness, unity, and majesty of God'. Hence, before accounting this a victory for Eusebes, the Christian, it is wise to examine his arguments to learn if his religion does promulgate 'the goodness, unity, and majesty of God', or if the final statement is an echo of the triumphant 'Q.E.D.' at the end of the less mature *Necessity of Atheism*. Between the writing of these two pamphlets Shelley had gained a wide acquaintance with the literature of scepticism; many of these books Harriet had read with him; some she knew only as he had expounded them to her. That she believed and disbelieved only because Shelley did was not true; she had early opposed her belief to his disbelief and had been vanquished in argument. Step by step she had followed the development of thought now presented in the dialogue. There is also no evidence that Eliza had yet found her brother-in-law's free-thinking in any way reprehensible. Whether by intent or neglect, Ianthe had not been christened.

In the dialogue the assault upon Deism is direct, that upon Christianity oblique. Eusebes' paeans of praise for Christianity, digested, become a firm foundation for disbelief; his defence makes a parade of all the weakest points in the church's position. The *defence* parallels and echoes the *attack* spoken in *Queen Mab* by Ahasuerus in answer to the question:

> Is there a God?—aye, an almighty God,
> And vengeful as almighty! . . .
>
> .   .   .   .   .   .
>
> . . . [his] name . . . dreaded . . .

Eusebes points to the injustice of salvation by faith; Ahasuerus presents this as an attack, Eusebes as a defence. Theosophus, the Deist, calls it unjust that God should condemn to hell all those who, having lived before Christ, could not have been enlightened. Eusebes counters with ironic disparagement of Democritus, Pliny, Lucretius, Euripides; and of Anaxagoras, Pythagoras, and Plato, monotheists but not, because of early birth, Christian. Blandly Eusebes infers their eternal suffering in hell—God would not have used hell as a vain threat merely to frighten men; damnation therefore must be actual. By his approval Eusebes demonstrated the irrationality of such belief.

Eusebes' high praise of Christianity stresses its approval of humility but not of other qualities 'which have engaged the admiration of mankind'. He assumes that all Christians live by their creed and are other-worldly, humble, charitable, and chaste. The Christian despises this world in order to inherit the world to come.

Eusebes attacks Theosophus's deistical belief in a creative

deity rather than in the Law of Necessity, the 'Mother of the World'. Eusebes declares

The laws of attraction and repulsion, desire and aversion, suffice to account for every phenomenon of the moral and physical world. A precise knowledge of the properties of any object, is alone requisite to determine its manner of action. Let the mathematician be acquainted with the weight and volume of a cannon ball, together with the degree of velocity and inclination with which it is impelled, and he will accurately delineate the course it must describe, and determine the force with which it will strike an object at a given distance. Let the influencing motive, present to the mind of any person be given, and the knowledge of his consequent conduct will result.

Harriet could well have pondered the possible results of this thinking. Not being a mathematician, a philosopher, or a psychologist, she did not translate this theory into terms of conduct, nor even Eusebes' reasoning that order and disorder are only relative terms:

All . . . is abstractedly neither good nor evil because good and evil are words employed to designate that peculiar state of our own perceptions, resulting from the encounter of any object calculated to produce pleasure or pain. Exclude the idea of relation, and the words good and evil are deprived of import.

Harriet thought she believed this; Shelley wholeheartedly did.

At the end, in the same breath with which Eusebes asks Theosophus to choose between Atheism and Christianity, he points out that such wise men as Bacon, Newton, Locke, and Hume had disproved 'the existence of God', and that

The Christian Religion, then, alone, affords the indisputable assurance that the world was created by the power, and is preserved by the Providence of an Almighty God, who, in justice, has appointed a future life for the punishment of the vicious and the remuneration of the virtuous.

It should be noted that the God of Eusebes is the Old Testament anthropomorphic God of wrath, and it is the literal truth he upholds, the either-or acceptance of narrow belief or denial of belief.

Such a piece of writing was not calculated to make Shelley's father relent; it was the son's answer to the terms of reconciliation; far from recanting he was offering a more powerful and

effective plea for free-thinking. He was not moderating his ideas
—or making the slightest pretence.

Because he was writing what concerned him deeply, with a
sympathetic and harmonious family, the weeks in Edinburgh
were happy ones, or would have been had he not been harassed
over finances. Aside from his own needs, he had committed
himself to Godwin. Accepting the theory that property belonged
to him whose need was greatest, he was determined to 'save'
Godwin. It angered him that Eliza opposed his grandiose plan
for pulling Godwin out of the financial morass (which was his
natural habitat). That Eliza was fundamentally right in her
opposition only made his affection for her sour into hatred. In
the hinterland of his over-active mind there lurked a faint suspicion of the impossibility of the task. Harriet had commented
upon the change in Godwin, no longer a Socrates, but an un-
impassioned man. Shelley fought against this disillusionment,
preferring to believe himself deceived in Eliza for whom his
feelings had now run the full course: admiration, unity of outlook, affection, disillusionment, hatred. His affection for his
father had faded under disagreement and disapprobation; his
father had become a tyrant, and an ugly, ungenerous bigot.
Elizabeth Hitchener had descended from the enlightened sister
of his soul to the Brown Demon. Eliza Westbrook now became
a 'loathsome worm'. It would have afforded Eliza a grim satisfaction if she could have read over his shoulder as he wrote to
Godwin a few years hence (7th August 1820):

I have given you within a few years the amount of a considerable
fortune, and have destituted myself for the purpose of realising it of
nearly four times the amount. Except for the *goodwill* which this
transaction seems to have produced between you and me, this money,
for any advantage that it ever conferred on you, might as well have
been thrown into the sea. Had I kept in my own hands this £4,000
or £5,000 and administered it in trust for your permanent advantage, I should have been indeed your benefactor. The error, however,
was greater in the man of mature years, extensive experience, and
penetrating intellect than in the crude and impetuous boy.

'Crude and impetuous' were terms he would not have brooked
from Eliza in 1813 when, returned to London, he busied himself with Godwin's affairs. Godwin's diary recorded daily meet-

ings with him; in December he was penning letters to money-lenders from Godwin's address, 41 Skinner Street.

Harriet, Eliza, and Ianthe had returned from Scotland with him, and Peacock had gone his own way. Shelley's antipathy to Eliza smouldered, blazing into fury in early spring. By March 1814 he had forgotten the years of harmony when Eliza had kept the household in order, managed their meagre finances cleverly, sewed a scarlet cloak for Harriet, shared lodgings, cottages, gracious houses, the discomforts of hasty journeys by land and sea, the literary plans, the schemes for aiding the Irish, the Welsh, the world; he could see her now only as an obstruction, an intruder:

I certainly hate her with all my heart and soul. It is a sight which awakens an inexpressible sensation of disgust and horror to see her caress my poor little Ianthe, in whom I may hereafter find the consolation of sympathy. I sometimes feel faint with the fatigue of checking the overflowings of my unbounded abhorrence for this miserable wretch. But she is no more than a blind and loathsome worm, that cannot see to sting.

In contrast to Eliza, Cornelia, Mrs. Boinville's daughter, was the 'reverse of everything bad', having inherited 'all the divinity of her mother'. Eliza might have had a 'sensation of disgust' had she seen the verses enclosed for Hogg's perusal—though Shelley labelled the stanza 'a delirious vision' with 'no more reality than the colour of the Autumn sunset'. It might have referred to either Cornelia or her mother, but would seem to be addressed to the daughter:

> Thy dewy looks sink in my breast;
>   Thy gentle words stir poison there;
> Thou hast disturbed the only rest
>   That was the portion of despair!
> Subdued to Duty's hard control,
>   I could have borne my wayward lot;
> The chains that bind this ruined soul
>   Had cankered then—but crushed it not.[5]

Refusal of sympathy, of complete approval, was to Shelley like a blast from the North Pole. Harriet could not remain loyal to her sister without creating in him the feeling that he was on

sunless terrain. Mrs. Boinville five days before had told Hogg
that Shelley was hunting for a house in Bracknell

resolved to leave off rambling. . . . Seriously I think his mind and
body want rest. His journeys after what he has never found have
racked his purse and his tranquillity.[6]

What he had never found was a proper place in which to live
where he could exert that influence for good he held to be life's
end; a place like Nantgwillt, with an income large enough to
support the spread of his liberal ideas; and he had never found
his ideal woman.

Harriet was obviously not ready to repudiate her sister with
whom she was currently staying at their father's in London,
Shelley going back and forth to Bracknell. He had on the 16th
of March told Hogg that he had been staying for the past month
with Mrs. Boinville, but this is an obvious inaccuracy. Six days
later in London, taking Godwin with him, he made application
for a licence to remarry Harriet, as he had always meant to do
when he came of age. He stated under oath that he was 'of the
Parish of Saint George Hanover Square', and that his 'usual
abode hath been in the said Parish of Saint George Hanover
Square for the space of Four weeks last past'. He could not have
been both in Bracknell and resident in the Parish of St. George's
Church. Since the purpose of the remarriage was to insure the
validity of a union contracted when they were under age and
had not fulfilled the residence requirements of Scotland, it is
unlikely that the Westbrooks would have permitted any falsity
of statement. Shelley must have spent considerable time with
Harriet at her father's. Moreover, he had to be in London to
raise money, most of which was intended for Godwin; on the 4th
of March he negotiated with London money-lenders; he was to
sell a post-obit bond for £8000 for less than one-third its value:
£2593, 10 shillings. On the 13th he wrote from Bracknell to his
father—perhaps to avoid Eliza's eyes—saying that unless his
grandfather helped him he would have to sell post-obit bonds.
His grandfather did not assist him.

On the 24th of March Shelley and Harriet were remarried
at St. George's Church. Whatever the friction over Eliza their
mutual affection remained; Shelley had railed against Eliza

without a word against Harriet, though he implied that Harriet
wished Eliza to remain. He had written in his verses of 'Duty's
hard control', but he had not yet accused Harriet of freezing
his heart. If love had wavered, it was renewed by the ceremony
of remarriage, and Harriet soon knew that there would be
another child at Christmas time. There is no record of the house
they moved into at Bracknell; Eliza went with them, but
shortly after the middle of April took her departure, Harriet
accompanying her to London whence she would go to Southampton. Her absence did not solve much for Shelley; he was
greatly harassed, and Harriet must have missed her sister very
much. Eliza had taken responsibility for Ianthe, and for the
household; even with servants, Harriet was forced to spend
more of her time in domestic matters, leaving Shelley free to
join the Boinvilles; when he was not reading Italian poetry and
entering into long discussions with them, he was off to London
to tire himself out with money-lenders. Left much alone, in
the early weeks of pregnancy, not yet nineteen, she was not
adroit enough to cope with and dispel Shelley's moods of
despondency, to detach him either from Mrs. Boinville and
Cornelia or from Godwin. With no immediate prospect of a
settled home, with the money that could have secured Nantgwillt
borrowed to appease Godwin's creditors, Harriet understandably listened to Eliza's advice and delayed her return from
London.

In April, May, and June, Shelley wrote out his mixed emotions in poems, the first of which was addressed to himself:

Stanzas—April, 1814

Away! the moor is dark beneath the moon,
  Rapid clouds have drank the last pale beam of even:
Away! the gathering winds will call the darkness soon,
  And profoundest midnight shroud the serene lights of heaven.

Pause not! The time is past! Every voice cries, Away!
  Tempt not with one last tear thy friend's ungentle mood:
Thy lover's eye, so glazed and cold, dares not entreat thy stay:
  Duty and dereliction guide thee back to solitude.

Away, away! to thy sad and silent home;
　Pour bitter tears on its desolated hearth;
Watch the dim shades as like ghosts they go and come,
　And complicate strange webs of melancholy mirth.

The leaves of wasted autumn woods shall float around thine head:
　The blooms of dewy spring shall gleam beneath thy feet:
But thy soul or this world must fade in the frost that binds the dead,
　Ere midnight's frown and morning's smile, ere thou and peace
　　may meet.

The cloud shadows of midnight possess their own repose,
　For the weary winds are silent, or the moon is in the deep:
Some respite to its turbulence unresting ocean knows;
　Whatever moves, or toils, or grieves, hath its appointed sleep.

Thou in the grave shalt rest—yet till the phantoms flee
　Which that house and heath and garden made dear to thee ere-
　　while,
Thy remembrance, and repentance, and deep musings are not free
　From the music of two voices and the light of one sweet smile.

Not distinguished for clarity, the verses betray a despondency
arising from two different affections, that for his home with
Harriet, 'sad and silent' in her absence; and that for Mrs.
Boinville and Cornelia, especially, it would seem, the latter.
Here, too, is the despair of peace this side of the grave which was
to recur most poignantly toward the end of his short life. These
verses bear a striking resemblance to those written years hence
to Jane Williams, 'The serpent is shut out of Paradise', also
written in April; then, too, his home was 'cold' and he could
find no rest. It was the Shelleyan pattern, one he could never
escape. In April 1814 either by Mrs. Boinville's decision or his
own, dictated by his sense of duty, he was compelled to withdraw from the charmed circle of unworldliness, poetry, and
refinement where life was lived much as he had planned it for
Harriet and himself. The combination of ultra-refinement and
bohemianism there contrasted with the dull ordered regularity
of the Westbrook household such as Eliza had no doubt tried
to impose upon the Shelleys.

　Influenced by her sister, Harriet had let Shelley feel her dis-

approval, her hurt pride perhaps over his devotion to the Boinvilles, certainly over his reckless absorption in Godwin. As she
remained friends with Mrs. Boinville later on, when Mrs. Boinville refused to receive Shelley, she presumably saw nothing
wrong in his relations with Cornelia. Her own close companionship with him had been interrupted by his absorption in his
Italian studies with Cornelia, and even more by his vexatious
dealings with money-lenders, trying to secure a very large sum
of money for Godwin, ever more insistent. Domestic peace had
also been disturbed by the struggle between Eliza and Shelley
for Harriet's loyalty. Though Eliza had been forced to withdraw, she had not lost her hold upon Harriet.

The sense of guilt, seen in the verses of April as a dull back-
drop, pervades the two poems of May (to Harriet) and of June
(to Mary) which closely resemble each other in mood, metre,
and pattern. The lines dated at Cooke's Hotel, London, in May
were a direct appeal to Harriet, to her love for him, a tribute
to her gentle nature, a witness to his love for her; it is also a cry
of *Peccavi*:

> Thy look of love has power to calm
>   The stormiest passion of my soul;
> Thy gentle words are drops of balm
>   In life's too bitter bowl;
> No grief is mine, but that alone
> These choicest blessings I have known.
>
> Harriet! if all who long to live
>   In the warm sunshine of thine eye,
> That price beyond all pain must give,—
>   Beneath thy scorn to die;
> Then hear thy chosen own too late
> His heart most worthy of thy hate.
>
> Be thou, then, one among mankind
>   Whose heart is harder not for state,
> Thou only virtuous, gentle, kind,
>   Amid a world of hate;
> And by a slight endurance seal
> A fellow-being's lasting weal.

L

> For pale with anguish is his cheek,
>   His breath comes fast, his eyes are dim,
> Thy name is struggling ere he speak,
>   Weak is each trembling limb;
> In mercy let him not endure
> The misery of a fatal cure.
>
> Oh, trust for once no erring guide!
>   Bid the remorseless feeling flee;
> 'Tis malice, 'tis revenge, 'tis pride,
>   'Tis anything but thee;
> Oh, deign a nobler pride to prove,
> And pity if thou canst not love.

There is no record of Harriet's reaction to this or to the April poem, or under what circumstances they were shown to her; they were in her possession. They disprove Godwin's horrid hints about her conduct at this time. In the second stanza it is specifically stated that if she scorns 'all' who love her, then he himself is 'most worthy' of her scorn—he was remembering her rejection of Hogg's proffered love, and, seemingly, his own great love for her. The 'slight endurance' is, of course, her forgiveness. He was pleading with her to put aside resentments, to turn a deaf ear to Eliza, and to grant him, if not love, pity (which is akin to love).

The first two stanzas are not immediately clear, and have been subject to misconstruction. Shelley was giving voice to a fear of having lost her love; alone, he grieves that the blessings of her love *have been* his; it is the Horatian use of the perfect tense, expressing a cessation—in this case of Harriet's calming 'look of love', her 'gentle words'. She had not, however, ceased to love him, though she may not, as his altercations with Eliza had intensified, have manifested this clearly to him. While she fretted over the separation from Eliza, over the lack of a settled home, over the pouring of money into Godwin's bottomless well of debt, an unforeseen threat to her peace had arisen.

In June she was much alone in Bracknell while Shelley was in London, dining daily with the Godwins; from the 8th to the 10th he was with her in Bracknell; from the 18th to the 25th, yielding to Godwin's persuasion, he stayed in London, lodging in Fleet Street where he was not known, in order to avoid his

creditors. Mary Godwin was now at home. Having no inkling
of her husband's interest in Mary, Harriet, to escape loneliness,
joined the Westbrooks in Bath about the 25th of June,[7] intending
to rejoin Shelley when he had concluded dealings with money-
lenders and given Godwin the proceeds. It was at this time that
Shelley let his emotions overflow into verse, using the same
stanza that had voiced his plea to Harriet in May; his life
which then depended upon Harriet's love, now depended upon
Mary's:

I

Mine eyes were dim with tears unshed;
   Yes, I was firm—thus wert not thou;—
My baffled looks did fear yet dread
   To meet thy looks—I could not know
How anxiously they sought to shine
With soothing pity upon mine.

II

To sit and curb the soul's mute rage
   Which preys upon itself alone;
To curse the life which is the cage
   Of fettered grief that dares not groan,
Hiding from many a careless eye
The scorned load of agony.

III

Whilst thou alone, then not regarded
   The [   ] thou alone should be
To spend years thus, and be rewarded,
   As thou, sweet love, requited me
When none were near—Oh! I did wake
From torture for that moment's sake

IV

Upon my heart thy accents sweet
   Of peace and pity, fell like dew
On flowers half dead;—thy lips did meet
   Mine tremblingly; thy dark eyes threw
Their soft persuasion on my brain,
Charming away its dream of pain.

V

We are not happy, sweet; our state
　　Is strange and full of doubt and fear;
More need of words that ills abate;—
　　Reserve or censure come not near
Our sacred friendship, lest there be
No solace left for you and me.

VI

Gentle and good and mild thou art,
　　Nor can I live if thou appear
Aught but thyself, or turn thine heart
　　Away from me, or stoop to wear
The mask of scorn, although it be
To hide the love thou feel for me.

There is a strong resemblance between these stanzas and
those of the preceding month to Harriet; there is the same plea
to the loved one to be herself, to avoid scorn, to grant pity; in
both the person addressed is gentle and virtuous and kind, and
her words calm him. The term 'friendship' for love Shelley used
repeatedly; he had used it in poems to Harriet—it implied the
highest love. It included, but was not restricted to sexual love.
What Shelley had felt for Harriet and now felt for Mary was
friendship intensified by sexual love. In both poems he appealed
for help in this dark world where he was grief-stricken and
forlorn. In the third stanza of the lines to Mary he indicated
that his love and Mary's had gone beyond the limits of restraint;
in the fifth stanza he banned 'reserve or censure', which is
fairly explicit. Godwin later said the date was the 26th of
June.

Until the 4th of July Harriet heard with sufficient regularity
from her husband; then his letters stopped. By the 7th she was
seriously perturbed; he had been in danger of arrest for debt;
he might be ill; he might have been attacked—she knew that he
feared that he was being followed in London, and he had been
attacked in Keswick and at Tanyrallt. She appealed to Hookham with whom Shelley was sure to be in touch. Dating
her letter from 6 Queen's Square, Bath, the 7th of July, she
wrote:

MY DEAR SIR

You will greatly oblige me by giving the enclosed to Mr. Shelley. I would not trouble you but it is now four days since I have heard from him which to me is an age. Will you write by return of post, and tell me what has become of him, as I always fancy something dreadful has happened if I do not hear from him. If you tell me that he is well, I shall not come to London; but if I do not hear from you or him I shall certainly come as I cannot endure this dreadful state of suspense. You are his friend and you can feel for me.

I remain yours truly,

H. S.

Since their marriage nearly three years ago they had seldom been apart. She had always accommodated herself to him; they had settled down again and again, only, as she wrote to Mrs. Nugent, to pull up stakes suddenly. She had not complained. Shelley had praised her modesty of desire to Fanny Godwin:

How is Harriet a *fine lady*? You indirectly accuse her in your letter of this offence—to me the most unpardonable of all. The ease and simplicity of her habits, the unassuming plainness of her address, the uncalculated connexion of her thought and speech, have ever formed in my eyes her greatest charms.

Harriet had not changed since that was written at the end of 1812. Now she was approaching her nineteenth birthday, and her third wedding anniversary; in December her second child would be born; if it were a boy Shelley, and perhaps his father, would be most happy.

Shelley received the letter she had enclosed in hers to Hookham, having come to the bookshop with Godwin. His reply was to ask her to come to London at once; on the 14th of July, bringing Ianthe with her, she arrived. The Shelley she now met was not her eager, enthusiastic, loving husband, but a man possessed by emotions he could neither control nor conceal. He asked of her a forbearance, a strength of mind, a magnanimity, and an understanding that would have been remarkable in a much older wife.

The happiest years of Harriet's life had come to a cruel close.

CHAPTER VI

This is a Vampire

I sang of the dancing stars,
  I sang of the dædal Earth,
And of Heaven—and the giant wars,
  And Love, and Death, and Birth,—
    And then I changed my pipings,—
Singing how down the vale of Menalus
  I pursued a maiden and clasped a reed:
Gods and men, we are all deluded thus!
                              Hymn of Pan

O N the hundred-mile journey by carriage from Bath Harriet had for company her sister, her child, and her worried thoughts. From the letter which Shelley wrote to her immediately after their first interview in London it is apparent that only then did she learn of his involvement with Mary Godwin, and of his wish for the termination of their marriage. It is also apparent that, whatever shock she sustained as he made his tumultuous declarations, she kept firm control of her tongue, and gave the impression of strength as he turned to her for consolation, in urgent need of her consent to and approval of his proposed action. Peacock and Hookham were always to remember his maddening dilemma, still deeply attached to Harriet while a fierce passion for Mary flamed within him. Though later in his satirical novel *Nightmare Abbey* Peacock portrayed comically the conflict of Scythrop (Shelley), torn between love for the beautiful, accomplished, coquettish Marionetta (Harriet) and love for the learned Stella (Mary), at the time he was a sympathetic and understanding friend to both Harriet and Shelley; and though he liked Harriet and did not like Mary (he did not yet know her, but they were never to be

at ease with each other) he realized that Mary's intellectual
superiority met Shelley's requirements more nearly than Harriet's; when at this time he reminded Shelley of his fondness for
Harriet he was answered:

Every one who knows me must know that the partner of my life
should be one who can feel poetry and understand philosophy. Harriet is a noble animal but she can do neither.[1]

This was unfair; Harriet had entered into his discussions with
Peacock and others; she had a lively, receptive mind, not, however, a creative mind; she could not herself write poem or essay
or continue discussion into the higher reaches of abstract thinking. She was what Shelley had made her, a free-thinker in
religion, in political and social philosophy, an intelligent listener
to abstract discussions, a helpful critic of his writings, the sharer
of his hopes and his efforts. She had not realized before that he
required of her qualities she did not possess, an intellectuality
greater than hers, than that of any woman he was ever to know;
that his ideal wife was a female Peacock combined with the facile
grace, the conversational ease, the unconventionality, and the
delicate femininity of Mrs. Boinville and her daughter. Shelley
had not yet realized that the wife of his dreams did not and
could not exist except in novels: she was Luxima in *The Missionary*, she was Constantia in *Ormond*. Few men and no women he
ever knew in life could give him the intellectual stimulation he
required—Peacock did, and most of all, Lord Byron. To Harriet
in July 1814 he explained his imperative need of this, and his
belief that he would have it from Mary Godwin.

That Shelley had believed what he had often said vocally and
in poems to Harriet, that his love for her was permanent,
eternal; that neither of them had anticipated an end to their
mutual love; that the news was a profound shock to her, is
attested in his letter of 14th July:

MY DEAREST FRIEND
    Exhausted as I am with our interview, and secure of seeing you
to-morrow at 12, I cannot refrain from writing to you.
    I am made calm and happier by your assurances. It is true that
my confidence in the integrity and disinterestedness of your conduct

has ever remained firm; but I dreaded lest the shock might inflict on you some incurable unhappiness; lest you should doubt the continuance of my affection for you, lest you should see, what I so deeply felt, nothing but misery and despair.

My spirit turned to you for consolation, and it found it; all that vulgar minds regard as so important was considered by you with consistent and becoming contempt. Feeling still persuaded that my affection for you was undiminished, you offered to my view and anticipated for yourself that pure and lasting happiness which is the portion only of the great and good.

For this, dearest Harriet, from my inmost Soul, I thank you. This is perhaps the greatest among the many blessings which I have received, and still am destined to receive at your hands. I loathed the very light of day, and looked upon my own being with deep and unutterable abhorrence. I lived—Mary too consented to survive—I lived in the hope of consolation and happiness from you, and I have not been deceived.

I repeat (and believe me, for I am sincere) that my attachment to you is unimpaired. I conceive that it has acquired even a deeper and more lasting character, that it is now less exposed than ever to the fluctuations of phantasy or caprice. Our connection was not one of passion and impulse. Friendship was its basis, and on this basis it has enlarged and strengthened. It is no reproach to me that you have never filled my heart with an all-sufficing passion; perhaps you are even yourself a stranger to these impulses, which one day may be awakened by some nobler and worthier than me; and may you find a lover as passionate and faithful, as I shall ever be a friend affectionate and sincere!

Shall I not be more than a friend? Oh, far more—Brother, Father of your child, so dear as it is to us both, for its own sake and because we love each other.

Mrs. Boinville deeply knows the human heart; she predicted that these struggles would one day arrive; she saw that friendship and not passion was the bond of our attachment. But I derided her short-sighted prophecies—I! who was so soon to be the object of their completion.

Can your feelings for me differ in their nature from those which I cherish toward you? Are you my lover whilst I am only your friend, the brother of your heart? If they do not, the purest and most perfect happiness is ours. I wish you could see Mary; to the most indifferent eyes she would be interesting only from her sufferings, and the tyranny which is exercised upon her. I murmur not if you feel incapable of compassion and love for the object and sharer of my passion.

If you want to draw on the Bankers before I see you, Hookham
will give you the checks.

Adieu. Bring my sweet babe. I must ever love her for your sake.
Ever most affectionately yours,

P. B. SHELLEY[2]

Come at 12.

Shelley's trepidation at their meeting could not have ex-
ceeded hers as she read this lengthy plea for her understanding,
for her to regard him as no longer her husband, but an affectionate friend. From her self-control he had wrongly deduced a
non-existent composure; she fell ill, to his consternation and
Eliza's; pathetically she told Mrs. Nugent (but not until later)
that whereas her will to live was not strong after this great
shock, her constitution was, and hence she survived. Shelley,
understandably in a state of excitement, had little comprehension of her plight; since she had assented to his principles he
hoped she would readily put them into practice; an harmonious
triangle was what he had in mind.

Harriet was well aware that their love had not been at first
sight or like the usual Gothic romance; it had, however, developed like that of Eloise and Fitzeustace in *St. Irvyne* and it
had been very deep. As for the 'tyranny' to which Mary had
been subjected and her 'sufferings', Harriet had a right to be
sceptical; she knew the shortcomings of Mrs. Godwin, the discomforts of the Skinner Street household, the naggings, the
discontents, the lack of order, the impecuniousness, the ever-
present threat of arrest for debt. These distresses Mary had
escaped by a long sojourn in Scotland; at home they were, after
all, the normal course of life. Harriet did not know—or believe
—that Godwin was tyrannical toward Mary or that he opposed
her union with Shelley—had he not advocated free love openly?
Godwin, however, like the most conventional of fathers, had
been outraged; he had called Shelley 'seducer' (Harriet applied
this term to Mary), and had exacted promises from Mary and
Shelley that they would no longer meet. Harriet kept her temper
more successfully, the most adult and dignified of them all in
these troubled days. Before Harriet collapsed in illness there
were many meetings: Harriet and Shelley; each alone and both

together with Godwin, Mrs. Godwin, Mary; and all of them together. Mary promised to give Shelley up; Shelley flourished
a bottle of laudanum, urging Mary to join him in death; when
he took an overdose his life was saved by Godwin and a doctor,
walking him all through one night. The exact sequence of illnesses, interviews, protestations, promises, is uncertain as diary
entries were inserted later and were often distorted; and the
Godwins, to exculpate themselves, coloured events with their
imagination. With Harriet bedridden for a fortnight there was
only a week for these frenzied meetings. It was not until autumn
that Shelley wrote his feverish account to Hogg and Harriet her
temperate one to Mrs. Nugent.

Before July ended matters came to a crisis; very early on the
morning of the 28th Shelley, with a post-chaise, waited around
the corner from 41 Skinner Street—did he recall waiting for
Harriet on an August morning nearly three years ago? Having,
like the heroine of a novel, left a note for her father, Mary
joined him, but returned to fetch forgotten treasures: the manuscripts of her juvenilia, regarded by them both as writings of
importance. And then they were off for Dover and the continent, taking with them Mary Jane Clara Clairmont (soon to
become 'Claire'), Mary's dark, vivacious, talkative step-sister,
eight months her junior, who came for the lark. Shelley was
not disconcerted; he had never expected to live alone with one
companion, but in a group. The elopement of Shelley and
Mary, though most certainly the result of the emotional stress
of a compelling love, was not a sudden unprepared dash for
freedom; it was a calculated tourist trip. At the time there
was peace with France, and travel, previously restricted, was
popular; they were in the full sweep of the tourist tide. The
industry with which their journal was commenced and continued with an eye toward publication betrays coolness. It was
not for nothing that Mary was the daughter of writers, and she
did not doubt the validity of Shelley's exalted estimate of her
genius—it was to flower in one deathless novel, *Frankenstein*,[3]
and in her brilliant editing of Shelley's poems.

They had not been gone long before an ugly rumour spread,
reaching Harriet's ears: that Godwin had 'sold' his two daugh-

ters, a slander hard to disprove since Shelley's borrowing of a fantastic sum at exorbitant interest for the discharge of Godwin's debts could not have escaped notice. Harriet was tempted to believe the slander. Yet she was still confident, or tried to be, of Shelley's love, believing he would return from this escapade repentant. His finances were in an exigent state, his income small—if he gave Miss Hitchener her due and Peacock what had been promised him, Shelley had exactly nothing for income, since Mr. Westbrook would not continue his allowance for Shelley's use. It was unlikely that his father or grandfather, who had been adamant when he had lived quietly with his wife and child, would contribute to the extravagance of foreign travel with Mary and Claire. Harriet could only wait; wait for her husband's penitent return; wait for the birth of her child, who, if a boy, would be heir to the Shelley title and wealth.

Harriet sent for Peacock. To him she described Mary in unflattering terms; whereupon he asked what, then, had attracted Shelley? With sharp insight Harriet answered, her name, her descent: as the daughter of Mary Wollstonecraft, of whom Shelley held an exalted view, and of Godwin, she had magnetic attraction for him.[4] Shelley had told Harriet that he and Mary had regularly met at the grave of her mother; propriety would not have permitted Harriet to relieve her resentment by saying, 'Like mother, like daughter'. Harriet, like any normal wife, blamed the other woman. Shelley had given her to understand that Mary had declared her love first, even as earlier he had put the onus upon Harriet. His first elopement had been a chivalrous 'rescue' of Harriet who had 'threatened suicide'. He now told Harriet that Mary had threatened suicide if he rejected the overpowering love she confessed to him. It may be that both Harriet and Mary had felt the force of love sooner than Shelley; there is nothing to prove this. Mary had been under no misapprehensions; when she met him first, in October 1812, he was a happily married man; when she met him again in the spring of 1814 he was in London apart from his wife and child only to arrange the extrication of Godwin from his chronic financial embarrassment. Though Mary had been much given to daydreaming, she had had no way of gauging her susceptibility; if she dreamt of romance, its hero would have been Byron, whose verses she read and memorized, and wrote on the fly-leaf of the copy of *Queen Mab* given her by Shelley. Mary saw herself as an amalgam of the father she inordinately adored and the mother he had idealized for her. Harriet's summing up was shrewd: Godwin was the great bond between Mary and Shelley; his reverence for and his effort to succour him first won her admiration.

The brief courtship of Shelley and Mary, shortly before his twenty-second, her seventeenth birthday, was a chapter in a turgid novel, a compendium of those Shelley had written and those he had most admired. It was more or less modelled upon Charles Brockden Brown's *Ormond*,[5] whose hero had been happy in the love of the beautiful Helena until he met the intellectual Constantia. (Ormond, an anti-matrimonialist, had overcome Helena's objections to a free union, convincing her of his constancy.) Shelley never forgot; he used the two names continually; in his eyes now Harriet was Helena, Mary, Constantia; later in his poems Mary was Helen and Claire became immortal as Constantia, singing. In *Ormond* Helena was, like Harriet, beautiful, intelligent, with a sweet singing voice and a pliant disposition. In time she ceased to stimulate Ormond's mind in abstract discussion, and hence to inspire him to creative invention. With Constantia, whose mind was quick to comprehend, his own mind expanded. Pitying Helena, he was honest with her: she had lost his love, which necessarily he felt for the superior person, Constantia. Realistic and ruthless, he saw no future for Helena but suicide. Though in 1814 Shelley's letters to Harriet echoed Ormond's to Helena, Shelley was not ruthless, and he did not now or at any time contemplate her suicide.

Harriet *could* be happy; she had only to trust him, keep in close communication with him as her most interested and devoted *friend*, accept Mary as his *wife*, and in time she would herself meet some one who would be the perfect lover for her. There was no chasm for Shelley between theory and practice. He expected Harriet to be the woman of the future, independent and divorcible, but it was only the early nineteenth century; Harriet was still in love with her husband; there was no future for her as a restricted inhabitant of her father's narrow home. Neither of them could have secured divorce, which was difficult indeed, and divorce permitting remarriage all but impossible— it would have to go first through the Ecclesiastical Court, and, if favoured, to the House of Lords; marriage was believed indissoluble. Shelley did not feel the need of legal divorce—he pronounced it himself; writing to Harriet, 'I am no longer your husband', he declared himself united with Mary.

Knowing that while Harriet lived she could never marry Shelley, why did Mary elope with him? That she suffered from her position in illicit union, having much respect for convention and social standing, is evident in her journals, her letters, her behaviour. The conditions of her home were not unbearable; it was an exciting atmosphere, for distinguished men were often there: Coleridge, and Charles Lamb, and Francis Place, and William Blake; Aaron Burr from America; Humphry Davy, the scientist who remarked that it was not often so much brainpower was in one room as when he, Coleridge, and Godwin were together—(Godwin appreciated Davy's brains, though he deprecated using them for chemistry).[6]

The household was ill run and duns were at the door, but the life of the mind was free. There were always books in the making, and Mary, allowed in her father's study among his friends, felt herself a participant, even if silent, in the workings of powerful minds. Early on, her father had used her as reader for the children's books he published in the ill-starred venture into which he had plunged his wife. Mary was, as she recorded, 'nurtured on dreams of glory'. Of young men she had had no experience until Shelley poured for her the heady wine of unadulterated admiration; as the child of her parents he saw her as brighter than he—never vain of his own talents, he thought her as much beyond him as he was beyond Harriet; *she* would instruct *him*. He was, of course, mistaken.

The magic of his praise combined with the magic of his personality. She would not have meant, any more than he did, to fall in love. She was farther removed from his normal social sphere than Harriet, the schoolmate of his sisters; he had met Mary in unfamiliar Bohemia, through his hero-worship of her father. Between her father and Shelley's there was a wider gap than between Mr. Westbrook and Mr. Shelley; when circumstances obliged these two to meet there was a modicum of mutual respect, neither overstepping the line which divided the country gentleman, the future baronet, from the city man whose wealth had been earned, not inherited. Mr. Shelley would have been nonplussed at a meeting with Godwin, the Devil's disciple. Though she may well have been impressed by the Shelley title and estates, Mary would not have been influenced by this, having been taught to pay highest respect to the intellect; Godwin was never a materialist. He preferred to be solvent; but he did not covet wealth. Mary knew that when Shelley did inherit, it would be Harriet who would become Lady Shelley. She knew, too, that living with Shelley without legal sanction she would meet rebuff—but not, she thought mistakenly, from her father. United with her, Shelley would have added motive for generous provision for her father, a generosity which endeared him to her, for Mary was never free from anguished concern for her father's well-being.

Added to all else, there was the urgency of their love which had found fulfilment in late June, resulting in her pregnancy. The date is pinpointed by Godwin's letter to his friend, John Taylor, and by an entry in Mary's *Journal*: Godwin wrote that Shelley, meeting Mary constantly at her mother's grave, first thought of 'seducing' her on the 26th of June; on the 4th of August Shelley wrote in the *Journal*:

Mary told me that this was my birthday; I thought it had been the 27th June.

Whether or not Harriet knew of Mary's pregnancy, Mary knew of hers, and of Shelley's hope for a son.

While Shelley with Mary and Claire made merry on the continent, meticulously recording their impressions of foreign places and people, starting novels (*Hate*, *The Idiot*, and *The Assassins*) Harriet was unhappy, physically not well, lonely, in the midst of Londoners gaily celebrating the peace. Napoleon was confined to Elba, and London was in an ebullient mood. In April Napoleon's abdication had brought the Tsar of Russia

and the King of Prussia to add grandeur to the public spectacles
—had Harriet stayed with Eliza there in order to see them? In
August, the first month of her solitude, London rioted joyously;
wherever crowds were there were strolling performers, acrobats,
musicians, entertainers of all sorts; Hyde Park's revelry could
be heard in Chapel Street. The London parks were brightened
by a rash of 'Follies'; there was a miniature fortress, a Temple
of Concord, a Chinese bridge with a blue-and-gold pagoda.
There was a mock naval battle fought on the Serpentine in
which the Americans (England and the United States were at
war) were soundly beaten. There was a balloon ascent that
proved man's conquest of space travel: the balloonist stayed
aloft three-quarters of an hour, travelling several miles to land
in Essex marshes. At night there were fireworks bursting into
stars of brilliant colours. The Temple of Concord revolved, dis-
playing triumphant Peace, defeated Discord. The happiness of
the multitude, the joy over the end of war and tyranny, made
more poignant the private grief of Harriet.

In her father's home Harriet would not have had much sympathy for her continued love for her errant husband. It was two
weeks before she heard from him, a letter starting 'My dearest
Harriet' and continuing:

I write to you from this detestable town; I write to show that I do
not forget you; I write to urge you to come to Switzerland, where
you will at least find one firm and constant friend, to whom your
interests will be always dear, by whom your feelings will never wil-
fully be injured.[7]

The detestable town was Troyes; he went on to describe the
war-devastated country through which they had passed, assuming that she would want to hear of 'our adventures', of which a
detailed account would be sent her if she did not join them; he
would gladly find her 'some sweet retreat' in the mountains
where she would be near him—and, of course, near Mary and
Claire. He asked her to bring the deed of separation preparing
at his lawyers and a copy of her marriage settlement; but, he
went on, as if the separation were the minor matter, 'What shall
be done about the books?' The query, razor-edged, assumed
correctly that they would both want them and reinforced the

finality of their parting. Though he concluded, 'Ever most affectionately yours', there was nothing here to foster hope; in the months to come hope was to blossom and wither again and again.

Harriet did not go to Switzerland; had she done so she might have been stranded there; Shelley, Mary, and Claire went wandering off to arrive back in London penniless six weeks after the elopement. He was forced to appeal to Harriet, in order to pay the ship captain and the coach driver and the cost of a night's lodging. Hearing his step upon the stairs, Harriet could momentarily believe that he had come back to her; she was quickly undeceived. While Mary and Claire waited below in the coach, for two hours Shelley was with Harriet; Mary recorded the fact in her *Journal*, but not her thoughts or feelings; Shelley, she wrote, was able to discharge the immediate debt, and to get his clothes; and they then went to the Stratford Hotel to dine and go to bed. Whatever was said in those two hours, Harriet was in the end forced to yield. 'Poor Mary', Mary wrote; and the long wait must have been hard for her; poor Harriet, her hopes crushed, as her husband expressed no remorse for her unhappy weeks while he had enjoyed foreign travel and a new romance; instead he asked for her selfless sympathy for his plight, and for money. The money she finally gave him may have come from his bankers, but her position was precarious, and she was to remain dependent upon her father; when at last an allowance was arranged it was not large, and no provision was made for the children. In addition to his bounty to Godwin, Shelley was now supporting Mary and Claire.

The autumn of 1814 was an unhappy time: for Harriet, relinquishing hope while still feeling anguished love for her husband; for Shelley, often in hiding from creditors, meeting Mary on Sundays when the law against debtors was in abeyance, saddened by Harriet's determined refusal to accept what he regarded as his divorce and remarriage; for Mary, in dingy lodgings with the omnipresent Claire, suffering the discomforts of poverty, not unknown to her, and the new ones of pregnancy; for Godwin, still dependent upon the bounty of his daughter's lover and deeply grieved over his daughter's position (and the

The Battle on the Serpentine, 1814

gossip it caused); for Mrs. Godwin upon whom fell the reproach of the upbringing of the two girls; for Fanny, torn between love of Godwin—whom she believed to be her father—and love of Shelley and Mary, used as a messenger to importune Shelley for funds (Godwin would receive neither Shelley nor Mary), scolded and penalized for being kind to Mary. Gentle Fanny feared lest harm come to Mary and Shelley; she tried to defend Mary to Mrs. Godwin, Mrs. Godwin to Mary. Alone of the three girls Fanny had consideration for Mrs. Godwin and felt some affection for her; she had no great love for her, but she would not have her misrepresented. Claire alone was buoyant; the irregular life suited her; she found excitement in giving way to her stormy moods, keeping Shelley up more than half the night, screaming with nightmares, and supplanting him in Mary's bed. She replaced Harriet as Shelley's pupil, more volatile, more stubborn, and more exciting—and her singing voice, though untrained, was lovelier than any he had known. Mary he regarded as intellectually adult; Claire needed guidance, her mind and her behaviour being disorganized. Harriet had not had this nuisance value; she had too equable a temper, too conciliatory a nature, to keep her husband's mind preoccupied with her. Claire's volatility fascinated Shelley; he never lost interest in her. Her presence (and Shelley's interest) did not add to Mary's happiness.

As for Harriet's, that was irretrievably shattered. She made a valiant effort to retain the interests she had shared with Shelley, following the trend of world affairs, concerned over tyranny, war, injustice; she kept in touch with former friends, the Nanneys, Mrs. Boinville, the Newtons, Peacock. She did not turn to Hogg. News of Shelley she sought from Peacock, with whom he took refuge to escape his creditors. She worried about his health, urging him to wear flannels, and not to wash his head in cold weather; she did not trust Mary to guard his precarious health. His letters scolded her for insufficient sympathy with Mary who had 'renounced all' for him, at the same time that he praised Mary to her for her disregard of convention. Fearing to lose him entirely, Harriet temporized; if in one letter she inveighed against him, or Mary, or Godwin, she retracted in

M

the next. His letters to her bear a striking resemblance at times to those he had written to his irate father three years ago. Then he had asked: 'Are you a Christian?' and had exhorted Mr. Shelley to live up to his faith; so now he asked Harriet: 'Are you above the world, and to what extent?' admonishing her to live up to his principles which she had accepted. As earlier he had attributed all blame to his father's stubbornness, so now he blamed Harriet for their worsening relations. He blamed her for relying upon her sister for advice instead of her husband who was a 'worthier and better' guide for her; for her breach of faith in showing his letters to Eliza, for her reproaches to him when he had *not* injured her. He reminded her that, though swept by a 'violent and lasting passion for another', he was still trying to be useful to her. He asked, he said, little of her, but that she be generous and kind in her estimate of Mary and see her as 'the noblest and the most excellent of human beings'. He had, indeed, a frantic desire that Harriet should think well of Mary and of him. If she would not, he threatened to lose interest in her:

Consider how far you would desire your future life to be placed within the influence of my superintending mind: whether you still confide sufficiently in my tried and unalterable integrity to submit to the laws which my friendship would create between us; whether we are to meet in entire and unreserved faith or allow our intimacy to subside. On you these things depend.

Affectionately yours
P. B. SHELLEY[8]

Had Harriet accepted Shelley's difficult terms—his tutelage and friendship in return for her concessions—she might have reshaped love into friendship and found a modicum of contentment. It was not an acceptable pattern in the early nineteenth century, and her family would not have countenanced such flaunting of custom; a wife did not become her husband's friend, and that of the woman with whom he lived openly. Instead Harriet tried to convince Shelley that *she* was his true love, his passion for Mary spurious and transient. And as he was inclined to blame Eliza for having promoted their union, she blamed Godwin for promoting his with Mary.

His anger was the greater because he had confidently expected Godwin to approve; but Godwin had been horrified that his daughter should have taken a young man away from his wife and children; Godwin's theories of free love were for a perfected society. In 1805 Godwin's friends, appealing to Thomas Jefferson for an American subsidy (it was not given) to promote Godwin's educational books for children, had pointed out that he did not mean his advanced ideas to be put into practice in an imperfect society; he could be relied upon to inculcate moral ideas in the young mind. His agony over his daughter was acute; the more bitter because his radical theories could be quoted against him. Neither he nor Mary Wollstonecraft had had any ties, or had done harm to anyone when they had lived in free union; they were mature people nearer forty than thirty—Mary and Shelley were not in the same category.

Harriet had consulted a lawyer, which offended Shelley—she did not trust him to provide for her. Fearing that he had lost her good will, which he ardently desired to retain, he let his anger rise, reminding her of the harmony in which they had lived together when she believed in him:

I was an idiot to expect greatness or generosity from you, that when an occasion of the sublimest virtue occurred, you would fail to play a part of mean and despicable selfishness. The pure and liberal principles of which you used to boast that you were a disciple, served only for display. In your heart it seems you were always enslaved to the vilest superstitions, or ready to accept their support for your own narrow and worldly views. You are plainly lost to me for ever. I foresee no probability of change.

'Vilest superstitions' included for him the sanctity of marriage. Utterly sincere in his horror, he was still capable of skilful tactics, transferring the blame of selfishness from himself to her —*he* would not 'willingly' cause *her* the slightest pain. In her reply, in which she explained her visit to the lawyer as only to ask advice, she made such strictures against Mary as roused him to further ire, reminding her how with him she had scorned the opinion of the world:

Your contumelious language toward Mary is . . . impotent and mean. You appeal to the vilest superstitions of the most ignorant and slavish of mankind. I consider it an insult that you address such cant to me.

Yet he yearned for her approval:

Harriet, if you still continued what I once hoped you would never cease to be, if you deserved my affection, with what eagerness would I devote myself to your pleasure. Desert the selfish and the worldly wretches with whom you seem to pride yourself in making common cause, and I will be your friend, not in the vulgar sense of friend, but in the most emphatic meaning of the word.

.   .   .   .   .

If you feel yet any ambition to be ranked among the wise and good, write to me. I am hardly anxious to hear from you, as I despair of any generosity or virtue on your part. How happy I should be if I have done you injustice.

A postscript explained that he was penniless and could give her nothing. On the 3rd of October he again put the onus of strained relations upon her, seeing 'little hope of any advantage . . . to either of us from our intercourse', and praising himself for having continued to see her, to write to her, to have her on his mind:

although united to one perfectly adapted to my nature by a deep and lasting affection, you should have perceived that I continued to be mindful of your happiness, that I would have superintended the progress of your mind, and have assisted you in cultivating an elevated philosophy, to which without the interest I have taken in your improvement, it is probable that you never would have aspired. . . .

I am united to another; you are no longer my wife. Perhaps I have done you injury, but surely most innocently and unintentionally, in having commenced any connexion with you.

These were harsh words; he added a long postscript in a softened tone, showing solicitude over her coming confinement, expressing confidence for her safety as she was in the care of a skilled physician. He added: 'I am in want of stockings, hanks, and Mrs. W.'s posthumous works'.

The stockings and handkerchiefs were sent; Mrs. Wollstonecraft's books Harriet wished to retain. His next letter, of the 5th of October, repetitively protested that he was her 'friend in every sense of the word'—she had been his wife, she was the mother of his children. Unctuously he said he agreed that he was not the brother of her soul, participating in her feelings, tastes, opinions. But she had not said this; she had said that he

THIS IS A VAMPIRE

had changed, had lost his high resolve; it was a neat turning of the tables on his part. They did not lose contact; they sympathized with each other's illnesses, hers a threatened miscarriage, his an attack of lung trouble. On the 12th of October he promised that eventually he would provide for her support, though he could not yet; he offered to come to her if it would 'amuse or benefit' her. She had, he said, forbidden him to call upon her. She may have felt too keenly the strain of their meetings. He expressed regret at her dejection, and concluded tenderly: 'Believe me, dear Harriet, most anxiously yours, P. B. S.'

The kindly solicitude of this letter is belied by that written two days earlier to Hogg, a self-exculpatory romantic version of his separation from Harriet and union with Mary. It was an apology for not having written sooner, and also something of a boast of amatory success—Hogg was still a bachelor. He asked Hogg to

rejoice that after struggles and privations which almost withered me to idiotism, I enjoy a happiness the most perfect and exalted that it is possible for my nature to participate . . .⁹

His staying in early spring with Mrs. Boinville had opened his eyes—here he says 'two months', but at the time he had written Hogg 'one month'; neither was accurate. 'The contemplation of female excellence is the favourite food of my imagination', he continued, and cast aspersions on Harriet and Eliza without naming them, by praising the 'mildness, the intelligence, the delicacy of a cultivated female' as having unaccustomed charm for him, 'a strange contrast to my former friendless and deplorable condition'. It is true that he was at that time at odds with Eliza, but not with Harriet whom he was about to remarry; yet he now believed that

I suddenly perceived that the entire devotion with which I had resigned all prospects of utility or happiness to the single purpose of cultivating Harriet was a gross and despicable superstition. Perhaps every degree of affectionate intimacy with a female, however slight, partakes of the nature of love. Love makes men quicksighted, . . .

Certainly he had not devoted himself entirely to the cultivation of Harriet; he had devoted himself to Irish nationalism; to the embankment, to Godwin; he had written pamphlets and broadsides; he had bombarded people with these and with argumentative letters; he had written *Queen Mab*, a long poem, and *A Refutation of Deism*, an intricate exposition of free thinking; he had made speeches in Ireland and in Wales; he had extended his own reading on a vast scale. If he had so devoted himself exclusively to his wife's education, his father would have had less to complain of. This was an attempt at self-justification; so was the excuse that his love for Cornelia revealed the inadequacy of Harriet (Mary had not yet entered his life). Moreover, the early March visit to the Boinvilles could hardly have produced the revulsion against his marriage, 'as if a dead and living body had been linked together in loathsome and horrible communion'; for though he wrote sad verses on duty's taking him from the sweet presence of Cornelia in April, in May he wrote his verses to Harriet whose look of love calmèd him.

To Hogg he admitted having felt most intensely the 'voluptuousness' of spring as he walked—he says forty miles—from Bracknell to Field Place. But the love that he now wished to confess to Harriet was no longer for Cornelia, but for one who had been responsive to him, and 'already were the difficulties surmounted that opposed an entire union'. This distorts the calendar of events which he records more properly in saying that it was in June he was in London almost constantly at Godwin's and there met 'his daughter Mary'. Expatiating upon her loveliness of character and her intellectuality, in terms of excessive admiration, he told of experiencing a sense of inferiority to her 'intellectual nature', and at the same time an ardent passion for her. He hesitated to transgress a real 'duty', but she dispelled his 'delusions' and confessed her love. They were cruelly treated, their departure delayed, until they felt compelled 'to disregard all considerations but that of the happiness of each other'. He declared himself, at the end of an incredibly long letter, to be remade, restored to virtue, living in 'pure and celestial felicity'.

Against this rather fanciful and embroidered recital should be put two letters of Harriet's to Mrs. Nugent, 26th August and 20th November. A month after Shelley's departure for the continent with Mary, Harriet was bravely trying to piece together her life, retain her interest in the world, and keep in touch with friends. She uttered no strictures against her husband and did not mention Mary:

MY DEAR MRS. NUGENT

I am afraid you will think I am not sincere when I tell you what pleasure the sight of your hand writing caused me. I think as you do with the greatest horror on the present state of things, giving the Slave Trade to France for seven years; can anything be more horrible. Peace has been dearly purchased at this price. I am dreadfully afraid America will never hold out against the numbers sent to invade her. How senseless all these rejoicings are; deluded beings they little know the many injustices that are to ensue. I expect France will soon have another Revolution. The present King is not at all fitted to govern such a Nation. Mr Shelley is in France; you will be surprised to find I am not with him but times are altered, my dear friend, & tho' I will not tell you what has passed still do not think that you cloud my mind with your sorrows. Every age has its cares; God knows I have mine. Dear Ianthe is quite well, she is fourteen months old, & has six teeth. What I should have done without this dear Babe & my Sister I know not. This world is a Scene of heavy trials to us all. I little expected ever to go thro' what I have but time heals the deepest wounds & for the sake of that sweet Infant I hope to live many years. Write to me often my dear friend, you know not what pleasure your letters give me. I wish you lived in England that I might be near you. Tell me how you are in health. Do not despond tho' I see nothing to hope for when all that was virtuous becomes vicious & depraved. So it is. Nothing is certain in this world; I suppose there is an other where those that have suffered keenly here will be happy. Tell me what you think of this. My Sister is with me. I wish you knew her as well as I do. She is worthy of your love. Adieu dear friend. May you still be happy is the first wish of your ever faithful friend

H. SHELLEY

Ianthe is well & very engaging.

The cause of her sorrow is not definitely stated beyond the fact that she is not with her husband in France. Three months later she unburdened her heart, giving her version of Shelley's defection; as Harriet was not given to exaggerations of fact or to fiction-writing, her relation of the development of love between Shelley and Mary must have been built upon Shelley's account to her. In revealing to Hogg and to Harriet that Mary had been the first to declare love, Shelley was excusing himself, as he had in his accounts of Harriet to Hogg and Miss Hitchener. His letters were echoing his Gothic novels. Some of the phrasing in Harriet's is so unlike her usual style as to make the attribution to Shelley's narration fairly safe:

MY DEAR MRS. NUGENT

Your fears are verified. Mr. Shelley has become profligate & sensual, owing entirely to Godwin's *Political Justice*. The very great evil that book has done is not to be told. The false doctrines there contained have poisoned many a young & virtuous mind. Mr. Shelley is living with Godwin's two daughters—one by Mary Wollstonecraft, the other the daughter of his present wife, called *Clairmont*. I told you some time back Mr. S. was to give Godwin £3000. It was in effecting the accomplishment of this scheme that he was obliged to be at Godwin's house, & Mary was determined to seduce him. She is to blame. She heated his imagination by talking of her mother & going to her grave with him every day till at last she told him she was dying in love for him, accompanied with the most violent gestures & vehement expostulations. He thought of me & my sufferings & begged her to get the better of a passion degrading to him as herself. She then told him she would die—he had rejected her & what appeared to her as the sublimest virtue was to him a crime. Why could we not all live together? I as his Sister, she as his wife? He had the folly to believe this possible, & sent for me, then residing at Bath. You may suppose how I felt at the disclosure. I was laid up for a fortnight after. I could do nothing for myself. He begged me to live. The doctors gave me over. They said 'twas impossible. I saw his despair, the agony of my beloved sister; & owing to the great strength of my constitution I lived; & here I am, my dear friend, waiting to bring an other infant into this woful world. Next month I shall be confined. He will not be near me, no, he cares not for me now. He never asks after me or sends me word how he is going on. In short, the man I once loved is dead, this is a vampire, his character is blasted for ever. Nothing can save him now. Oh! if you knew what I have Suffered your heart would drip blood for my miseries. When may I expect to see you? Do tell me, my dear friend, & write soon. Eliza is at Southampton with my darling babe; London does not agree with her. Will you enquire for a family of the name of Colthurst in Dublin? There is one Son & daughter growing up living with the mother. I want the direction as I know them very well. Adieu my dear friend may you be happy is the best wish of her who sincerely loves you

H. SHELLEY

She judged him harshly, yet forgivingly; he was a 'vampire', not the man she had loved. He no longer concerned himself with her, or let her know how he was; this was a poor return for her generosity shown him a month ago—which she did not mention to Mrs. Nugent—when he had appealed to her in piteous and affectionate terms, certain of her love for him. He had written vividly to move her to help him:

MY DEAR HARRIET

I cannot raise money soon enough. Unless you can effect something I must go to prison, and all our hopes of independence be finished. I see no resource. I must hide myself til the 6th and then if you can raise no money, go to prison to save my bail.

Direct to me still at Pancras, and tell me when I can hope to have a sum from you, and what that sum can be. I depend wholly on you. My own exertions have all failed. I tell you again and again that we must both be ruined if I cannot quiet Chartres. And I know not whether, in the event of my going to prison, my estate might not be sold for a mere trifle to benefit my creditors.

Write to me and send the money soon. Send what you can get, if in no other manner, by little and little. I should not have the conscience to press this matter so ungracefully if your danger was not almost equal to my own.

Write quickly . . . send a porter with the letter. If possible, let it contain the £30. I am certain to repay it in a fortnight.

These vexations have induced my antient illness. I am perfectly free from danger but so exhausted as scarcely able to walk. This however does not matter. I have not a friend in the world who can assist me. My endeavours have been in vain.

If once in prison, confined in a damp cell, without a sixpence, without a friend (for I have mortgaged my income to Mr Hookham), I must inevitably be starved to death. We have even now sold all that we have to buy bread. I am with a friend who supplies me with food and lodging, but I think you will shudder to hear that before I could sell the last valuable Mary and her sister very nearly perished with hunger. My dear Harriet, send quick supplies.

Very affectionately yours,

P. B. SHELLEY

He was so sure of her kindness and charity that he wrote to Mary as he finished his doleful plea:

I have written an extremely urgent letter to Harriet to induce her to send money. . . .

.   .   .   .   .

My beloved Mary, fear not. Have confidence in the fortunate issue of our distresses.[10]

It was disingenuous of Shelley to put forward Chartres' bill for the carriage as if it were the only bill against him; he had a mountain of debts, many from before his marriage; and surely Harriet was in no way responsible for the support of Mary and Claire. He had not been contributing to Harriet's support, constantly in letters saying that he could give her nothing yet, and the money he asked of her he must have expected her to get from her father; or else to borrow it as he could not. In sending the £30 Harriet must have been moved not by the plight of Mary and Claire, but by the pathetic picture Shelley painted of himself, scarcely able to walk, soon, unless she helped, starving in a damp prison cell. His situation was difficult, yet not as desperate as he presented it; far from being too weak to walk he was moving about, going to and from Peacock's to meet with Mary. Entries in her *Journal* show considerable ambulatory activity for him day after day—she rode in a coach to meet him. In spite of poverty they bought books, a guinea spent on one visit to a bookshop. Only a week earlier they had bought three seats in a box at the Drury Lane Theatre to see *Hamlet* and had not stayed until the end, being displeased with the performance. Claire's diary records that the three of them spent the night at the Stratford Hotel, surely not an economical procedure. Harriet would not have known of all the extravagances; she did, however, hear of Shelley's borrowing another fortune for Godwin (£1200). Distressed, she did not keep silent; Mary complained that she was trying to 'ruin Papa'. Harriet had no reason for furthering schemes for his benefit, and many for wishing to restrain Shelley's generosity to him, while she was dependent upon her father; if by tongue and pen she expressed scornful disapproval, she was thereby relieving slightly her painful resentment of her own plight. To Mary and Shelley criticism of Godwin was nothing short of *lèse-majesté*. Though Shelley was bitter over Godwin's refusal to receive him or Mary, he would brook no aspersions from Harriet; he retained his reverence for Godwin as the author of *Political Justice* (he was re-reading it with Mary and Claire), and as the father of Mary. In spite of difficulties, or because of them, his love for Mary burned bright.

In letters he scorned Harriet for deserting his wisdom for the prudential morality of Eliza. Warning her that if she did not continue under his guidance an emancipated lover of learning she would sink to the level of the commonplace, he renounced friendship with her:

There are probably many and very excellent persons in the world who are capable of being to you as the brother of your soul, who can participate your feelings, your tastes, and your opinions. You justly remark that I am not that person. I shall watch over your interests, mark the progress of your future life, be useful to you, be your protector, and consider myself as it were your parent; but as friends, as equals, those who do not sympathise can never meet.

Poor Harriet! she was unwilling to accept so complete a separation; she had not wholly given up hope. She had tried to make him understand that she grieved over the change in him; it was he who was not living by his bright ideals, who was diverted from philosophy and poetry to money-raising. She had been stung to the quick by his saying that he had conferred benefits upon her; she received a quick disclaimer:

Harriet, you mistake,—you obstinately mistake me. I never stated that I had conferred pecuniary benefits on you or that I derived from such sources a claim to your confidence and regard.

Pecuniary benefits warranted no regard, his to her, had there been any, her father's to him—this was not what he had in mind:

I had hoped that the more substantial benefits of intellectual improvement, and the constant watchfulness of a friendship, ill understood, it seems, would not have been degraded by so mean and common a mistake.

I perceive that your irritated feelings have led you into this injustice towards me. If my friendship is thus rejected, I cherish little hope of any advantage arising to either of us from our intercourse.

Harriet was not mistaken in feeling a note of condescension; Shelley regarded her as beneath Mary. For him nobility was of the mind; he ranked Godwin, son of a poor dissenting minister, above the Duke of Norfolk, the first duke of the realm, whom he had rebuffed as his father's mediator. Peacock, son of a

London glass merchant, was his closest friend. Had Harriet's mind been as flexible and original as his own—if it had been the equal of Mary's—he would have honoured her if she had been the daughter of a chimney-sweep. If, in addition to having a mind as capable as Mary's, she had been the daughter of two free-thinking authors, as Mary was, he would have put her on a pedestal. Now he indicated that he would be relieved to end even a tenuous friendship. Though in his verses to her and in his first letter, 14th July, he had referred to the 'blessings' she had conferred upon him, these were forgotten; he talked only of *his* kindness to *her* in continuing interest in her.

News of the birth of a son came to him from Hookham. Born a month prematurely on the last day of November, his advent was a source of pleasure to his father. Mary, understandingly bitter—looking forward to the birth of her child (who would be illegitimate), unable to gloss the fact that Shelley had other ties, that her position was irregular—coloured the item in her *Journal* with her resentment; it was rare for her to register emotions, as she did on the 6th of December:

A letter from Hookham, to say that Harriet has been brought to bed of a son and heir. Shelley writes a number of circular letters of this event, which ought to be ushered in with ringing of bells, &c., for it is the son of his *wife*.

The same day a letter came from Harriet to say that the child was a week old; Mary scornfully recorded the signature, under-lining it: 'from a *deserted wife*!' Mary was too young, too op-pressed by her own physical and emotional problems, to want to understand Harriet's, or to have the compassion she at long last, almost a quarter of a century hence, realized as Harriet's due.

On the 7th of December Shelley went to his lawyer's—the birth of a son secured to his line the succession of title and entailed estates—and then to Harriet. Mary was obviously not happy over this, but for her the paramount worry was over her father's precarious finances; Shelley had also on this day to borrow £100 for Godwin's immediate relief. On the 20th Mary was angered over a letter from Harriet 'who threatens Shelley with her lawyer'; the next day Shelley wrote in the *Journal* of

his arranging for a loan yielding £1000, at a future cost of £3000;
Harriet's demands were an impertinence, Godwin's sacrosanct.

Harriet's unhappiness over Shelley's visit was not only from
the accentuation of her loneliness, but from Shelley's evident
change from idealist to materialist, a lamentable debasement of
his character. She poured out her sorrows to Mrs. Nugent on
the 11th of December:

MY DEAREST MRS. NUGENT
I have been confined a fortnight on Wednesday. Ianthe has a
Brother. He is an eight months Child, & very like his unfortunate
Father, who is more depraved than ever. Oh my dear friend, what
a dreadful trial it is to bring children into the world so utterly help-
less as he is, with no kind Father's care to heal the wounded frame.
After so much suffering my Labour was a very good one from Nine
in the morning till Nine at Night. He is a very fine healthy Child
for the time.—I have seen his Father; he came to see me as soon as
he knew of the event but as for his tenderness to me none remains.
He said he was glad it was a Boy because he would make Money
cheaper. You see how the Noble Soul is debased. Money now & not
Philosophy is the grand Spring of his Actions. Indeed the pure &
enlightened philosophy he once delighted in has flown. He is no
longer that pure & good being he once was nor can he ever retrieve
himself.

Still under the influence of Shelleyan thought, anxious to use
her life for others, she sought to make life easier for Mrs.
Nugent, suggesting that when she came to Ireland to retrieve
possessions left there, Mrs. Nugent return with her; she would
be happy to relieve her of the harsh necessity of making her own
living; she would do everything to make her happy, her own
happiness having fled; 'I live for others'. The illness of the baby,
Charles, had increased her woes, and her outlook was dark:

I really see no termination to my Sorrows. As to Mr. Shelley I know
nothing of him. He neither sends nor comes to see me. I am still at
my Father's which is very wretched. When I shall quit this House
I know not. Everything goes against me. I am weary of my life. I am
so restrained that life is scarcely worth having . . . at nineteen I could
descend a willing victim to the Tomb. How I wish those dear children had never been born. They stay my fleeting Spirit when it
would be in another State. How many there are who shudder at
death. I have been so near it that I feel no terrors. Mr. Shelley has

much to answer for. He has been the cause of great misery to me &
mine. I shall never live with him again. 'Tis impossible. I have been
so deceived, so cruelly treated that I can never forget it. Oh no, with
all the affections warm, a heart devoted to him, & then to be so
cruelly blighted. Oh Catherine you do not know what it is to be left
as I am, a prey to anguish, corroding sorrow, with a mind too sensitive to others' pain. But I will think no more. There is a Madness in
thought. Could I look into futurity for a short time how gladly
would I pierce the veil of Mystery that wraps my fate. Is it wrong,
do you think, to put an end to one's sorrows? I often think of it—all
is so gloomy and desolate. Shall I find repose in another world? Oh
grave, why do you not tell me what is beyond thee? Let me hear
from you soon, my dear Friend. Your Letters make me more happy.
Tell me about Ireland. You know I love the green Isle & all its
Natives. Eliza joins in kind love to you. I remain your sincere but
unhappy friend

H. SHELLEY

It was only a few months since she had come from Bath to hear
her husband's dreadful news; in the first months of misery the
birth of her child offered some slight hope of his return to her
and her children; he had always been eager for a large family
to educate in his ideas. Mary was hurt at his jubilation; Harriet
found it based upon sordid motives. Sadly Harriet renounced
all hope, and resolutely tried to divert her mind from a death
wish; she reminded herself of her love for Ireland, how she had
declared herself to be at heart Irish. She would divert her
thoughts to the larger troubles of the world.

Yet in the narrow life in her father's home she had little outlet
for her wider interests; and no news of Shelley, of whom she
thought wistfully. Peacock, her usual informant, was not available; he had involved himself with two women, Marianne de St.
Croix, with whom he talked of marriage and emigration to
America (with Shelley's financial aid), and 'Charlotte' erroneously supposed to possess a fortune. Led by the latter into
extravagances, he was now detained in a debtors' prison.
Harriet would not have viewed the matter with the amused
detachment of Shelley who a week earlier, when both he and
Mary were angry over Harriet's sending her creditors to him,
had gone to see Marianne and learned that Peacock was living
with 'a rich heiress' who

is very miserable; God knows why. Shelley is, on her account and
that of Miss de St. Croix, who is miserable on her own account.

Mary sent Peacock £2. Peacock was not likely to have confided
in Harriet the cause of his failing to communicate with her.
Hookham, the other mutual friend, was not one to give her
detailed information of the odd Shelley household: Mary, advanced in pregnancy, diligently studying; Claire with her ebul-
lience and her moods of depression; Hogg, who had first met
Mary in November 1814, taking his place as part of the family,
pleased at having Mary receptive to his proffered love where
Harriet had been resentful. Hookham, when he had called on
the Shelleys on the 16th of December, after the birth of Charles,
had been, according to Mary, 'nasty'. His sympathies were
with Harriet; yet he never escaped the fascination of Shelley's
friendship.

Of Mary's amatory dalliance with Hogg, her acceptance of
gifts from him, her netting of purses for him, their exchange of
jejune love letters, Harriet was surely ignorant; had she known
she might not have realized that Mary's engaging in a love duet
with Hogg was a conscientiously cultivated emotion, or that his
served as balm to his self-esteem, wounded by her own rejection
of his love.

News of Shelley reached Harriet that necessitated their meeting again: at the end of the first week of January his grandfather,
Sir Bysshe, died. A year ago this event might have brought
something of a reconciliation between Shelley and his father,
now Sir Timothy; at least the financial benefits would have
established Shelley, Harriet, and their children at Nantgwillt.
Though there was no narrowing of the breach between them,
Shelley and his father came to an agreement that materially
bettered the son's position. By June 1815 his tangled finances
had been straightened, and a regular income of £1000 a year
allotted to him, of which £200 a year was assigned to Harriet;
his large and her moderate debts were paid, but no provision
was made for the children.

In April, after much persuasion, Harriet agreed to produce
the infant Charles in the Court of Chancery to settle certain
matters about the estate of Sir Bysshe. Mary's bitterness over

the legitimacy of Harriet's children whereas her own were not
entitled even to the name of Shelley—they were Godwins—
coloured her references to Harriet in the *Journal*; Harriet was
'selfish' and 'nasty', her debts were an impertinence, while the
demands of Godwin and even of his stepson, Charles Clairmont,
were Shelley's proper concern. The right of her son to title and
fortune did not afford satisfaction to Harriet; rather did it constitute a threat to her peace of mind lest he be removed from
her and her relatively plebeian family. Her fear of this gave
Shelley an advantage in their negotiations.

On the 26th of January she had taken the children to be
christened at St. George's, Hanover Square, the church in which
her parents had been married, in which she had been christened,
and in which ten months ago she had been re-married to
Shelley. In the baptismal record the children appear as Eliza
Ianthe, born the 23rd of June 1813, and Charles Bysshe, born
the 30th of November 1814, 'the children of Percy Bysshe &
Harriet Shelley, Chapel Street, Gent'. Under other circumstances it would have been a source of pride to Harriet and her
father to have the gentle birth of the children on record.

For Harriet the death of Sir Bysshe had meant only the minor
security of a fixed income so that she was no longer wholly
dependent upon her father; for Mary it had meant a change to
a way of life more gracious and secure than any to which she
had been accustomed. In August Shelley and Mary were established in a charming small house at Bishopsgate, in a leafy lane
just outside Windsor Forest, giving Shelley the sense of open
space of Field Place, of Cwm Elan, of Nantgwillt.

Six months before this, on the 22nd of February, Mary's first
child, a girl, had been born; it lived slightly less than two weeks.
Surviving birth in lodgings and removal six days later to other
lodgings, seemingly gaining steadily in strength, it died on the
6th of March. Mary's laconic entry in the *Journal* reads:

Find my baby dead. Send for Hogg. Talk. A miserable day. In the
evening read "Fall of the Jesuits." Hogg sleeps here.

Like Harriet's son it was an eight months' child; the 22nd of
February was slightly less than eight months from the 27th of

June. Had it been conceived after the elopement it would have been less than a seven months' child. Such an infant would not have been likely to survive even under ideal conditions. It may have been 'overlaid', a sufficiently common occurrence when babies were kept in bed with mother or wet nurse (Mary 'suckled' her child) feeding at will. Mary's early pregnancy is indicated variously: she had been repeatedly indisposed on the road from London to Dover, seasick on the crossing to Calais (Shelley and Claire were not, yet Shelley had been seasick between Ireland and Holyhead), and the infant with only her inexpert care had lived twelve days. The readiness with which she conceived is attested by the fact that her second child was born eleven months after the first.

How much Shelley confided to Harriet is uncertain. He called upon her frequently in the spring of 1815. Hogg was in attendance upon Mary, reading Ovid's love poetry with her. Mary, in spite of Hogg's lovemaking, was unhappy over Claire's absorption of Shelley's time, and eager to have her sent away. Her departure finally occurred on the 13th of May when Shelley saw her off to Lynmouth, where he had been idyllically happy with Harriet. He seems to have felt no incongruities: he had thought of securing Nantgwillt for himself and Mary, a place which he had coveted for himself and Harriet, and where he had anxiously watched at her sickbed. Mary, rejoicing over the banishment of Claire, entered in her *Journal* the recipe for a purge,[11] a vulgarity Shelley did not continue; instead he made a jesting entry, a burlesque of hers, his containing human blood, gunpowder, putrefied brain, and mashed grave worms to which Mary added, 'I begin a new Journal with our regeneration'. Whatever the stresses and strains, the jealousies and consolatory flirtations, Shelley's complacency over Mary and Hogg, Mary's lack of complacency over Shelley and Claire, Harriet's hopes for Shelley's return to her proved vain; he did not swerve from his attachment to Mary; her influence dominated him, and much as he enjoyed the presence of Claire, he consented to her banishment.

The year 1815 had its bright moments for Harriet—Napoleon's overthrow was now final; Sir Bysshe's death had sent Shelley to her as his legal wife. On the 10th of April 'Shelley

N

passes the morning with Harriet, who is in a surprisingly good humour' (Mary's *Journal*); on the 21st, Mary recorded, he went to her in the afternoon and the next afternoon he was again with her, somewhat nettled by her. On the pleasant morning visit he may have taken to her a copy of a new monthly Journal, *The Theological Inquirer or Polemical Magazine*,[12] which appeared for seven months that year, March to September, devoting an inordinate amount of space to Shelley; his name did not appear, nor did that of the editor (except pseudonymously as 'Erasmus Perkins, M.A.'). 'Perkins' referred to himself in other publications as a Unitarian clergyman who had stood beside Daniel Isaac Eaton at his trial for blasphemous libel—at the time Shelley was writing his fiery defence of Eaton, Harriet in a letter spoke approvingly of a clergyman who had supported Eaton. The elusive 'Erasmus Perkins' was an Irishman, George Cannon. Shelley disliked him intensely but he connived with him over the publication—its first—of *Queen Mab*, and of *A Refutation of Deism* in its entirety. The latter appeared in the March and April issues; *Queen Mab* in four issues, March, April, May, and July. The editor was determined to introduce Shelley's writings to the public, an interest he continued for years in England and America. Both poem and prose which began in the first issue were most familiar to Harriet, their composition associated with her. Omitting passages the authorities might have pounced upon as subversive, the reviewer of *Queen Mab* quoted a full third of the poem, with the parts omitted given in a running summary, the whole lengthy and extremely laudatory, with sufficient of the poem to constitute a publication (previously it had been only 'printed'). 'F', the reviewer (he was R. C. Fair, a minor versifier and journalist), published in the July issue a fervid 'Ode to the Author of *Queen Mab*'. In May a contributor, signing himself 'Eunomus Wilkins', in an article on Giordano Bruno, in whom Shelley was deeply interested, quoted the opening lines of Canto VII of *Queen Mab*:

> I was an infant when my mother went
> To see an atheist burned . . .

a passage of some length, as referring to Giordano Bruno, and went on to pay tribute to 'the inimitable author of *Queen Mab*'.

It would surely have been a source of satisfaction to Harriet to see published so much of the poem dedicated to her—though the dedication was not quoted—as its inspiration, and the prose dialogue composed in those charmed weeks in Edinburgh, the culmination of the 'happiest years' of her life. Both were in the voice of the Shelley she knew, admired, and loved; there was in them nothing of the heartless mercenary the Godwins were making of him; here was his true voice, impassioned for the triumph of freedom and virtue. *Queen Mab*, re-read, recalled the places described, the hills and the sea, Devon and Wales; the fervour of Shelley's hatred of injustice, his eager desire to reform the world. The turmoil of his life with Mary, Claire, and Hogg now kept him from such writing. Hogg, Harriet knew, was sceptical of such endeavour; Mary's deepest concern was for her father, to whom she was always over-devoted; and the children of radicals are wont to be suspicious of aspiring idealism; to them conservatism is romantic. Many years later, defending herself against criticism, Mary wrote that unlike her parents and Shelley, she had not supported reform or liberalism. Shelley's enthusiasms were not to be regained until, in 1816, he came in contact with Byron, then writing the third canto of *Childe Harold*.

Harriet could not have known that Shelley's idealism would be resurgent. In 1815 she found the Shelley she had known and believed in harassed and debased. She retained the *Notebook* into which he had written his poems, some of them in his writing, some in hers. She had copied there the sad stanzas to her, those of May 1814; and after these she wrote two stanzas, dating them 'Stanmore 1815'. Whether these are lines Shelley read or recited to her on one of their April meetings, or were her attempt to express her own feelings is uncertain. These lines, and many loving poems to her, few of them as yet published, she could read and re-read in her lonely hours:

> Full many a mind with radiant genius fraught
> Is taught the dark scowl of misery to bear,—
> How many a great soul has often sought
> To stem the sad torrent of wild despair!

'Twould not be Earth's laws were given
To stand between Man, God & Heaven,—
To teach him where to seek and truly find
That lasting comfort, peace of mind.

                              Stanmore, 1815[13]

This sounds like a lament for both Shelley, the genius bowed
down with cares, and for herself.

His long poem *Alastor or The Spirit of Solitude*, published early
in 1816, emphasized for Harriet the change in him. Shelley's
father, having read his copy, wrote, on the 27th of February,
to his solicitor, Whitton:

P. B. has published a poem with some fragments, somewhat in his
usual style, not altogether free from former sentiments, and wants
to find out one person on earth the Prototype of himself.

This is not without dry humour or penetration; Sir Timothy
shrewdly apprehended his son's perpetual search for a counter-
part, his Platonic other self, the embodiment in an earthly
woman of that which he was finally to realize existed only in
the ideal world. Sir Timothy perceived, too, that his reforming
ardour had cooled. This latter point Mary emphasized, in her
note on the poem, in editing it more than a decade after
Shelley's death:

Alastor is written in a very different tone from *Queen Mab*. In the
latter, Shelley poured out all the cherished speculations of his youth
—all the irrepressible emotions of sympathy, censure, and hope, to
which the present suffering, and what he considers the proper destiny
of his fellow-creatures, gave birth. *Alastor*, on the contrary, contains
an individual interest only. A very few years, with their attendant
events, had checked the ardour of Shelley's hopes . . .

Harriet still valued that ardour, those hopes.

Reviews of *Alastor* were not laudatory. Harriet could find
echoes in it of *Queen Mab* and 'Retrospect: Cwm Elan', but it
was not, like these, a happy poem. There is a superficial resemblance in places to *Queen Mab*: the lonely poet wanders in
remote places where Shelley had been only in heightened imagination; Athens and Tyre, shown to Ianthe by the faery Mab,
and beyond these Arabia, Persia, the Vale of Cashmire, the
'lone Chorasmian shore'. In the fixed Shelleyan pattern he had

been driven from his 'cold fireside and alienated home' by
loneliness, as Shelley himself had been driven from his family to
Harriet, from Harriet to Mary, and as he was to be in the future,
which Harriet could not foresee, from Mary to Emilia Viviani
and to Jane Williams. In *Alastor* the poet's dreams of love are
embodied first in 'an Arab maiden' who brings him food and
in sleepless love watches over his slumber, at dawn returning to
the 'cold home' of her father; and second, in the Vale of Cashmire, by 'a veiled maid'. This vision, unlike that of the Arab
maiden, is completely realized; the descriptive lines picture the
definite physical union of a passionate woman and a dazzled
man. If the poem is autobiographically based, this suggests a
contrast between the conventionally modest Harriet and the
passionate Mary. It is worth noting that both maidens are the
active lovers, the Arab shy, the other ardent.

In spite of bursts of lyricism and felicitous passages the poem
remains what its title indicates, the tale of a tortured poet who
dies alone and unheard, a gentle creature bruised by a world
'profuse of poisons', where 'heartless things' are done. Haunted
by the premonition that his life would be brief Shelley grieved
to see his impassioned thoughts fall upon barren ground. *Alastor*,
written when hope was low, is little more than an obscure
lament.

The Dæmon of the World, published with it, was a heavily cur-
tailed, emasculated revision of *Queen Mab*, devitalized, its magic
muted. It had been a winged rhapsody, a paean of joy springing
from love. The revision is pedestrian, no *cri de cœur* but a
laboured patchwork; gone are most of the ringing lines, the
swift movement, the breathless emotion; no longer is man 'of
soul and body, formed for deeds/Of high resolve'; no longer
does 'every heart contain perfection's germ', and though
Ianthe's spirit still stands 'on an isolated pinnacle' it is now
fixed there 'serene and inaccessibly secure', rather like a butterfly specimen. Part II is more faithful to the earlier text, but is
less coherent and forceful, its three hundred and nine lines
pieced together from Sections VIII and IX (reversed). Omitted
are the vivid enunciations of aspiration and the fiery denunciations of the evils of commerce, tyranny, and religion; Ianthe is

not exhorted to a 'life of resolute good'. The poem is, as Shelley labelled it, a 'Fragment'.

Of the short poems included, one was well known to Harriet, the autobiographic 'April, 1814' stanzas of sadness where death only offers peace. Two poems were sonnets, one to Wordsworth lamenting his apostasy from liberalism, the other 'Feelings of a Republican on the Fall of Bonaparte', wherein the tyrant seemed less a foe to virtue than is 'old Custom, legal Crime/And bloody Faith, the foulest birth of Time'. 'Mutability', four stanzas on the transience of life, contained the Stoic consolation: 'the path of its departure still is free'. In 'A Summer-Evening Churchyard, Lechlade', death is mild and 'terrorless as this serenest night'. 'Oh! there are spirits of the air', asks sadly:

> Ah! wherefore didst thou build thine hope
> On the false earth's inconstancy?

These were sad poems, keyed to the spirit of *Alastor*, even the sonnet on Napoleon's fall a lament. They do not reflect the perfect happiness or the heightened poetic power Shelley had anticipated as the result of his union with Mary Godwin. Compared with the exultant joy of *Queen Mab* their tone was black with gloom. 'A Summer-Evening Churchyard', in musical lines, has an almost hypnotic invitation to death. There was in the volume *Alastor* little to awaken a reader to the joy of life.

CHAPTER VII

Is it wrong?

Thus solemnized and softened, death is mild
And terrorless as this serenest night:
Here could I hope, like some inquiring child
Sporting on graves, that death did hide from human sight
Sweet secrets, or beside its breathless sleep
That loveliest dreams perpetual watch did keep.
                                    A Summer-Evening Churchyard

S OON after the publication of *Alastor* circumstances brought Shelley to London; two matters required his stay in town: the concluding phase of the lawsuit begun the preceding year over Sir Bysshe's estate, which involved the infant Charles (now in his second year), and the need of another large sum of money for Godwin. It was spring and he was alone, as he had been in 1811 and 1814. In 1811, expelled from Oxford, separated from Hogg, in disfavour with his family, he had found comfort with Eliza Westbrook and Harriet. In 1814, temporarily apart from Harriet, he had found comfort with Mary Godwin. Then he had been assiduously wooed by Godwin, dining daily at Skinner Street. In 1816 he was not welcome there, and Godwin made no attempt to alleviate his loneliness. Claire, recently returned from a trip to Ireland with her brother, was not available as constant companion, having embarked upon an exciting adventure of her own. Like Godwin, she depended upon Shelley for funds; in nine days in March he wrote cheques for her to the sum of forty-one pounds, an amount by no means negligible when Harriet received only fifty pounds a quarter. Claire's brother, Charles Clairmont, also continued to dip his hand in Shelley's purse as he travelled about seeking to settle upon some occupation. Shelley seemingly found it impossible to refuse any member of the Godwin family.

He could be firm with Harriet. Mr. Westbrook had tried to obtain, from him or from his father, at least half of the cost of the children's support. Some months earlier Mr. Westbrook, with his solicitor Desse, had called upon Whitton to inform him of Shelley's refusal, and of his counter-demand for the custody of the children. This led the Westbrooks to swift retreat. Whitton was told that the children would not be given up to Shelley and that, if he persisted in his demand, the case would be taken to court where custody would be denied him because of his anti-religious principles. Desse asked if, to avoid the publicity of a suit, Sir Timothy would agree to support one child, Mr. Westbrook to support the other. Whitton, ever careful of his clients' purses, answered with a firm refusal. He had, however, learned from Shelley's solicitor, Longdill, that unless Harriet signed the deed of separation (which she refused to do) and/or surrendered the children, her allowance would be stopped.

Whitton did not approve of Shelley's attitude, but his concern was for his client, Sir Timothy, whom he advised not to get involved in his son's affairs, as only discomfort could result; he was himself having trouble to keep the peace between the two solicitors, Desse and Longdill. It was in December 1815 that Whitton made the suggestion that Desse and Longdill should select a mutually acceptable guardian for the children as a compromise (presumably the expense would fall upon Mr. Westbrook). At some time in the year 1816 the children were put in the care of the Rev. John Kendall, vicar of Bud-broke, in Warwickshire. The Westbrooks were considering the welfare of the children; Ianthe did not thrive in London, and Charles was a delicate boy. It may be that they, and not the lawyers, chose the guardian, thinking to place the children where Shelley could not find them. No suit was brought against Shelley, and no more requests were made for their support. Sir Timothy and his lawyer agreed that Shelley *should* provide for them; he did not.

Nothing, however, deterred him from lavish borrowings for Godwin's benefit; even Fanny prodded him, believing it his duty and privilege to relieve Godwin's anxieties, as insistent as the idolizing Mary that Shelley should act promptly and generously in order to leave Godwin free to put his mind upon his forthcoming novel. That Shelley might want to put his mind upon something beside post-obit bonds did not interest Godwin. He did urge haste but for his own sake; Shelley, however, had a vein of prudence that made him seek less exorbitant terms than those first offered. Negotiations with the money-lender Bryant were therefore prolonged.

The other matter that required Shelley's presence in London —Mary remained at Bishopsgate—was the lawsuit to restrain his father from selling a considerable amount of valuable timber, the purpose being not to prevent the cutting or the sale, but to have Shelley's rights defined by the court; he expected a share of the profits. The presence of Charles was again obligatory, and Harriet was not co-operative. The year before Shelley had himself fetched the child—Mary wrote in her *Journal* on the 21st of April 1815: 'Shelley goes to Harriet to procure his son, who is to appear in one of the Courts'. In 1816 it became necessary to force the issue. On the 2nd of March Whitton wrote to Desse that he had procured an order for the Messenger of the Court to 'apprehend' the infant Charles and produce him in court. This order, Whitton wrote, he would be obliged to enforce 'unless Mrs. Shelley will make it unnecessary by bringing the child to Court without further trouble'. Harriet had little choice but to take him. Whitton subsequently informed Sir Timothy that Shelley was in court, unhappy over the verdict which permitted the sale of the timber without compensation to him.[1]

The existent letters written by Shelley in the spring of 1816 are merely those to the money-lender and to Godwin. Mary's *Journal* is missing, from the 13th of May 1815 when she wrote, 'I begin a new Journal', to the 21st of July 1816. It cannot, then, be known how frequently Shelley and Harriet may have met in the spring of 1816, or what powers of persuasion he used after the issuance of the court order (the order remained among the Whitton papers, not, apparently, having been served); or whether, seeing Harriet in court, Shelley felt a wish to be on friendly terms with her. Some relief from his perturbation, from his loneliness he might have sought—she had in the past had a calming influence upon him. If now he came to her tired and disheartened, she would have found it hard to resist him. He was without feminine companionship, away from Mary, not welcome at Mrs. Boinville's or the Newtons'. Harriet was still his legal wife, and still lovely. In a note to *Queen Mab* (V, 189) he had said, in deploring the law's putting control upon 'the involuntary affections of our nature', 'Love is inevitably consequent upon the perception of loveliness'. Between the Court order of 2nd March and the hearing in late April there was a period of over six weeks during which Harriet's consent had to to be won, and kept firm.

But Mary came to town, and on the 5th of May Shelley, Mary, and Claire were off to the continent, and as in 1814 Harriet was left alone. Shelley had planned to go to Italy and Hogg was to have gone with them. Though he was with them on their last night in London he was not told of their imminent departure and was again surprised to have been ignored. They had slipped away secretly without warning Sir Timothy or Whitton, both of whom were disturbed since Shelley's presence was necessary for the settling of certain legal matters. Shelley had yielded to Claire's importunities; they turned not to Italy but to Geneva.

Claire, seeking a romance of her own more exciting than her share in Mary's, had laid siege to Lord Byron, handsome, fascinating, popular poet, the world's great lover, celebrating the ladies he had loved each in a verse tale. No one could have failed to hear of Lady Caroline Lamb's scandalous pursuit of him, and her rage when he finally escaped from her. He had married in January 1815, and brought his bride to a house that was not very far from where Harriet now lived with her father. In slightly less than a year Lady Byron had taken her infant daughter to her parents; and in January 1816, a separation was arranged. When Claire wrote her bold letters, demanding an interview, Lord Byron was in a difficult situation. There were rumours of mad behaviour to his wife, of improper behaviour with his half-sister, Augusta Leigh. Society, in one of its recurrent moods of virtue, cast off its idol. Byron, at first unwillingly, had accepted the distraction of an interlude with the vivacious

Claire. Though she protested that she would rather be his 'male companion', his devoted attendant, than his mistress, she had from the first pleaded for an assignation; and before he left England she was exultantly pregnant by him. Though she took Mary to see him (she suggested that he might be interested in her, too) she did not confide her relationship with him in urging Shelley and Mary to follow him to Geneva.[2] Shelley had not yet met Byron; Claire was, however, right in expecting the two poets to become friends.

Harriet, as in 1814, turned to old friends. To Mr. Newton in early June she wrote offering to help him with his dying wife and his children.[3] Her affectionate message to her favourite among the children shows that she had continued to see them. She offered to send fruits from London such as they could not get in the country where they now lived. Peacock, kind as always, was acting as her intermediary with Whitton, in her effort to secure an increased income; hers was insufficient to permit her to have a home of her own. Mr. Westbrook, Shelley assumed, had continued his £200 allowance, but that may have been wholly allocated to the children—they were boarding in the country; the fees for their board and care in 1817 were exactly that amount. Shelley, in the long months when he could give her nothing at all, wrote that he did not wish her to be dependent on her father; yet he expected Mr. Westbrook to provide for the children, whom, vaguely, he planned to have with him in time. Meanwhile Harriet's twenty-first birthday, the 1st of August, was approaching, when she would be able to transact her own affairs. Peacock in June obtained from Whitton information of a step she could take to increase her income: as legal wife she would have certain rights when Shelley came into his inheritance; according to Whitton she could buy an annuity by signing away her future rights; he did not advise her to do so, but it was a possibility. It is so much in line with Shelley's own resort to post-obit bonds that one wonders if he had suggested it. Apparently she took Whitton's advice against this.

Again she was forlorn in London while Shelley, Mary, and Claire were off for a journey through France to Switzerland.

They were living more opulently than in 1814, and were before long established in a villa on the lake, outside Geneva, fairly close to Byron's. It was a happy summer for all, the two poets stimulating each other, their poems written at this time echoing each other, so that it is difficult to say with certainty which phrases, verses, rhythms, figures of speech, ideas, were first voiced by Byron or Shelley.

For Harriet the summer could have been only one of mounting fear. Gossip may well have reached her, for Byron was fair game; and the Shelley household, too, was vulnerable. English travellers avidly spread gossip of Byron's literary and amatory affairs. One, Lord Glenbervie, wrote in his *Journal* what he heard of Lord Byron:

He is now living at a villa in the Savoy side of the lake with that woman, who it seems proves to be a Mrs. Shelley, wife to the man who keeps the Mount Coffee House.[4]

Here is a double confusion which does, however, connect the offending Claire with Shelley, and Shelley with the Westbrooks. Other travellers told other tales, all seeping back to England.

How much of this reached Harriet's ears is uncertain; inevitably she would have been aware of some rumours. Her own position was increasingly wretched. She had no word from Shelley when he came to London, alone, in early September. He remembered her on the 24th when he signed his will, in which he left two legacies to Claire, one to Harriet, one each to Ianthe and Charles, and the remainder of all that was not entailed of his future inheritance to Mary. Without seeking Harriet he set about securing a house in Marlow, where Peacock lived. It was not far from Eton or from Bracknell; Shelley was returning to the scenes of his youth at Eton, and those of his last months with Harriet.

Early in October Fanny Godwin wrote that Harriet had been in Bracknell and had said unkind things about Shelley and Mary. Mrs. Godwin had recently been to Bracknell where she heard this from a lodging-house keeper. Fanny knew that Shelley and Mary gave little credence to anything Mrs. Godwin said, but there *might* be something in this. It might be servants' gossip; Fanny knew that Shelley and Mary were not circumspect; they carelessly left letters about where servants could and undoubtedly did read them. She advised them earnestly to keep only foreign servants who would not fraternize with the villagers. Ironically she approved of the nursemaid brought from Geneva, with whom both Mary and Claire were friendly, but who was to be, in later years, party to the blackmailing of Shelley.

But it was Fanny herself who now became the subject of gossip. Having always believed herself Godwin's daughter, she had been unprepared for the revelation that she was the illegitimate child of Mary Wollstonecraft. Mrs. Godwin, presumably in a mood of exasperation, had told her the truth, adding that Shelley and Mary, whom Fanny defended, made mock of her colourless character. Mrs. Godwin apparently, like most dominating people, despised those who never opposed her; it deprived conquest of its pleasure. It was the more cruel if Mrs. Godwin believed what she said, that Fanny was from the first in love with Shelley. Fanny at the moment was happily wearing a watch brought her from Switzerland, a token, she had thought of the love Shelley and Mary had for her. Suddenly she belonged to nobody. Her mother's sisters in Ireland had warmed and cooled toward her, offering her a home with them to help with their school, and then withdrawing the offer, lest, in view of gossip about Mary and Shelley, her presence should be detrimental.

Pretending that the Wollstonecrafts had sent for her, Fanny left Skinner Street on the 7th of October. No one bothered to see if she had enough money for the journey. Shelley was at Bath whither Mary and Claire had gone on their return to England, to remain until after the birth of Claire's child. They believed, or pretended to believe, that the Godwins knew and suspected nothing, although it was usual for Claire to come to see them, and to stay with them at times. Godwin, who gathered gossip readily, must have developed a deaf ear. In Bath, gossip attributed the paternity of Claire's child to Shelley. Again he had sent her to a place associated with Harriet; Harriet had been at Bath when his romance with Mary had developed. Fanny did not go to see them, as she might have done had Mrs. Godwin not broken her faith in their love for her. From Bristol she wrote a letter they found 'alarming', and a similar one to Godwin, who went in search of her, as did Shelley. But she had gone on to Swansea where, at the Mackworth Arms, she quietly put herself to sleep. The Swansea paper, *The Cambrian*, on the 12th reported the 'melancholy discovery' of the body of a young woman, and on the 19th, the verdict at the inquest: 'Found dead', this in spite of an empty laudanum bottle beside the bed, and a suicide note. There was a kindly tendency to return a verdict that would permit burial in consecrated ground; 'suicide' required burial at the crossroads with a stake through the heart. Any one definitely 'genteel' (the paper referred to her as 'a most respectable female') was given the benefit of the doubt. Fanny had torn off and burned the signature on her letter; the 'G' on her stockings, the 'M. W.' on her stays were not revealing. In her reticule she had only 'a red silk handkerchief, a brown berry necklace, and a small leather clasped purse, containing a 3s. and a 5s. 6d. piece'. She had also her new watch. Her note was printed in *The Cambrian*:

I have long determined that the best thing I could do was to put an end to the existence of a being whose birth was unfortunate, and whose life has only been a series of pain to those persons who have hurt their health in endeavouring to promote her welfare. Perhaps to hear of my death will give you pain, but you will soon have the blessing of forgetting that such a creature ever existed as . . .

Surely she was quoting Mrs. Godwin who often complained, from her earliest days with Godwin, that she had ruined her health toiling for the family, a fact Godwin rather complacently accepted. Fanny, gentle, uncomplaining, and self-sacrificing, could not resist hoping that her death would pain Mrs. Godwin (and others). It did indeed. Godwin shunned his friends, lest someone speak of her, and a year later had not let Charles Clairmont, who was abroad, know of her death.

Shelley was sufficiently under Godwin's domination to obey his hysterical command not to reveal her identity but leave her body unclaimed. And so Fanny had not even a modicum of respect in death. She who had been a merry child, beloved by her mother, petted by Godwin, had long since become a shadow. Godwin had sent her to prod Shelley, Mrs. Godwin with surreptitious gifts of baby-linen to Mary. No one tried to give her any life of her own. It was as if she had never been.

Yet Godwin's turning from grief was his attempt to live up to his principles: it was not reasonable to show grief; it was not reasonable to expose oneself to unpleasant publicity; life went on and should be lived in the intellectual sphere. But he had rather incongruously developed respect for the conventionalities of outer decorum. Mary who felt genuine grief, whereas Claire was affected only because it was the first time any 'acquaintance' of hers had died, entered in her *Journal*:

A miserable day. Two letters from Papa. Buy mourning.

An odd item; Godwin who had urged secrecy, had apparently decreed the wearing of mourning. One does not wear this outward show of loss for a day or a week, and others, besides the nurse Elise, would have known for whom it was worn.

Four years ago, in October 1812, Harriet had first met Fanny. To Fanny, Harriet had appeared 'a fine lady'; she had worn a silken gown such as Fanny had never owned, she had a magnetic husband, she had moved about the country while Fanny had been a stay-at-home, too useful to be spared. Now Harriet was the problem-child in her father's home, like a naughty schoolgirl who had not done well at her lessons. Most women managed to hold their marriages; husbands were often faithless, but they came back, and at least made a pretence of living with their wives. Any father would have felt that if his daughter had been clever she would not have let another woman capture her husband's person.

Harriet's meetings with Shelley in 1815 and 1816 had not awakened him to his proper responsibilities. If she knew of Fanny's death—and it was rumoured around London—her own despairing thoughts would have deepened. Her many happy memories could not sustain her, memories of gay light-hearted days when the unexpected was likely to happen; when with Shelley she had moved from cottage to villa to hotel to lodgings to proper house: Edinburgh, Keswick, Dublin, Devon, Wales, Ireland, London, Bracknell, years brief in time but crowded with ardent living. She had been the guest of the Duke of Norfolk, of the Calverts, the Nanneys, the Southeys, the Newtons, the Godwins; and Peacock, too, had been her friend as well as Shelley's. Life had been full of high-minded endeavour and practical help to the poor everywhere they had been. She had sung with Mrs. Nanney; she had listened to her husband's public speaking; she had been his companion in all his activities, and he had called her the inspirer of his verse. Life had been an enchanted garden where she walked with her Prince Charming; now the garden was choked with weeds and thorns.

Hogg had not come to comfort her; it is doubtful if he would have been welcome. He had remained her admirer as long as she was Shelley's. He wrote to her and received letters from her. At Bracknell his interest was sufficiently apparent for Mrs. Newton to twit him. When she ceased to be Shelley's, his interest ended; he turned quickly to Mary. His novel, written in 1812 when he was separated from Shelley and Harriet, published in 1813, and reviewed by Shelley in 1814 (read first with Harriet and then with Mary), was Hogg's attempt to sublimate his love of Harriet. In the novel, the *Memoirs of Prince Alexy Haimatoff*,[5] Alexy is a compound of Hogg and Shelley, or rather an idealization of himself in the image of Shelley. It was his only excursion into fiction except for his imaginative *Life of Shelley*. Alexy, like Shelley, was irresistible to women, as Hogg longed to be and was not. Hurt by Harriet's refusal, he dreamed of possessing lovely ladies, all remarkably resembling Harriet. Alexy's first love died, still innocent; the succeeding emotional experiences were more satisfyingly erotic; with them Hogg soothed his pride. The fourth and briefest episode was a three-day basking in the perfumed voluptuousness of a sultaness, a contrast to the cold control of Harriet whom she resembled in appearance. The second love had been an exquisite Greek girl first seen dancing at the Parthenon (Hogg had not been to Athens and did not know how steep the climb); meeting Alexy nightly at the Temple of Minerva, she did not reject his advances. Carried off by his tutor, Alexy consoled himself with a Circassian slave girl, who died. The fifth and final love, whom Shelley criticized as a coquette and a coward, was an English girl who converted Alexy to the Toryism of her father, whom she had refused to defy by marrying Alexy at once. All these loves had exquisitely lovely mouths, musical voices, and delicate complexions, vermilion melting into snow, transfused with transparent blushes. The bosoms of all five, actually observed or only fondly imagined, were perfect in shape and ivory in tint. The descriptions were built upon Hogg's memory of Harriet's beauty. But Hogg had changed allegiance and was happy to find Mary receptive to his love-making. There is nothing to indicate that he and Harriet ever met after Bracknell.

Peacock and Hookham, though friendly to Harriet, and not liked by Mary, were none the less more often in Shelley's company than hers. And the very qualities which had been of advantage in the restless days with Shelley, disqualified her for life in her father's dull home where there was little to interest her. She was too young for the friends of her parents or of Eliza. Her beauty could serve only to attract those whom, as a married woman, she could not encourage. Her cordiality had little scope. Shelley, going to and fro between London and Bath, and to Marlow where he stayed with Peacock to supervise the renovation of the house he had leased, did not try to see her; he was preoccupied with other cares. In Bath he had provided two sets of lodgings, one for Mary with little William, born the preceding January; one for Claire who pretended to be a married woman—in those days one could always claim a husband 'abroad'—as she awaited the birth of her child.

It is not known if Harriet had gone to help the Newtons in the summer, if she ever went to Wales to help 'poor, dear Mr. Nanney' when his wife was ill, as she had offered; or if she ever went to Ireland to gather up things left there, and to see Mrs. Nugent. About the time Shelley returned from Geneva she left her father's home. If Mr. Westbrook, as is likely, was paying the children's board in Warwickshire, he would not have been giving her an allowance; she would have been dependent upon the moderate sum of £200 a year, on which she could afford nothing more elegant than lodgings near Hans Place, at 7 Elizabeth Street, Brompton, not far from Chapel Street. Her reason for leaving her father's was now more than a desire to

o

escape from a stifling environment; and her family may either
have readily acquiesced in, or suggested her retirement for the
time being, with no suspicion that she might be thinking of
suicide.

In a letter to Mrs. Nugent in January 1815, Harriet, de-
pressed after the birth of Charles, had meditated on suicide;
was it wrong? She had always taken a philosophical interest in
suicide, discussing it freely, as was the habit of the times, and as
Shelley himself did. His interest had been more practical than
hers; in 1810 and 1811 he had carried laudanum and pistols
about in his wild despair over the desertion of his cousin Harriet
Grove and of his sister Elizabeth; in 1814 in his dilemma over
his wife and his new love he had taken an overdose of laudanum;
he had invited Mary to die with him even as in earlier years he
had played with the idea of 'setting off for the unknown' with
Hogg. In 1822, shortly before his own death, he was to ask a
friend to procure sufficient prussic acid for him.

Suicide was a common enough subject of conversation and a
common enough occurrence. In 1813 when Harriet had herself
been at the peak of her happiness, Mme de Staël's essay on
suicide, a somewhat apologetic explanation of her failure to
commit suicide in the day of her exile, was published in London
in both a French and an English edition. Her essay analysed the
motives that led others to do so, motives that varied among
different peoples, the English being led to suicide by loss of
esteem. Harriet had indeed lost esteem; she was a deserted wife.
She was weary of her life. The temporary alleviation of sorrow
and loneliness from renewed contact with Shelley in the spring
had had sad consequences. She was a burden to her family; she
had no place in their world or in Shelley's. Like Fanny Godwin,
she felt unneeded; she was of no use to any one—Eliza had
always superintended the children's upbringing; and at the
moment they were in Warwickshire. Harriet knew that the
Shelley heir would not be left with the Westbrooks; sooner or
later the Shelleys would claim him. Already Shelley had asked
for the custody of Ianthe.

Early in September a friend of her father's, a Mr. Alder (a
plumber, probably an employer of working men and not him-

self a worker) accompanied her to Elizabeth Street and installed her in lodgings. According to the landlady she had lived quietly and properly, but seemed to be in low spirits and not well, for she spent much time in bed; the landlady thought she was pregnant. On the 9th of November she had had her dinner served early, about four in the afternoon; she ate little, and was gone when the maid returned to clear away. She had recently paid her rent, in advance. She was known as Mrs. Smith, and said that her husband was abroad. The Westbrooks were sufficiently worried over her disappearance to ask Mr. Alder to have all the adjacent ponds dragged.

It was over a month later, on the 12th of December, that *The Times* contained a short item:

On Tuesday a respectable female, far advanced in pregnancy, was taken out of the Serpentine River and brought to her residence in Queen Street, Brompton, having been missed for nearly six weeks. She had a valuable ring on her finger. A want of honour in her own conduct is supposed to have led to this fatal catastrophe, her husband being abroad.

Queen Street and Elizabeth Street were the same. 'A want of honour' was the usual reason for the suicide of young women; one has only to read the journals and newspapers of the period to learn how common seduction was, how real life and the sentimental novel went hand in hand. But in this case 'far gone in pregnancy' might have been an error, the body swollen from long immersion, had it not been fact. It is unlikely that the body could have been in the Serpentine undiscovered for over a month; yet if Harriet was alive between the 9th of November and the 10th of December where was she? If the body was in the water, would the 'valuable ring' have stayed on her finger? Harriet did own such a ring, still existent.

The detractors of Harriet built up a story, fostered by Godwin, of her having lived with a military officer; but men do not take as mistresses women far gone in pregnancy. Putting the sin earlier and postulating her desertion contradicts the known fact that she lived at her father's until September, as her sister testified. But nothing can clarify the mystery of the month between her disappearance and the finding of the body. Nor can the manner of her death be known. Did she, like Mary Wollstone-craft, carefully soak her skirts before entering the water? (many a young unfortunate did so to keep her appearance modest, as much as to weight her clothes). Did Harriet go directly from her scarcely tasted dinner to the river near by? Was Harriet Shelley this Harriet Smith—who was also twenty-one and had been married for five years?

There were, of course, rumours. Fanny Godwin had been only an obscure girl, yet her death was variously reported: people said she had died in Ireland, of a fever; Charles Lamb a few weeks after her death was telling his friends that she had taken her own life, which was true; before a year was out a gossiping lady was telling all London that Fanny had hanged herself, which was utterly false. While Godwin busied himself spreading a manufactured story to the discredit of Harriet, the Westbrooks kept dignified silence. Harriet's descendants—the only direct descendants of Shelley—have no letters to or from Shelley; no picture of her, no record of her burial. Ianthe's children never heard the name Shelley spoken in their home. The Notebook of Shelley's early poems, including many to Harriet (not yet published), was and is preserved. Eliza West-brook, unlike the friends and acquaintances whose memories were astonishingly full and fresh, kept silent even when Shelley's rising fame brought a spate of reminiscences and memoirs. The one point of agreement between the Westbrooks and the Shelleys was this obscuration of the true facts.

Except for the evidence given at the inquest 'on the body of Harriet Smith' it is difficult to separate the true from the fabri-cated, the forged and the altered letters; and entries in diaries are suspect. Godwin's entries in his diary, on Harriet's death, are later entries. It was to the advantage of his daughter to colour the truth.

There is mystery surrounding the so-called 'suicide letter' from Harriet to Eliza. The heading 'Sat-Eve' has been assumed to refer to the day of her disappearance, which was a Saturday; but there is no evidence to support this; the letter was not men-tioned by the landlady, the maid, or Mr. Alder. Surely the maid, finding Harriet gone, or the landlady when she did not return,

would have found such a letter? (Fanny left hers on her bedside
table). If it had awaited discovery by Mr. Alder he would have
given it to Eliza. If so it is difficult to understand how so intimate and painful a letter could have left Eliza's hands. There is
no reference to it in Shelley's letter to Eliza. It was not used in
the Court of Chancery where it might have served the Westbrook case—yet they would not have wanted the suicide to go
on record. Its pathos is genuine; and though the handwriting
differs in many points from the indubitably genuine letter to
Mr. Newton in June 1816 (now in the British Museum), it has
been considered authentic; written in agitation it might differ
from carefully penned letters; that is a problem for the handwriting experts. It was a century after Shelley's death (a centen-
nial is a good time for disclosures, when interest is high), in the
year 1922, that the 'suicide letter' was published in the April
issue of the *Cornhill Magazine*, presented to the public by W.
Courthope Forman who declared that it had recently made a
'mysterious reappearance'. The books and manuscripts of his
collector brother, H. Buxton Forman, had just been sold, this
letter among them. It was re-sold at the A. Edward Newton sale
(1941) since when it has remained in private hands. Mr.
Courthope Forman provided, on a small sheet of white paper,[6]
something of a history of owners which probably still exists with
the letter. Fortunately Newton published a photostat of half of
the letter, the remainder appearing in the catalogue of the sale.
Though comparison with the letter of June 1816 raises questions, one is impelled to give it credence:

To you my dear Sister I leave all my things as they more properly
belong to you than any one & you will preserve them for Ianthe.
God bless you both

Sat-Eve

My dearest & much belo^D Sister

When you read this let^r I shall be [no] more an inhabitant of this
miserable world. Do not regret the loss of one who wld never be
anything but a source of vexation & misery to you all, belonging to
me. Too wretched to exert myself, lowered in the opinion of everyone,
why should I drag on a miserable existence embittered by past re-
collection & not one ray of hope to rest on for the future. The
remembrance of all your kindness which I have so unworthily

repaid has often made my heart ache. I know that you will forgive me because it is not in your nature to be unkind or severe to any; dear amiable woman, that I had never left you, oh! that I had always taken your advice—I might have lived long and happy, but weak & unsteady have rushed on my own destruction. I have not written to Bysshe—oh no, what would it avail? my wishes or my prayers would not be attended to by him & yet should he see this perhaps he might grant my last request to let Ianthe remain with you always; dear lovely child, with you she will enjoy much happiness, with him none. My dear Bysshe, let me conjure you by the remembrance of our days of happiness, to grant my last wish: do not take your innocent child from Eliza who has been more than I have, who has watched over her with such unceasing care. Do not refuse my last request, I never could refuse you & if you had never left me I might have lived but as it is I freely forgive you & may you enjoy that happiness which you have deprived me of.

There's your beautiful boy. Oh! be careful of him & his love may prove one day a rich reward. As you form his infant mind so you will reap the fruits hereafter. Now comes the sad task of saying farewell—oh! I must be quick. God keep & watch over you all—you, dear Bysshe, and you, dear Eliza. May all happiness attend ye both is the last wish of her who loved ye more than all others. My children —I dare not trust myself there. They are too young to regret me & ye will be kind to them for their own sakes more than for mine. My parents, do not regret me; I was unworthy your love & care. Be happy, all of you. So shall my spirit find rest & forgiveness. God bless you all is the last prayer of the unfortunate   Harriet S⸗

Harriet here gave sufficient reasons for ending her life; and characteristically took responsibility for her action in rushing on her own destruction. Her letter addresses the two she loved most dearly, her sister, and her husband. There is nothing in this letter that suggests any guilty conduct. Harriet had never sufficiently imbibed Shelley's ideas of free love to have permitted her to enter into extra-marital relationships with an easy conscience. She had resisted Hogg's advances; she had uttered strictures against the conduct of Mary and Shelley which he had promptly labelled 'cant', shocked at her sharing of 'vulgar prejudice' over the sanctity of marriage, the sinfulness of free love. She had consistently refused to sign the deed of separation, upholding the view of marriage as indissoluble.

Shelley had gone to Marlow on the 5th of December; a week

Facsimile of Harriet's 'Suicide' Letter, 1816
(See pp. 197-8)

To you my dear Sister I leave all my things as they more properly belong to you than any one 'Upon oi'r preserve them for Ixuthe Godbeppe both My dearest Irunchbed Sister

When you read this lett. It shall be more an inhabitant of this miserable world. don't regret that to pofor who could never be anything but a source of vexation & misery to you oh! talking -ing to me. Tho entitled to exact myself toward in the opinion of everyone why should I decay on a miserable existence embitterd by past recollections. And on ray of hope to out on farther future. the remembrance of all your kindness which I have so unworthily repaid has often made my heart ache. I know that you will forgive me because it is now in your interests. be unkind to never to any dear amiable woman that I had never left you oh! that I had always taken your advice. I might have lived and be happy but seach & wortently have rusked or my own destruction I have not written to Byshe. And what would it avail my written or my prayers would not be attended to by him & yet I should like see him perhaps he might grant my last request to let Ianthe remain with you always dear lovely child, with you she will enjoy much happiness with him none   My dear Byshe let me conjure you by the remembrance of our days of happiness to grant my last wish do not take your innocent child from Elge who has been more than Frene, who has watched over her with such unceasing care. Don't refuse my last request I never could refuse you. If in life you had never left me I might have lived but not now in Ippeely forgive you & may you enjoy that happiness which you have destroyed next.

later he was visiting Leigh Hunt in London; both Shelley and Hunt wrote to Mary on the 12th, neither having seen the notice in *The Times* or, if they had, not connecting it with Harriet. Shelley reached Bath the evening of the 14th; if Mary's *Journal* entry is correct Hookham's letter sent on the 13th, which should have reached Bath the 14th, came on the 15th:

MY DEAR SIR,—It is nearly a month since I had the pleasure of receiving a letter from you, and you have no doubt felt surprised I did not reply to it sooner. It was my intention to do so, but on enquiry I found the utmost difficulty in obtaining the information you desired relative to Mrs. Shelley and your children.

While I was yet endeavouring to discover Mrs. Shelley's address, information was brought to me that she was dead—that she had destroyed herself. You will believe me that I did not credit the report. I called at the house of a friend of Mr. Westbrook; my doubt led to conviction. I was informed that she was taken from the Serpentine river on Tuesday last apparently in an advanced state of pregnancy. Little or no information was laid before the jury which sat on the body. She was called Harriet Smith and the verdict was *found drowned*. [actually *found dead*.]

Your children are well, and are both, I believe in London.

This shocking communication must stand single and alone in the letter which I now address to you. I have no inclination to fill it with subjects comparatively trifling; you will judge of my feelings and excuse the brevity of this communication.

Yours very truly,

T. HOOKHAM JUN.[7]

Though Hookham had often called upon Shelley and Mary he had not concealed his disapproval. The tone of this letter suggests that he was restraining himself from harsher words.

Mary's entry in her *Journal* reads:

Sunday, Dec. 15.—Draw. A letter from Hookham with the news of the death of Harriet Shelley. Walk out with Shelley. He goes to town after dinner. Read Chesterfield.

Shelley rushed from Bath to London as Harriet had at his bidding two and half years ago. Neither he nor Mary was as calm as her entry implies; her letter to him two days later is full of anxiety over his agitated state. Shelley in his letters to her and to others tried, like Godwin, to restrain emotions and be reasonable; he gave vent to his feelings in vituperation of the Westbrooks. His natural medium for emotional expression was verse; the stanzas he wrote (erroneously dated April 1815 instead of December 1816) belie the pretence of calm; their importance in his estimation is shown by the fact that he rewrote them twice —in 1817 when the revolving year recalled the deaths of both Harriet and Fanny, and in 1819 when the three-year-old William died.[8] These verses are not a factual picture of a body lifted from the river, hair and clothing sodden. In other poems he did not shrink from morbidity of detail; here he avoided it. He described the body lying on the ground; was this poetic licence? or was it the account given to him by Eliza or by Desse, the Solicitor? If Eliza's, would it have been an accurate account, or one tailored to make it more grim, more of a reproach to him?

The scene evoked is a desolate one, a chill, dreary atmosphere for a chill, dreary death. Harriet's hair, a 'poet's dream', so beautifully neat in other days, was tangled as poor Harriet's life had been. That once dear head lay exposed to the winter wind, all colour drained, that which had been warm and glowing, a pallid corpse:

> The cold earth slept below;
> 　Above the cold sky shone;
> 　　And all around,
> 　　With a chilling sound,
> From caves of ice and fields of snow
> The breath of night like death did flow
> 　　Under the sinking moon.
>
> The wintry hedge was black,
> 　The brown grass was not seen;
> 　　The birds did rest
> 　　In the dark thorn's breast,
> Whose roots, beside the pathway track,
> Bound hard the soil and many a crack
> 　　The black frost made between.
>
> Thine eyes glowed in the gleam
> 　Of the departing light;
> 　　As a starry beam
> 　　On a deep dark stream

Shines dimly—so the moon shone there,
And it shone through the strings of thy tangled hair,[9]
    That shook in the blast of night.

The moon made thy lips pale, beloved;
    The wind made thy bosom chill;
        The night did shed
        On thy dear head
Its frozen dew, and thou didst lie
Where the bitter breath of the naked sky
        Might visit thee at will.

This is valid emotion, a regret that could scarcely be voiced; to Peacock only did Shelley reveal the cause of the gloomy moods that from time to time swept over him: 'I was thinking of Harriet', he apologized. However much he excused himself, he was a prey to a feeling of guilt, which coloured various poems, notably *Julian and Maddalo*, as Mary's does her novels, notably *Falkner*.[10]

The act of suicide is more often than not like the tossing of a pebble in a pond; the ripples widen, and disappear. But Harriet's death was not that of the wife of an anonymous young man; she had been the wife of one destined to live timelessly among the great poets. Upon his early poems she had been a happy influence; upon his later ones her shadow was cast. Early on she had reflected upon social injustice; Shelley fanned that interest and fashioned its form. Because he encouraged her thinking, because he became her guide, her lodestar, because with him the springtime of her life blossomed into early and brief summer, because without him the summer withered into bitter hopeless winter, her life came to an abrupt close four months after her twenty-first birthday. An added sorrow, a bitterness that would once have been a joy, made continuance in life intolerable, and strengthened and stiffened her longing to leave 'this woful world'.

Shelley sent for Peacock, who had no wife, and who offered what was needed, understanding and quiet sympathy. Shelley kept his feelings under control by concentrating on the contest over the children. Once only did Peacock witness an outburst, and Peacock was not psychologist enough to see its significance.

They had gone together to Marlow to supervise work on the house and gardens on West Street where Shelley, with Mary and Claire, were to live. They came upon a gardener lopping off the last branches of a holly tree, to sell on the Christmas market. In a rage Shelley discharged the man summarily—he had misshapen a beautiful tree.

CHAPTER VIII

These Poor Little Innocents

> Dearest when most thy tender traits express
> The image of thy mother's loveliness.
> *To Ianthe,* 1813

ONCE more Shelley turned his steps to 23 Chapel Street. He was not admitted. He was intent upon gaining possession of both of Harriet's children; Charles, as the Shelley heir after himself, he assumed would be yielded at once, but he feared that Eliza would wish to detain Ianthe. He transferred his agony of emotion over Harriet's suicide to his anxiety over the children. Godwin had answered Mary's letter at Fanny's death, by asking with acidity what good she thought such expressions of sympathy did? Shelley followed his teaching and example; he would not give expression to futile regrets. He vented his spleen on the Westbrooks and preserved an outward calm. To Mary he wrote of what was of most interest to her, the possibility of marriage; to Claire of what was of most interest to her, the possibility of a larger income (Claire apparently had queried if now he would have free the income allotted to Harriet; he disillusioned her). To Eliza he wrote of what was of most interest to her, the fate of the children.

He wrote, as he thought, most reasonably. Forgotten were the vituperations he had written to Hogg, forgotten those just written to Mary, forgotten the cold formality of his references to 'Miss Westbrook' in his letters to Harriet; this letter began, 'Dear Eliza'; it closed, 'I remain, dear Eliza, yours very truly', and a postscript apologized for having inadvertently offended her by applying to his attorney. He had certainly had some communication from her or her father or Desse. He asked no questions about Harriet; the tone of the letter was conciliatory. It is of Ianthe that he speaks, never doubting that the boy

would be surrendered. His letter understandingly did not mollify Eliza or dispose her to accede to his wishes:

Before you receive this letter Mrs. Boinville will probably have informed you of my resolution with respect to Ianthe. My feelings of
duty as well as affection, as a father, incite me to consider every
moment of absence and estrangement from these beloved and unfortunate children, as an evil, the sense of which has been increased
to agony by the terrible catastrophe which is the occasion of this
address. You will spare me and yourself useless struggles on this
occasion, when you learn that there is no earthly consideration
which would induce me to forego exclusive and entire charge of my
child. She has only one parent, and that parent, if he could ever be
supposed to have forgotten them, is awakened to a sense of his duties
and his claims, which at whatever price must be asserted and performed.

I called on you twice yesterday. I wish I had found you at home.
I designed to have communicated intelligence which I am aware is
painful to you, in a manner the least painful. As it is, allow me to
assure you that I give no faith to any of the imputations generally
cast on your conduct or that of Mr. Westbrook towards the unhappy
victim. I cannot help thinking that you might have acted more
judiciously, but I do not doubt that you intended well.

My friend Mr. Leigh Hunt will take charge of my children and
prepare them for their residence with me. I cannot expect that your
feelings towards the lady whose union with me you may excusably
regard as the cause of your sister's ruin should permit you to mention
her with the honour with which Ianthe must be accustomed to
regard the wife of her father's heart. To deal frankly with you, I
cannot believe that you will refrain from inculcating prepossessions
on her infant mind the most adverse to my views. I do not think the
worse of you for this; perhaps you would have the generosity to curb
the feelings that would lead to this effect, but I cannot consent that
days and weeks should pass, and that what I consider my duty and
the happiness of my child should depend on your forbearance.

I had the strongest wish to consult your feelings in this affair. And
I cannot but think that they should be best consulted by immediate
compliance. Nothing can shake my resolution. The lapse of a few
weeks would only render the execution of it more distressing to you.
As to Ianthe, a child's sorrows are over in a few hours.

Mr. Hunt will attend any appointment you may be pleased to
make for delivering the children to his care in my behalf. I should
feel most happy in complying with any request which you might
make that is consistent with that agonizing and impatient sense of

duty, which will not endure the absence of my child. I can sincerely say, that I should eagerly seize any occasion of convincing you that I bear no malice.

I purposely omit adverting to the event from which the occasion of this letter springs. All parties, I imagine, suffer too deeply to find any consolation in the unnecessary display of their sensations.

I remain, dear Eliza,

Yours very truly,

P. B. SHELLEY

I may as well say—tho' I dare say Mrs. B. has told you as much—that my applying to my attorney on this occasion was founded entirely on error.[1]

A Godwinian letter, this. He was aware of his vulnerability since he had practically ignored his children. He had early on in the separation written to Harriet that it was sad to be deprived of Ianthe. Harriet could hardly avoid knowing that her children would rank in his estimation far below those of Mary, grandchildren of William Godwin and Mary Wollstonecraft. Eliza now would have wanted to save Ianthe and Charles from a household where they would be stepchildren. Reasonable as Shelley's stress upon *duty* was—he had had no contact with them to awaken love—it must have rung coldly on Eliza's ear. As he exonerated the Westbrooks from blame for their conduct toward Harriet, which he pronounced 'injudicious' but well-intentioned, he apparently had had some communication from them; he was not, he said, listening to 'any of the imputations' (indubitably gossip had spread many), probably because he knew why they had consented to or advised Harriet's going into lodgings. He did not even hint at any impropriety in Harriet's conduct; her 'ruin', for which Eliza might 'excusably' blame his union with Mary, was her suicide. Eliza's sympathy for Shelley's advanced views had long since vanished; her affection for the children, largely under her care, had strengthened. She would not under any circumstances have enjoyed turning them over to a regimen of vegetables and cold baths; she would not have believed that the children would be happy, or their 'sorrows' from parting with a loving aunt and grandparents 'over in a few hours'.

Neither Eliza nor her father was amenable to reason; Shelley was not admitted at Chapel Street, and could not influence Eliza, as of old, by his personal pleading. Mr. Westbrook acted swiftly and effectively to protect the children: by settling upon them the sum of £2000, he made them wards of the Court of Chancery; he then in their behalf petitioned the court to appoint him their guardian and restrain their father from taking possession of them. Whitton, the Shelley family solicitor, tried in vain to persuade Shelley not to contest, fearing the publicity and the possible consequences. He was, as he wrote to Sir Timothy, certain that the Lord Chancellor would regard Shelley as 'totally unfit' to have custody of the children. Whitton was impressed by the amount of Westbrook money lavishly bestowed upon Shelley children when 'any sum, however small, would have been sufficient'.

Whitton felt it his duty to inform Sir Timothy that against Shelley there would be produced a copy of *Queen Mab*, the printed *Letter to Lord Ellenborough* (a defence, he explained, of a publisher convicted of selling blasphemous works), and several letters from Shelley to his late wife. Shelley meant to counter the charges by saying that the action against him stemmed only from a feeling of resentment, and that the Westbrooks were 'equally unfit with himself to have the care of infants from the turpitude of their own conduct'. Whitton expressed his own opinion that Eliza was 'unworthy and Mr. Westbrook is unequal to the care whatever his will may be'. Hence he believed that 'the Lord Chancellor will look to you as the superintending protector of these little unoffending creatures', for whom a guardian must be found.[2]

Whitton had assured Sir Timothy that the impending action would be heard 'in his Lordship's private room in the hope that the ground of the application may not be made publick'. The privacy of the hearings did not, however, prevent publicity and *Westbrook* v. *Shelley* appeared in the newspapers: the *Globe*, the *Morning Chronicle*, the *Morning Post*, and the *Courier*, 25th January; Leigh Hunt's *Examiner* on the 26th reported the case from a friendly angle. As the case dragged on other notices appeared.

In a letter to Byron on the 17th of January 1817, Shelley, apprehensive, sought relief from his overwrought emotions:

My late wife is dead. The circumstances which attended this event are of a nature of such awful and appalling horror, that I dare hardly aver to them in thought. The sister of whom you have heard me speak may be truly said (though not in law, yet in fact) to have murdered her for the sake of her father's money. Thus did an event which I believed quite indifferent to me, following in the train of a far severer anguish, communicate a shock to me which I know not how I have survived. The sister has now instituted a Chancery process against me, the intended effect of which is to deprive me of my unfortunate children, now more than ever dear to me; of my inheritance, and throw me in prison, and expose me in the pillory, on the ground of my being a REVOLUTIONIST, and an *Atheist*. It seems whilst she lived in my house she possessed herself of such papers as go to support these allegations. The opinion of Counsel is, that she will certainly succeed to a considerable extent, but that I may probably escape entire ruin, in the worldly sense of it. So I am here, dragged before the tribunal of tyranny and superstition, to answer with my children, my property, my liberty, and my fame, for having exposed their frauds, and scorned the insolence of their power. Yet I will not fail; though I have been given to understand that I could purchase liberty by recantation. Indeed I have too much pride. . . .

His imagination was running a little too fast; Whitton in trying to dissuade him from contesting the Westbrook action, had undoubtedly stressed the danger of the exposure of his views, and Shelley immediately saw himself impoverished and imprisoned. The 'frauds' and the 'insolence' were those of the tribunal, that is, the law and the government, not the Westbrooks. He had almost lost sight of the children in his indignation at the charges brought by Eliza. Fear of failure to obtain custody of the children, through whom alone he could make amends to Harriet, once dearly loved, led him into exaggerations and distortions. It is doubtful if his statement that Fanny Godwin's death was a 'severer anguish' than Harriet's was more than a brave show, and a concession to Mary's feelings. Biographers, wishing to believe that he sprang full-formed from Mary Godwin's brow, have regarded it as a laudable sentiment.

Eliza was not trying to deprive him of his inheritance; why should she? it would devolve upon *Harriet's* son. Whatever her resentments she would not have wanted the children's father pilloried or imprisoned. She did most earnestly desire to prevent him from having his children to bring up in Godwinian radical-ism—and under Mary's influence; for she loved the children. She had not 'possessed herself' of poems and pamphlets; undis-tributed copies had been about Shelley's home and Mr. West-brook's. 23 Chapel Street had been Shelley's permanent address, and the repository of his books and various impedimenta.

Offered as evidence of Shelley's dangerous doctrines were *Queen Mab*, the *Letter to Lord Ellenborough*—in reality a noble plea for a free press and free speech—and ten letters, one to Eliza, nine to Harriet in which Shelley urged her to live with him and Mary, telling her she was no longer his wife, suggesting that she find another mate. Years later, after the death of Whitton's successor as family lawyer the letters came to Shelley's sister Hellen who, with her sister Margaret, was thor-oughly shocked.[3] When in 1929 Leslie Hotson sought and found transcripts imbedded in the records of the Court of Chancery and in 1930 published them, the public was shocked.

Shelley denied the charges against him: he had not deserted his wife; they had agreed to separate after the birth of Ianthe; he had yielded to her wish to have the children with her in view of their 'tender age', intending to take them himself when they were old enough. He denied that he was living in adultery, having married Mary Godwin on the 30th of December; Leigh Hunt in the *Examiner* sprang to his defence on this point, as if the ceremony had obliterated two and a half years. Shelley's counsel (Wetherell) dwelt lovingly upon this marriage with Mary; it proved that his actions differed from the opinions he expressed in *Queen Mab*, since, a professed anti-matrimonialist, he had married twice before he was twenty-five; anyhow *Queen Mab* was 'boyish and silly'. Basil Montagu, the well-known barrister engaged by Shelley, went further; the poem had never been published, it was merely something Shelley had written 'for his amusement'; it would not be read by his children.

Wetherell pointed out that Mr. Westbrook was disqualified as a possible 'guardian for Mr. Shelley's children' since he had kept a coffee-house; Eliza he blamed for having brought about Harriet's tragedy by manœuvring the marriage of Shelley, aged nineteen, and Harriet, aged 'seventeen'. Eliza was called 'illiterate and vulgar', which was far from the description that could have been given by the Calverts, the Southeys, the Nanneys, the Boinvilles. There would be other disadvantages to the children if they were left in the care of the Westbrooks: the children's material prospects would suffer and Mary's children benefit when Shelley came into his ample inheritance. Lord Eldon, in giving judgment, paid more heed to the *moral* welfare of the children, and their chances of eternal life; custody was awarded to the Westbrooks.

It was not until August 1818, more than a year and a half later, that guardians were finally appointed, Shelley's appeal against the judgment having been allowed. There had been much acrimony between the solicitors before a compromise was reached. The final decree placed the children with friends of Shelley's solicitor Longdill, a Dr. and Mrs. Hume. The plan for their education had been drawn up by Longdill: it was formed to curb childish tendencies, and natural impulses; to provide a regime of morning and evening prayers, grace before and after meals, and to turn them into conventional little conservatives. Charles was to be sent to school at seven; Ianthe was to learn at home French and sewing, music, literature (expurgated texts of Pope and Shakespeare), and dancing. Their father might see them once a month in the presence of a guardian; the Westbrooks once a month without a guardian present; Sir Timothy and Lady Shelley were given free access to them at any time.

Harriet had not foreseen this. Her last letter had admonished Shelley to be careful how he formed the infant mind of his son, surely a request not to subject him to Godwinianism? That he would never again see his children she would not have believed. Hookham's letter to Shelley had said that the children were in London. Had Harriet, one wonders, gone to Warwickshire to see them in November when she disappeared? or had she gone earlier and brought them back to Eliza? There are no clues. There was nothing detrimental to Harriet's 'honour' mentioned at any stage of the hearings. It was Shelley who was under fire. Lord Eldon pronounced him unfit for the custody of the children, not because of *Queen Mab* and the *Letter to Lord Ellenborough*, not because of his having lived with Mary Godwin in free union,

P

but because he had shaped his conduct on principles which were
not for the good of society, on which he would form his children's
minds. Shelley made no pretence of having changed his views.

The charges against Harriet's probity did not stem from
Shelley; if he could have substantiated them he could have made
use of them to bolster his case; they were pressed upon him by
Godwin who was desperately anxious to cover up the fact that
Mary had been living in adultery. He industriously spread tales
of Harriet's misbehaviour as a smoke screen. Claire Clairmont
years later supported Godwin's unfounded slander that Harriet
had been unfaithful to her husband *four months before* his elopement with Mary. Claire named the seducer: Major Ryan. Godwin had counted back from the birth of Charles Shelley (30th
November 1814), an eight months' child; if true, this made him
illegitimate. It was not true; the legitimacy of Charles was fully
established in 1822, when Shelley's death made it imperative
to ascertain the proper heir. At that time his grandfather took
charge of him; at the age of twelve he died, his grandparents'
love for him expressed by a tablet on the wall of Warnham
Church: 'Charles Bysshe Shelley, grandson of Sir Timothy and
Lady Shelley', as if he had had no intermediate parents.

Godwin besmirched Harriet to protect his daughter; Harriet
was dead and could not be seriously hurt; Mary was living and
needed reinstatement in the world. He changed from the first
accusation of misconduct in the spring of 1814 to that of
'repeated acts of levity', and then that she had 'latterly lived in
open connection with a Colonel Maxwell. Peace be to her
shade!' The pious ejaculation came ill from him as he added
that he had this from an 'unquestionable authority'; if he had
it from any one, it was from a notorious gossip, Tommy Hill.
He wrote to his wife that he did not tell Shelley of his having this
from Hill; even so, Shelley refused to consider the charge—to
Godwin's chagrin.[4] No one has seriously tried to trace the
colonel; vast efforts in research[5] produced two Major Ryans,
both Irishmen in the English Army, one conveniently overseas,
the other possibly the Mr. Ryan who dined with Shelley and
Harriet in London in 1813, and who called upon Shelley in
1815. Harriet mentioned him to Mrs. Nugent, writing as if he

were known to her. This would link him with an Irish patriot, a Dublin merchant who in 1805 had seized power in the Catholic Emancipation group, and as a self-appointed delegate had corresponded with Fox and the English Whigs. In January 1815 he wrote to Shelley and called at his lodgings, probably having obtained the address from Harriet—23 Chapel Street had in the past been Shelley's mailing address. Mary complained in her *Journal* twice during the first week in January that Harriet 'was sending her creditors here'. Charles Clairmont the next January wrote to Francis Place of Harriet's embarrassing Shelley financially in association with an 'Irish adventurer' carefully adding that the association was in no way 'criminal'.[6] Ryan either had bills of his own against Shelley—possibly for Harriet's purchases when they were in Dublin—or those of other merchants. He *may* have been trying to collect money for the Irish cause.

As Harriet had lived at her father's until September 1816, and then in lodgings, and as in the spring she had had to take Charles to court with Shelley present, there seems to be no time when she could have lived openly or secretly with any one. It would have been a relief to Godwin if he could have proved that she had been deserted recently so that the blame for her suicide did not rest upon Shelley or Mary. His defence of his daughter would seem less cruelly cold toward Harriet if he had not at the same time shown such smug satisfaction at his daughter's marrying above her station; he was awed at the thought of her as Lady Shelley, and felt that his home was hardly good enough for a visit from 'a future ornament of the baronetage', as he unctuously called her. Alas for his pride; he did not live to see his grandson inherit the title from the long-lived Sir Timothy; and his daughter never became Lady Shelley.

There remains the charge against Harriet made in the troublesome letter from Shelley to Mary written on the 16th of December 1816 (misdated 15th):

It seems that this poor woman—the most innocent of her abhorred and unnatural family—was driven from her father's house, and descended the steps of prostitution until she lived with a groom of the name of Smith, who, deserting her, she killed herself.[7]

It has never been proved that Shelley did write this; the sentence following has, however, his stamp:

There can be no question that the beastly viper her sister, unable to gain profit from her connexion with me, has secured to herself the fortune of the old man—who is now dying—by the murder of this poor creature.

The outburst against Eliza was an understandable burst of anger; Mr. Westbrook, however, was not dying; he lived until 1834. That Harriet had become a prostitute and then the mistress of a groom is fantastic. She had resisted Shelley when he proposed a free union; when she had resisted Hogg Shelley had himself said that her prejudice against sexual freedom was 'interwoven with the fibre of her being'. The calendar of events in 1816 is her defence: the Chancery suit in March and April; the offer to go to the Newtons' aid in June; the visit to Bracknell probably in August; lodgings alone in Brompton from September to November.

The letter upon which this charge rests is shaky evidence. Controversy still rages over its authenticity, each of two copies, similar but not identical in content, different in format and punctuation, having its vehement defenders and detractors. One, given to the Bodleian in 1892, by Lady Shelley, the daughter-in-law of Mary, came from a group of letters in Mary's desk when she died in 1851, letters unsorted and unmarked. In 1845–1846 Mary had been an eager customer of a man who, starting as a collector of and dealer in genuine manuscripts and letters, especially of Byron and Shelley, was unmasked in 1852 as a clever and unscrupulous forger. Calling himself Major George Byron, he posed as the son of Lord Byron and a Spanish lady. Sir Percy also bought from him, and so did the publisher Moxon who in 1852 had swiftly to withdraw a volume of Shelley *Letters*, with an introduction by Robert Browning, when one of the letters was identified as an essay by Francis Palgrave. The fact that Major Byron in his sales mixed the genuine with the spurious, and that he was an expert in handwriting forgery, made detection difficult, and Lady Shelley was not qualified to differentiate the true from the false letters. Besides she was interested in anything that belittled Harriet and in consequence raised Mary's stature.

The British Museum letter, in the Ashley Collection, has a more curious history, aside from having passed through the hands of Thomas J. Wise, discriminating collector, expert forger, maker of bogus first editions and thoroughly successful impostor. This copy has double postmarks, Bath and London, December 1816, Bath and London, March and April 1859. Its defenders have offered the ingenious but naïve explanation of its having gone through the post in 1859 (a year in which interest in Shelley biography was high), *caught up in someone's outgoing mail*; and coming to the Dead Letter Office since the addressee was not to be found. A clerk made a copy, sending it to Leigh Hunt as a friend of the family, but Hunt did not offer to buy—he died that year, and may not have spoken of it to Sir Percy. Eight years later in 1857 Mr. John Tilley, secretary of the General Post Office in London, presented it to a distant cousin of Shelley's. Spencer Shelley wrote of it to Lady Shelley who assured him that it was another forgery—she knew of at least three—as the original was with the family. She added that she did not suspect Peacock of forgery as he would have wanted to suppress anything detrimental to Harriet. It did not occur to her that Hogg might possibly have had a hand in the hoax, if hoax it was. Hogg had earlier been on most affectionate and intimate terms with her; invited to write the official biography of Shelley, he had outraged Sir Percy and Lady Shelley with his first two volumes, published in 1858 before this letter was 'discovered' in the Dead Letter Office. Sir Percy and Lady Shelley had prohibited further volumes, and had withdrawn from him all sources in their possession which had been freely open to him. He affronted Lady Shelley by leaving in the offending *Life of Shelley* his dedication to her; in his continuation of affectionate letters to her he seems intentionally mischievous. He would have delighted in drawing a red herring across her path. It is pure speculation to attribute to him the re-posting and perhaps even the fabrication of this letter, but there is no likelier clue.[8]

Both copies have been defended each as the original by the

THE HUNT LIBRARY
CARNEGIE INSTITUTE OF TECHNOLOGY

claim that Mary's letter of the 17th of December answered it point by point, which is not wholly true. Mary's reference to a parcel sent by Shelley was a response to a postscript of Shelley's which occurs only in a copy of the letter which is an obvious forgery—the copy at Lehigh University. This suggests an original from which Major Byron drew for his copies, none an exact transcription.

Mary's postscript refers to Shelley's animadversion against Eliza:

How it would please me if old Westbrook were to repent in his last moments and leave all his fortune away from that odious Eliza.

She expressed an affection for Ianthe and Charles and an eagerness to see them, which was belied by her telling of Claire's teasing the year-old William by constantly reminding him that he would be displaced as eldest child and be served third at table. She sorrowed for Fanny whom she could now have had in her home. She did not mention Harriet.

It seems unlikely that she would have paid no attention to such a shocking statement as the descent to prostitution and the living with a groom. She had little or no sympathy for Harriet, but she was not merciless; she had inherited her mother's sensitive nature. Such a fall, even if not followed by suicide, would surely have distressed her—even under these circumstances when Harriet's tragedy meant a double joy for herself, marriage to Shelley, and renewed contact with her beloved father. In the absence of any comment in her letter there is at least a chance that the statement may not have been in the letter she received.

Naturally Mary was excited over her own prospects; naturally she wanted to excise Harriet from Shelley's life, minimizing her influence, and, in later years, omitting the dedication of *Queen Mab* until protests from Hogg and Peacock forced its return. But always a sense of guilt was woven into the novels she wrote, and finally, more than twenty years after Harriet's death, she wrote in her *Journal*, 12th February 1839:

Poor Harriet, to whose sad fate I attribute so many of my own heavy sorrows, as the atonement claimed by fate for her death.

This entry, blacked out in the manuscript *Journal*, was printed in Lady Shelley's *Shelley and Mary*, then carefully excised by her; but one copy escaped the scissors.[9] In her adulation of Mary, her adoration of Shelley, she could permit no one, least of all Mary, to show sympathy for Harriet. This compendium of Shelley papers, journals, and letters, over 1243 pages, privately printed, carefully annotated by Lady Shelley to reinforce her interpretations, seems somewhat haphazard and all-inclusive; but Lady Shelley selected, suppressed, destroyed material in order to present a poet with character consonant with the feminized portrait by Amelia Curran, with the most perfect wife (Mary) with whom he had lived in absolute harmony and happiness. She could not understand the true poet, his poems, or his life—or his aspirations for a socialized world where men and women would walk free and equal.

Harriet had understood; she had grieved to see his aspirations dimmed. In their contact in 1816 she had found traces of the Shelley she loved. Legally he was still her husband; the attraction they had had for each other had not wholly vanished. 'Love', Shelley had said in a note in *Queen Mab*, 'is inevitably consequent upon the perception of loveliness.' If Harriet was, when she died, in an advanced stage of pregnancy, the child must have been conceived in the early spring, in April, when Shelley was in London, alone and lonely. The situation is one not unknown in today's world of divorce, two people overcome by memories of love. Shelley had never believed in exclusive love; he had accepted Mary Wollstonecraft's definition of chastity as faithfulness to one love at a time. He disapproved of promiscuity, but love 'grew bright gazing on many truths', and permanence was not one of its qualities.

If this was so, his departure for Geneva in May would have left her in a difficult position of which he would have been ignorant. Her father, forced to support two children, would not have been sympathetic; Eliza would have been even less so. They may have urged Harriet to retire to hide her condition; the choice may, however, have been her own. In her letter to Eliza she expressed the wish that she had followed Eliza's advice—could this have been against renewed contact with

Shelley? Was this the destruction into which she had rushed? Was the conduct of the Westbrooks which Shelley called injudicious but well-intentioned, the countenancing of or compelling her retirement into lodgings? Pregnancy would explain her leaving her father's home for a dull life in lodgings where she spent most of her time in bed. A young woman in normal health would not have done so, nor would her family have permitted this.

Confirmation comes from the highly esteemed lawyer, Henry Crabb Robinson, an indefatigable diarist who knew everyone in the literary world, who heard all news, all gossip, and sifted it cautiously. Godwin was always a thorn in his flesh, though he credited him with having awakened his mind; reading *Political Justice* as a young man he had determined to shape his life for social usefulness. The man himself he found improvident and importunate, but he could not refuse him aid. Wearied by Mrs. Godwin's complaints and requests, he none the less credited her with such virtues as she had, and understood what irritated him, her boasting of husband and children, and her sensitivity to loss of prestige. The divorce she asked him to secure for Shelley was, he explained, impossible: Shelley had no grounds, and was himself living in adultery. Harriet's adultery, which Mrs. Godwin asserted as positive fact, he refused to believe. He went directly to an authoritative source of information, Shelley's defence lawyer in the suit for the custody of the children.

A brilliant barrister, Basil Montagu had not been a match for the more brilliant Sir Samuel Romilly, representing the Westbrooks, who had the stronger case. The hearing had been on the 24th of January 1817. Crabb Robinson recorded in his diary in November 1817 Montagu's answer to his query:

Montagu was employed by Shelley lately on the application to have his children taken from him by his late wife's father, on the ground that Shelley avowed atheism and lived in adultery with Godwin's daughter. It appeared that Mrs. Shelley, being pregnant, threw herself into the river and was drowned. It is singular that it was not suggested to Basil Montagu by Shelley that he was not the father of his wife's child. Mrs. Godwin had stated this to me as a fact. Basil Montagu thinks it improbable.[10]

Correctly Robinson gives the grounds of the Westbrooks' case, more concrete and less embracing than the grounds on which

Lord Eldon based his decision. He went to the essential point: who was the father of the unborn child? Mrs. Godwin, like her husband, was positive in her statement of Harriet's infidelity, both stopping at nothing in the desire, commendable in itself, to whitewash Mary. Their falsehoods seem to have been as deliberate as they were unscrupulous.

Montagu had no reason to tell anything but the truth to a good friend and fellow lawyer; his answer was cautious but entirely straightforward. He called Mrs. Godwin's statement 'improbable'. Shelley had not disclaimed responsibility for the pregnancy of Harriet. As a shrewd lawyer Montagu would have found a disclaimer of use in the defence of his client. The unfaithfulness of a wife, even a deserted wife, was not to be condoned. In his desperate desire to have his children under his care, Shelley did not stoop to this falsehood, turning a deaf ear to Godwin. (He had untruthfully stated that the separation from Harriet had occurred by mutual consent, a statement disproved by the letters given in evidence.) It must then be assumed that he knew it was possible for Harriet to have been pregnant by him. What Crabb Robinson found difficult to believe was not this, but Montagu's statement that Godwin had continued to take money from Shelley while he was living with Mary in illicit union. Unwilling to be unduly harsh in judgment of others he softened criticism:

when integrity is so hard to preserve under poverty we ought not to expect moral delicacy and refinement.

However much one is tempted to believe that Harriet was not pregnant, that she was not the Harriet Smith whose body was taken from the Serpentine, the evidence of Crabb Robinson, obtained from Basil Montagu, must be regarded as conclusive. She did drown herself, she was pregnant—by her husband. Godwin, a philosopher, suffered greatly under the reproach of Fanny's suicide; the Westbrooks, with less philosophy and more humanity, must have felt the reproach more keenly, a disgrace added to the sorrow for one truly loved, a daughter for whom their hopes had been high.

Two years earlier Harriet had felt reluctance to resume life after the birth of her son. The circumstances of her life had not lightened but darkened. At twenty-one she could not face even her immediate future. In *Queen Mab* Ianthe's fears of death had been soothed. In the *Alastor* volume Shelley's poems had sung of easeful death, of life as the veil clouding reality.

The manner of Harriet's death is of less consequence than the manner of her living in those bright years, brief in time but long in experience, when she shared the development of a poet, an idealist, a reformer; when the world held the promise of a better future; when two young aspirants believed that by selfless efforts they might inspire others to work for a sinless and just society where hate, violence, poverty, and war would be outmoded, and love be the only law of this so lovely world.

It was the springtime of Shelley's life that was hers. For ever she lives in lines penned to and of her, and in the later verse where her sunshine and her shadow fall. *Queen Mab* is eminently her poem. Shelley's disparagement of it is often quoted, but it is not convincing. At the end of his life, in 1822, he gave it to a friend, pleased when he called it 'astonishing'. Near the end of the year 1817 he sent a copy of *Queen Mab* to a Mr. Waller with a letter saying that the poem was composed in early youth, and was full of errors 'as far as arrangement of imagery and language are concerned—But it was a sincere overflowing of the heart and mind, and that at a period when they are most uncorrupted and pure. It is the Author's boast that it constitutes no small portion of his happiness, that after . . . added experience and reflection the doctrines . . . to which the Poem is devoted, have gained rather than lost that beauty and that grandeur which first determined him to devote his life to the inculcation of them'.

The dedication to *Queen Mab* is Harriet's most fitting epitaph as the sharer of that 'sincere overflowing of the heart and mind' of Shelley's springtime.

NOTES

Chapter I—FAIR IN FORM AND PURE IN MIND

1. From the Register of Marriages, St. George's Church, Hanover Square, London. There is a discrepancy here: either John Westbrook was over twenty-nine in 1790, or less than eighty-eight at his death in 1834. The tombstone in the churchyard at Kingston St. Mary's, Somerset, reads:
   John Westbrook Es^r
   Formerly of the City of Westminster
   Who died at Walford House
   November 3^d 1834 AETAT 88.
2. The Baptismal Register, St. George's. The children were: Mary Ann 1781, Eliza 1783 (born 1782), Matilda 1792, Harriet 1795.
3. British Museum Add. MSS. 37496. Julian Edition, Vol. VIII.
4. Cecil, David, *Melbourne*, London, 1955.
5. The inscription reads:
   Timothy Shelley Es^q of Horsham in this County
   d. 11th March 1771 aged 70
   Joanna his wife Died 17th November 1770 aged 75.
6. Ingpen, Roger, *Shelley in England*, London, 1917; facing p. 16 are excellent pictures of Castle Goring.
7. Sumner, George Henry, *Life of Charles Richard Sumner*, London, 1876. Charles Richard Sumner became Bishop of Winchester and private chaplain to the household of George IV. Sumner entered Eton in 1802 and left in 1809; Shelley entered in 1804 and left in 1810. Shelley would have known of Sumner, two years his senior, a popular and prominent older boy. Unfortunately no copy of *The White Nun* is known to exist; Bishop Sumner's descendants kindly searched for a copy, but in vain. It is listed in Harcourt's *Bibliography of Eton*, London, 1898, and in Vol. VI of the *Dictionary of Anonymous and Pseudonymous English Literature*, London, 1926. Attention was first called to this novel in *The Times Literary Supplement* of 28th December 1946, by Henry Tyler.
8. Reprinted among the *Juvenilia* in the Oxford *Shelley*.
9. Shelley's novels have been variously reprinted in his prose works. Julian Edition, Vol. V.
10. British Museum Add. MSS. 37496; Julian Edition, Vol. VIII.
11. In the Library of St. John's College, Cambridge University, where permission was kindly given to consult both the volume of pamphlets and *The Necessity of Atheism*. *The Necessity of Atheism* was reissued in 1906 by the Rationalist Press Association. It is in Vol. V of the Julian Edition.
12. *Shelley in England*, from the Whitton papers.
13. Mary Shelley to John Bowring (later Sir John), 25th February 1826.
14. Hogg, Thomas Jefferson, *Life of Shelley*, first published 1858.
15. Peacock, Thomas Love, *Memoirs of Shelley*, Vol. III of *Works*, London, 1875. Originally published in *Fraser's Magazine*, June 1858, January 1860, and March 1862.
16. The letters are in the archives of Wheaton College, Norton, Massachusetts. Nancy Eaton wrote to Joseph Emerson in 1803: 'Some men desire a slave, some a toy, some indeed are more rational in their choice, but who but my lover wishes for a rational companion?' After marriage the Emersons boarded in order to give her more time for study.

Chapter II—A MARRIAGE IS MADE

1. *Shelley in England.*
2. Hogg, T. J., *Life of Shelley.*
3. Scott, Winifred, *Jefferson Hogg*, London, 1951. The letters are published in Walter Sidney Scott's first volume from the Hogg papers, *The Athenians*, 1943.
4. The author of *Adeline Mowbray* had herself declined Godwin's proposal of marriage, and became the wife of the painter, John Opie, one of whose best-known portraits is that of Mary Wollstonecraft which Harriet saw over Godwin's desk, and is now in the National Portrait Gallery, London. Aaron Burr took Keenan's copy of it back to America with him which, privately owned, has been exhibited in the New York Public Library.
5. *Political Justice*, Book VIII, chapter vi. This book was issued in a separate volume, George Allen & Unwin, London, 1890, 1918, and 1929. The extracts here are from this edition, pp. 101 and 102.
6. Undated, but soon after arrival at Cwm Elan. Hogg's *Life*.
7. Hogg's *Life*.
8. In *Shelley Memorials*, 1859, Lady Shelley said in a note on page 22: '. . . in a sad and evil hour for both, this girl "who had thrown herself upon his protection" and "with whom he was not in love" became his wife. These expressions are quoted from some published letters of Shelley's the authenticity of which I am not able to guarantee.'
9, 10, 11. These letters from *Shelley in England.*
12. This and the following letter, Julian Edition, Vol. VIII.

Chapter III—YOU WILL SEE HOGG

1. This presentation of Hogg is built up from many sources, first of all his *Life of Shelley* (1858) wherein Shelley is only the loom on which he wove his picture of himself; Shelley's letters to him which also idealize him, and those to Miss Hitchener; Crabb Robinson's references in his Diary to both the man and his *Life of Shelley*; Walter Sidney Scott's publications from the Hogg papers: *The Athenians* (1943), *Harriet and Mary* (1944), and *Shelley at Oxford* (1944), and the volume of letters from these, *New Shelley Letters* (1948); Winifred Scott's *Jefferson Hogg*, also from the Hogg papers (1951); and numerous biographies of Shelley. Finally his novel, *Memoirs of Prince Alexy Haimatoff*, which the title-page said was 'Translated from the original Latin MSS. under the immediate inspection of the Prince, By John Brown, Esq.'. It was reissued in 1952, Sidney Scott, ed.
2. The Rev. Mr. Terrot had probably heard of the Boinville ladies, too.
3. Shelley papers in the Horsham Museum, Horsham, Sussex.
4. Wickwar, William H., *The Struggle for the Freedom of the Press*, London, 1928. The Society for the Suppression of Vice and the Encouragement of Religion and Virtue was formed in 1802; by the end of 1803 it had over 800 members and had secured 700 convictions for blasphemous libel. In 1817 membership dropped; by 1828 there were only 240 members.
5. *Shelley in England.*
6. Hogg's *Life*. In a letter to Hogg (*New Shelley Letters*) Shelley blames himself for having exposed him to Harriet's charm by introducing him to her.

7. The material on the Duke of Norfolk is from several sources, but mainly from *The House of Howard*, London, 1907 (Brenan, G. and Statham, C. P.). Pertinent entries from the Duke's Diary appear in MacCarthy, *Shelley's Early Life*.

8. The description of Greystoke is indebted to *Follies and Grottoes* (Barbara Jones), London, 1953, p. 175; there is also a picture of one corner of Fort Putnam.

9. Dowden, Vol. I.

10. Southey, Robert, *Letters to John Rickman*, Boston, 1875; reprinted in White, N. I., I.

11. To Miss Hitchener, 27th Feb. 1812.

12. To Miss Hitchener, 18th March 1812. MacCarthy discovered this letter in the Public Record Office: 'Ireland. January to April, 1812. No. 655'. Also in Julian Edition, Vol. VIII.

13. Belittlers of Shelley have dismissed this speech as of fifteen minutes' duration. Delivery, with interruptions, would have required more nearly an hour; in MacCarthy it covers pp. 181-224 inclusive; in the Julian Edition, Vol. V, pp. 215-245 inclusive. Material on Ireland from various books on Dublin and Ireland, and from contemporary newspapers.

14. MacCarthy gives a full account of the correspondence, including Harriet's letter (which also is in the Julian Edition, Vol. VIII).

15. To Mrs. Nugent, 16th April.

16. From a photostat of the original letter in the Huntington Library, San Marino, California (HM 20178-20198, collection of letters Harriet Shelley to Catherine Nugent). Always misprinted 'agreeable' instead of 'sociable'. In the original letter 'sociable' is written over 'agre'.

Chapter IV—THE THIRST FOR ACTION

1. To Miss Hitchener.

2. The correspondence with Miss Hitchener has been consulted in the original letters, British Museum Add. MSS. 37496. This rhapsody was written across the first page of the letter; 'crossing' was commonly used to keep letters within the bounds of a single sheet folded to make the envelope like today's air-letters. Julian Edition, Vol. VIII, contains the correspondence.

3. Letters to Miss Nugent, with the exception of that quoted on p. 168 have been transcribed from the originals at the Huntington Library, San Marino, California: HM 20178-20198. They are available in the Julian Edition, Vols. VIII and X. The letter on p. 168 is in the British Museum (Ashley 5021).

4. Peck, Walter E., *Shelley*, Vol. I; first published by W. M. Rossetti in the *Fortnightly Review*, 1871.

5. Some pieces made for Shelley are in the possession of Mr. R. H. Ellis-Davies of Craig Wen, Caernarvon, whose grandfather bought them at the sale of Shelley's effects at Tanyrallt; they are owned by the family of the late Mr. Ellis W. Davies, M.P. Mr. R. H. Ellis-Davies kindly removed for me the glass plate over Shelley's signature on the sideboard, a signature believed to be genuine after having been collated with others. An inscription added at some later time is in error: 'This was made for Mr. P. B. Shelley whilst staying with Mr. Madox at Tanyrallt 1805'.

6. This letter ends with postscripts written on three sides of the address. At

the bottom: 'oh my Harriet nothing shall induce me desert thee, her,
who loves thee with her sincerest love'. Crossing two sides are these:

Percy I	this time
entreat	oh tell
thee	me
write	she
by every	is
post	better
a line	
will do	
lest	
Harriet	
needless	
never call	

7. The *Liverpool Daily Post* on the 20th of July 1960 headlined its article on
the Embankment: '£150,000 Portmadoc scheme'. It reported the in-
auguration of 'a major repair scheme', giving due credit to Madocks
for the building in 1811 of the main embankment. A charming contemporary print of the work of construction was reproduced. I am indebted to Dr. Eleanor Nicholes for this newspaper.

8. 'Only twice' in the original letter; misprinted 'once'.

9. Mrs. Godwin has been presented in pejorative phrases by Charles Lamb,
Francis Place, and other contemporaries, of whom Crabb Robinson was
the most patient with her. Fanny defended her to Mary; Mary had no
regard for her, and Claire, her own daughter, kept away from her. Godwin remained devoted to her, urging her to return whenever she left
him, as she did repeatedly; though he chided her, he enjoyed her company and was faithful to her. She was overworked and under heavy
pressures, struggling with poverty, debt, and a difficult husband who
withdrew to his study and appeared among his family only at stated
intervals. Not even the name of the father of her Clairmont children is
known, but she had attracted him long enough to account for two children almost three years apart. Her real name, as given at her second
marriage ceremony with Godwin (at the first she had called herself Mrs.
Clairmont, widow), was Mary Jane Vial, spinster. Claire's contempt for
marriage and her seeking a liaison with Byron may have resulted from
her discovery of her own illegitimate birth, and a desire to take pride
in it. This new information about Mrs. Godwin has recently appeared
in the Keats-Shelley Memorial Bulletin, Number XI, 1960, 'The Clairmont Enigma' by Herbert Huscher. Mrs. Godwin had moved in higher
social and economic circles before her marriage to Godwin.

10. Among the biographies of William Godwin two have been most useful:
C. Kegan Paul, *William Godwin: His Friends and Contemporaries*, 2 vols.
London, 1875, and R. Glynn Grylls, *Godwin and His World*, London,
1953. Henry Crabb Robinson's Diary as selected by Edith Morley and
published as *On Books and Their Writers*, London, 1938 (Vol. I) is invaluable for Godwin and Mrs. Godwin, their virtues and vagaries.
Godwin's letters have been included in biographies; some, e.g., 'The
Elopement of Percy Bysshe Shelley and Mary Wollstonecraft Godwin'
have been privately printed. Shelley's letters to Godwin are revelatory, as are some of Mary's letters to Shelley, and her novels, and her
Journal.

11. Dowden, Vol. I.

12. The best interpretation of the attack is given by H. M. Dowling in *Notes
and Queries*, July, September, and December 1954, and December 1955.

In March 1955 Mr. Dowling explained 'the Arrest for Debt' at Caernarvon.

13. From the Madocks papers, County Hall, Caernarvon; quoted by permission of Breese, Jones & Casson, Port-Madoc, and of the County Archivist, Caernarvon, Mr. K. Williams Jones.

14. Julian Edition, Vol. IX, note, p. 51.

15. From the original letter in the Caernarvon County Archives. As printed it begins, 'As Mr. Shelley' but it seems to be 'As Mrs. Shelly [sic]', as compared with the 'Mr. Shelley' further on in this letter. Quoted by permission of Breese, Jones & Casson, and of the County Archivist, Caernarvon.

Chapter V—THE HAPPIEST YEARS

1. Volney, Constantin François, *Ruins of Empires*, London, 1792; Paris, 1791.

2. Jones, Sir William, *The Palace of Fortune*, London, 1810. Shelley bought a copy in 1812.

3. *To Harriet* 1812.

4. Letter to Godwin, 18th March 1812.

5. *Stanza, Written at Bracknell*. March 1814; first published by Hogg.

6. Mrs. Boinville to Hogg, 11th March 1814; given in Julian Edition in a footnote on p. 86, Vol. IX.

7. Godwin recorded the date.

Chapter VI—THIS IS A VAMPIRE

1. Peacock, *Memoirs*.

2. Hotson, Leslie, *Shelley's Lost Letters to Harriet*, Boston, Mass., 1930. First published in the *Atlantic Monthly* they were issued in a single volume (1930) by the Atlantic Monthly Press in Boston, Faber & Faber, London. Permission to quote has been given by Mr. Hotson and by the *Atlantic Monthly*. These letters weighed heavily against Shelley in the lawsuit over the custody of the children.

3. The vitality of *Frankenstein* is attested not only by the sensational films that make use of the name but by the fact that it continues to be reprinted, with a new edition in a paperback in 1960. Started under the influence of Byron in Geneva 1816, or the combined influence of Shelley and Byron, when Mary was not yet nineteen, it is infused with some of Shelley's ideas. Frankenstein's scientific curiosity was Shelley's; his monster's moral corruption accorded with Shelley's (and Mary's) belief that lack of love froze the heart. It is the same Godwinian idea as in Coleridge's *Ancient Mariner*. The opening lines of Shelley's poem, *Lines Written Among the Euganean Hills* reflects upon it, and the lines 45-65 refer to the monster's death, unloved and alone in Arctic wastes.

4. Peacock, *Memoirs*.

5. Brown, Charles Brockden, *Ormond*, New York; first published in 1799. Ormond's Helena was 'beautiful, flawless, with a rosy complexion'. For all her desirable qualities she could not be 'the object of a genuine and lasting passion'; Constantia could, and as the superior woman, made a stronger appeal to his senses. He told Helena: 'I cannot help it; I make not myself; I am molded by circumstances; whether I shall love thee or not is no longer in my own choice'.

6. Paul, C. Kegan, *William Godwin: His Friends and Contemporaries*, London, 1876.
7. Julian Edition, Vol. IX.
8. This and following letters to Harriet, *Shelley's Lost Letters*.
9. *New Shelley Letters* prints the letter in full.
10. *Shelley and Mary*, I; Julian Edition, Vol. IX.
11. Recipe checked with contemporary medical dictionary.
12. Material in '*Erasmus Perkins*' *and Shelley*, Modern Language Notes, Vol. LXX, June 1955. The late Newman Ivey White first suggested that I engage in this bit of detection.
13. These stanzas, published here for the first time, appear with the permission of the Clarendon Press and of Mr. Neville Rogers. They are written in the Esdaile Notebook after the May 1814 stanzas; both poems are in Harriet's handwriting. The Esdaile Notebook is the only possession of Harriet's in the keeping of her descendants save for her wedding band of tiny diamonds and turquoises, Shelley's matching tie-clip, and Shelley's christening shirt. Ianthe Shelley married Edward Jeffries Esdaile of Cothelstone, Somerset; the Esdailes are the only direct descendants of Shelley. I am indebted to the great granddaughter of Shelley and Harriet for her hospitality, for permission to examine letters of Dowden to her father and for the information of the descendants who are Mrs. Lettice Worrall, her sister, her two sons, her granddaughter, her niece Mrs. Warmington, and her three daughters and one son. Mrs. Worrall writes: 'ten of us who actually have Shelley's blood in our veins, and there are *no* others'. My careful investigation of the claims of Americans who believe themselves in direct descent from Shelley has proved that the claims rest upon family myths or upon an ancestor named Skelly. Mrs. Worrall's statement is entirely correct.

Chapter VII—IS IT WRONG?

1. *Shelley in England*, Whitton papers.
2. Grylls, R. Glynn, *Claire Clairmont*, London, 1939, is the best account of Claire; her letters to Byron were kept by him, to appear in biographies of him, among his letters, and in Shelley biographies.
3. British Museum Add. MSS. 37232.
4. Lord Glenbervie's *Journal*, II, p. 160; first quoted in *Notes and Queries*, Vol. 155, July-December 1928, pp. 171-172. Also in *Notes and Queries* Byron's 'Lord Mount Coffee-house, the Irish peer/Who killed himself for love, (with wine)' *Don Juan*, I, cxlix.
5. Reissued in 1952 by The Folio Society, London, with an introduction by Sidney Scott.
6. The Julian Edition, Vol. X, in a note to this letter, p. 423, says: 'This letter was purchased in 1895 by Mr. G. Suckling, who has kindly given me a copy which he made before selling the original letter to Mr. H. Buxton Forman'. The note adds that the letter first appeared in the sale catalogue in 1920. In January 1922 W. Courthope Forman published it in the *Cornhill Magazine*, saying that it had made a 'mysterious reappearance' which he did not explain. It was resold at the A. Edward Newton sale (1941). Newton published a facsimile of part of the letter in his *The Greatest Book in the World*, Boston, 1924; the other half was printed in facsimile in the Newton Sale catalogue. Hence the writing can be compared with that of the June 1816 letter to Newton. The list of owners provided by W. Courthope Forman is not available for con-

sulting. I am indebted to Miss Elsa Forman, who obtained the information about this from the widow of W. Courthope Forman.

7. Hookham's letter, on gilt-edged paper (the gilt is barely visible today), is in the Berg Collection of the New York Public Library; I am indebted to Mr. John D. Gordan for permission to examine it.

8. I am indebted to Neville Rogers for this information.

9. The text of this poem (pp. 200-201) is that of Ingpen's careful transcript from the MS. on which Shelley crossed out the variant readings frequently printed. From the Ingpen Papers.

10. Mary Shelley drowned more than one heroine. In *Falkner* the gentle and beautiful heroine does not commit suicide but is overtaken by the tide while trying to escape from her kidnapper.

Chapter VIII—THESE POOR LITTLE INNOCENTS

1. Hotson, Leslie, *Lost Letters*.

2. *Shelley in England*, Whitton papers.

3. Houston, Mrs. [M. C.], *A Woman's Memories of World-Known Men*, London, 1883. Mrs. Houston, who up to this time (1833) had hardly heard of Shelley, met and became intimate with Hellen Shelley, then living with her sister Margaret at Field Place; Hellen would talk of her brother but warned Mrs. Houston not to mention his name in Sir Timothy's hearing. Hellen later on showed her letters of Shelley's which had been given her by the daughter of the family solicitor after his death (she named a Mr. Stedman). Mrs. Houston agreed with Hellen that the 'religious and other views' were abhorrent and repulsive, and worthy only of destruction. These were the letters presented in the case over the custody of the children, she thought. Mr. Stedman had then been dead for several years, but Hellen had apparently waited to get some other opinion. Mrs. Houston approved of the destruction.

4. *Shelley and Mary*, I, 201 B. Dowden in his copy (now in the British Museum) wrote in the margin about Godwin's letter to his wife in May 1817, in which Godwin expressed chagrin over Shelley's refusal to accept his statement even though he had not told him it came from Hill; Shelley had written to Godwin that the story was 'much exaggereated and that for the present explanation was superfluous'.

5. White, N. I., *Shelley*, Vol. I, 345-346, 674-676. Dowden gave the correct clue (Vol. I, p. 238) to a Dublin merchant prominent in the Emancipation movement but failed to follow it up, and omitted the reference in the revised one-volume *Life*. The full story is in the *Historical Sketch of the Late Catholic Association of Ireland*, 2 vols., London, 1829, by Sir Thomas Wyse.

6. British Museum Add. MSS. 35152. Dated 1815, this letter is post-marked 1816. Clairmont asked Place to aid Shelley in establishing him in a business venture; to disarm Place's prejudice against Shelley he defended him and Mary and called Harriet deliberately extravagant.

7. For discussion of this letter see *The Times Literary Supplement*, 1937: 20th, and 27th March; 3rd, 10th, 17th, and 24th April. Seymour de Ricci came to the defence against Sylva Norman and Graham Pollard. Robert Metcalf Smith's *The Shelley Legend*, New York, 1945, goes into the matter exhaustively. The exposure of 'Major Byron' as a forger was disturbing, but the exposure of Thomas J. Wise's chicaneries overshadows that.

Q

8. This ingenious conjecture comes from a sound, and a witty Shelley scholar.

9. In *Mary Shelley's Journal*, F. L. Jones, ed., Norman, 1952, this entry has a footnote stating that the excision in other copies was not made in the Yale University copy. It has been neatly cut from Dowden's copy in the British Museum, cut by Lady Shelley.

10. Robinson, Henry Crabb, *On Books and Their Writers*, Edith Morley, ed. London, 1938, Vol. I, p. 199. This significant entry for 2nd November 1817 in Crabb Robinson's voluminous diaries has largely escaped notice. Robert Smith quoted it in *The Shelley Legend* but missed its meaning. Highly charged with emotions, that book caused emotional outbursts against it; exposure of its faults tended to obscure its virtues.

BIBLIOGRAPHY

I

A PARTIAL LIST OF HARRIET SHELLEY'S READING TAKEN FROM HER LETTERS AND SHELLEY'S

Campbell, Thomas, *Gertrude of Wyoming.*
Coleridge, Samuel Taylor, *The Ancient Mariner; Remorse, a Tragedy.*
Drummond, Sir William, *Academical Questions.*
Godwin, William, *Memoirs of the Author of a Vindication of the Rights of Women; An Enquiry Concerning Political Justice.*
Jones, Sir William, *Palace of Fortune.*
Lawrence, Sir James Henry, *Love, an Allegory; Empire of the Nairs.*
Owenson, Sydney (Lady Morgan), *Patriotic Sketches of Ireland.*
Paine, Thomas, *Age of Reason; Rights of Man.*
Peacock, Thomas Love, *Palmyra.*
Robertson, William, *History of Scotland; History of America.*
Scott, Sir Walter, *Rokeby.*
Smith, Horace, and James, *Rejected Addresses.*
Southey, Robert, *History of Brazil; Curse of Kehama; Thalaba.*
Volney, Constantin François, *Ruins of Empires.*
Wollstonecraft, Mary, *A Vindication of the Rights of Woman; Posthumous Works.*
In Latin: Horace: *Odes*; Ovid: *Metamorphoses*; Virgil: *Georgics*; (selections from these).
Translations from Greek; various books bought for her with translations; read to her by Shelley: Homer, *Iliad* and *Odyssey.*
Novels:
  Adeline Mowbray (Mrs. Opie).
  Claire d'Albe (Mme Cottin).
  Empire of the Nairs, or the Rights of Woman (Sir James Lawrence).
  Fleetwood (William Godwin).
  The Missionary; The Novice of St. Dominick (Sydney Owenson, Lady Morgan).
  Memoirs of Prince Alexy Haimatoff (T. J. Hogg).
  Ormond (Charles Brockden Brown).
  St. Irvyne (Shelley).

II

LETTERS OF HARRIET SHELLEY

To Elizabeth Hitchener, originals, British Museum, Add. MSS. 37496.
To Thomas Hookham, 4 letters, Julian Edition of Shelley's *Works*, Vol. IX.
To J. Frank Newton, June 1816, British Museum, Add. MSS. 35252.
To a Mrs. Newman of Dublin, Huntington Library, HM 20175.
To Catherine Nugent, originals in the Huntington Library, HM 20178-20198, San Marino, California; British Museum, Ashley 5021.
To Eliza Westbrook, Julian Edition, Vol. X; facsimile partly in A. E. Newton's *Greatest Book in the World*, partly in the Newton Sale Catalogue.

LETTERS TO HARRIET SHELLEY

From Elizabeth Hitchener (also E. H. to and from Shelley), British Museum,
    Add. MSS. 37496.
From Shelley, *Shelley's Lost Letters to Harriet*, Leslie Hotson, ed., Boston,
    Mass. 1930.

OTHER LETTERS, JOURNALS

Browning, Robert, Original Letter, 12th Oct. 1883, to Edward Dowden
    concerning Harriet Shelley. British Museum, Ashley 5021.
Clairmont, Charles, Letter to Francis Place, concerning Harriet and
    Shelley, British Museum, Add. MSS. 35152.
Clairmont, Claire, MS. Diary in the British Museum.
Dowden, Edward, Letter to Mr. Esdaile; in the possession of Mrs. Lettice
    Worrall.
Hookham, Thomas, Letter to Shelley, December 1816, with news of the
    death of Harriet; original in the Berg Collection, New York Public
    Library, New York City.
Shelley, Percy Bysshe, Letter to Mary, December 15 (16), 1816, British
    Museum, Ashley 5021; the letter about Harriet and her death.
Westbrook, Eliza, to John Williams, original letter among the Madocks
    Papers, Caernarvon County Hall, Caernarvon, Wales.

III

GENERAL

Blunden, Edmund, *Shelley*, London, 1946.
Brenan, G., and Statham, C. P., *The House of Howard*.
Brown, Charles Brockden, *Ormond*, New York, 1799.
Brown, Ford K., *Life of William Godwin*, London, 1926.
Cameron, Kenneth Neil, *The Young Shelley*, London, 1951.
Carter, John and Pollard, Graham, *An Enquiry into the Nature of Certain
    19th Century Pamphlets*. 1934.
Cecil, David, *Melbourne*, London, 1955.
Cobbett's Political Register 1811–1816, passim.
Cole, Sonia, *Counterfeit*, London, 1955.
Cottin, Mme, *Claire d'Albe*, 1808.
Dacre, Charlotte (Rosa Matilda), *Zofloya, or the Moor*, London, 1806.
Dowden, Edward, *Life of Percy Bysshe Shelley*, 2 vols., London, 1886.
Dowling, H. M., *The Alleged Attempt to Assassinate Shelley*, and continuing
    articles, *Notes and Queries*, July, September, December 1954, and De-
    cember 1955.
Drummond, Sir William, *Academical Questions*, London, 1805.
Ehrsam, Theodore, G., *Major Byron*, New York, 1951.
Farrar, James Anson, *Literary Forgeries*, London, 1907.
Garnett, Richard, *Relics of Shelley*, London, 1862.
Garnett, Richard, Dowden, Edward, and Rossetti, W. M., *Letters about Shelley*,
    London, 1917.
Godwin, William, *An Enquiry Concerning Political Justice*, London, 1793;
    Fleetwood, 3 vols., 1805; *Memoirs of Mary Wollstonecraft*, 1798.
Godwin, William, *The Elopement of Percy Bysshe Shelley and Mary Wollstone-
    craft Godwin*, privately printed, Bibliophile Society, Boston, Mass. 1911.
Godwin, William, Appeal to Thomas Jefferson by Godwin's friends for a
    contribution for his publishment of the *Juvenile Library*, 6th September

1808; *William and Mary Quarterly*, Vol. 9, 2nd series, Virginia, 1929, pp. 127-128.

Grylls, R. Glynn, *Claire Clairmont*, London, 1939; *Mary Shelley*, London, 1938; *William Godwin and His World*, London, 1953

Hogg, Thomas Jefferson, *Life of Shelley*, 2 vols., 1858; *Memoirs of Prince Alexy Haimatoff*, London, 1813, reissued, Sidney Scott, ed., 1952.

Holbach, Baron Paul Henri d', *Le Système de la nature*; and *Le Christianisme déviolé* (Voltaire's copy, annotated by him).

Hotson, Leslie, *Shelley's Lost Letters to Harriet*, Boston, Mass., 1930.

Houston, Mrs. (M. C.), *A Woman's Memories of World-Known Men*, London, 1883.

Hughes, A. M. D., *The Nascent Mind of Shelley*, London, 1947.

Ingpen, Roger, *Shelley in England*, London, 1917.

Ingpen, Roger and Peck, Walter E., eds. *The Works of Percy Bysshe Shelley*, 10 vols., London, 1926–1930. *The Julian Editions.*

Jeaffreson, John Cordy, *The Real Shelley*, London, 1885.

Jones, Barbara, *Follies and Grottoes*, London, 1953.

Jones, Frederick L., ed. *Mary Shelley's Journal*, Oklahoma, 1947.

Jones, Sir William, *Palace of Fortune*, London, 1810.

Koszul, A. H., *La Jeunesse de Shelley*, Paris, 1910.

Lawrence, Sir James Henry, *Empire of the Nairs, or the Rights of Woman*, London, 1811; *Love, an Allegory*, London, 1802.

MacCarthy, Denis Florence, *Shelley's Early Life*, London, n.d. (1872).

Madocks, William, Papers in County Hall, Caernarvon, N. Wales.

Marshall, Mrs. Julian, *Life and Letters of Mary Wollstonecraft Shelley*, London, 1889.

Medwin, Thomas, *Life of Shelley*, London, 1847; *Revised Life of Shelley*, London, 1913.

Middleton, Charles S., *Shelley and His Writings*, London, 1858.

Norman, Sylva, *Flight of the Skylark*, Oklahoma, 1954.

Notes and Queries, passim.

Opie, Mrs. (Amelia), *Adeline Mowbray*, London, 1805.

Owenson, Sydney (Lady Morgan), *The Missionary*, 1811; *The Novice of St. Dominick*, 1812; *Patriotic Sketches*, 1807.

Partington, Wilfred, *Forging Ahead*, 1939.

Paul, C. Kegan, *William Godwin, His Friends and Contemporaries*, London, 1876.

Peacock, Thomas Love, *Memoirs of Shelley* (1855, 1869, *Fraser's Magazine*); *Nightmare Abbey* (1818); *Headlong Hall* (1815) in *Works*, London, 1875.

Peck, Walter E., *Shelley, his Life and Work*, Boston and New York, 1927.

Ricci, Seymour de, *Bibliography of Shelley Letters*, Paris, 1927.

Robertson, J. M. *A History of Freethought in the Nineteenth Century*, New York, 1930.

Robinson, Henry Crabb, *On Books and Their Writers*, Edith Morley, ed., London, 1938.

Rogers, Neville, *Shelley at Work*, Oxford, 1956.

Rossetti, William Michael, *Memoir of Shelley*, London, 1886.

Scott, Walter Sidney, *The Athenians, Harriet and Mary*, and *Shelley at Oxford*, 1943, 1944; *New Shelley Letters*, London, 1948.

Scott, Winifred, *Jefferson Hogg*, London, 1951.

Shelley, Harriet, Letters of, Julian Edition of Shelley's *Works*, Vols. VIII, IX, and X; *Letters to Catherine Nugent*, privately printed, London, 1889; in the New York *Nation*, 1881.

Shelley, Jane, Lady, *Shelley Memorials*, London, 1859; *Shelley and Mary*, privately printed, 1882.

Shelley, Mary W., novels of, *Frankenstein, Falkner, The Last Man, Lodore, Matilda, Valperga.*

Shelley, Mary W., Richard Garnett, ed., *Tales and Stories*, London, 1891.

Shelley, Percy Bysshe,
Alastor, London, 1816.
Queen Mab, London, 1813.
Posthumous Poems, London, 1824.
Poems (with Keats and Coleridge), Paris, 1829.
Poetical Works, 4 vols., London, 1839.
Poetical Works, Oxford Edition, 1933.
Poems, Julian Edition, 1926.
Address to the Irish People, 1812.
A Declaration of Rights, 1812.
Letter to Lord Ellenborough, 1812.
The Necessity of Atheism, 1811.
A Refutation of Deism, 1814.
St. Irvyne, 1811.
Victor and Cazire, Original Poetry by, 1810.
Zastrozzi, 1810.
Shelley-Rolls, Sir John C. E. and Roger Ingpen, *Verse and Prose from the MSS. of P. B. Shelley*, London, 1934.
Shelley, Sir Timothy, Letters, in the Horsham Museum, Horsham, Sussex.
Smith, Robert M., *The Shelley Legend*, New York, 1945.
Staël, Mme de, *Essay on Suicide*, London, 1813.
Sumner, George Henry, *Life of Charles Richard Sumner*, London, 1876.
The Theological Inquirer, or Polemical Magazine, Erasmus Perkins (George Cannon), ed., London, 1815, March-September.
The Times Literary Supplement, 1937: 20th, 27th March, 3rd, 10th, 17th April; Sylva Norman, Graham Pollard, and Seymour de Ricci on the authenticity of Shelley's letter to Mary, December 15/16, 1816.
Trelawny, Edward, Letter to Claire Clairmont on Lady Shelley's misrepresentation of Harriet, and other letters 1870-1875, British Museum, Ashley Library, 5022.
Twain, Mark (Samuel Clemens), *In Defence of Harriet Shelley*, New York, n.d. (after Dowden's *Life of Shelley*); in *Works; How to Tell a Story*, etc.
Volney, Constantin François, *Ruins of Empires*, London, 1792.
White, Newman Ivey, *Shelley*, 2 vols., New York, 1940.
White, N. I., Jones, F. L., and Cameron, K. N., *An Examination of The Shelley Legend*, Philadelphia, 1951.
White, W., *Calumnies of the 'Athenaeum Journal' Exposed*, London, 1852. *Letter to Mr. Murray on the Subject of the Byron, Shelley, and Keats Manuscripts*, London, 1852.
Wickwar, W. H., *The Struggle for the Freedom of the Press*, London, 1929.
Wollstonecraft, Mary, *A Vindication of the Rights of Woman*, London, 1792; *Letters to Imlay*, London, 1879.
Wood, Jacobus, volume of miscellaneous pamphlets, in the Library of St. John's College, Cambridge University, 1836.
Wyse, Sir Thomas, *Historical Sketch of the Late Catholic Association of Ireland*, London, 1829.

ADDENDA

The Ingpen Papers in the Rare Book Department, University of California Library, Berkeley, California, including letters from Sir John Shelley, Rolls, E. Dowden, R. Garnett, W. E. Peck, W. M. Rossetti, T. S. Wise, W. Withall, and others; notes, MSS., typescripts and proofs of *Shelley in England*, the *Julian Editions*, etc.; transcripts and photostats of Shelley MSS.; pictures of people and places; and a collection of various works of Shelley and of Shelleyana. There are also transcripts of three unpublished letters from Harriet to John Williams.

INDEX

PRINTED BY R. & R. CLARK, LTD., EDINBURGH